UNBEATABLE

UNBEATABLE

NOTRE DAME'S 1988 CHAMPIONSHIP
AND THE LAST GREAT COLLEGE
FOOTBALL SEASON

JERRY BARCA

ST. MARTIN'S PRESS ⚑ NEW YORK

www.stmartins.com

Library of Congress Cataloging-in-Publication Data

Barca, Jerry.
   Unbeatable : Notre Dame's 1988 championship and the last great college football season / Jerry Barca.
     p. cm.
   ISBN 978-1-250-02483-1 (hardcover)
   ISBN 978-1-250-02484-8 (e-book)
   1. Notre Dame Fighting Irish (Football team)—History.   2. University of Notre Dame—Football—History.   I. Title.
   GV958.N6B37 2013
   796.332'630977289—dc23

                               2013009265

St. Martin's Press books may be purchased for educational, business, or promotional use. For information on bulk purchases, please contact Macmillan Corporate and Premium Sales Department at 1-800-221-7945, extension 5442, or write specialmarkets@macmillan.com.

First Edition: August 2013

10 9 8 7 6 5 4 3 2 1

For my parents, Elizabeth Barca and Salvatore Barca, whose love and commitment to me gave me the life I have.

And for Beth; I am so blessed to share love and life with you.

CONTENTS

UNBEATABLE

CHAPTER 1

Unflinching

There is an appointed time for everything,
and a time for every affair under the heavens . . .
A time to love, and a time to hate;
A time of war, and a time of peace.

—Ecclesiastes 3:1, 8

Shrieks and frenzied screams ricocheted off the locker room walls in
a cacophony of rage and excitement. Tears rolled down some of the
young men's faces, an uncontrolled emotional response after launching into battle.

The days of the Notre Dame Fighting Irish playing the role of
the nice weakling had ended.

Leaving the field after pregame warm-ups, the Miami Hurricanes chose to go through a line of Notre Dame players, rather than
go around them. Miami met an unflinching Irish squad.

The Hurricanes, the No. 1 team in the country and the best
program of the era, had been the chief tormentor of the Irish in recent years. In the schools' previous two meetings Miami humbled
Notre Dame by a total score of 82–7. Flashy on-field celebrations
deepened the embarrassment doled out by the 'Canes.

Now Miami had traveled to Notre Dame Stadium, and the

showy, bullying antics would not be tolerated. When the 'Canes breached the Notre Dame warm-up line, a fight exploded on the ground separating the end zone and the stadium's lone tunnel.

"It was a melee. It wasn't like guys fighting in a bar where they want someone to break it up. We did not care if someone broke it up. We wanted to take them there," Notre Dame starting strong safety George Streeter said years later. "Quite frankly, for me, I wasn't paying attention to the score. I wanted to win the fight."

Stadium security and law enforcement officers stepped in to end it.

Both teams withdrew to their locker rooms.

Fifth-year senior Wes Pritchett, the middle linebacker who called the plays in the Irish defensive huddle, threw his helmet across the room.

Spit flew from Frank Stams's mouth as the outside linebacker pumped up the defense that had gathered around him.

Blood rushed to the hands of quarterback Tony Rice, who had just been throwing punches in the clash.

Joe Moore, Notre Dame's grizzled offensive line coach, who had graduated summa cum laude from football's old school, cracked a green slate chalkboard with a kick.

"The whole thing put me in a fighting mood," said Andy Heck, a quiet team captain and the starting offensive tackle.

The room grew quiet when head coach Lou Holtz addressed the team. The words that came out of his mouth were unexpected, a character departure, and they recharged the enraged atmosphere that had been subdued by his presence.

The skirmish with Miami made the statement that Notre Dame would no longer be pushed around. At the time, the Fighting Irish had not even reached the midpoint of the season.

By the end of the 1988 campaign, this Notre Dame squad would leave a path of battered All-American quarterbacks in its wake, give birth to legends, restore the school's stature in the game, win a national title, and accomplish something no other team in the history of college football has done.

CHAPTER 2

The Ashes

In fifth grade Gerry Faust whistled the Notre Dame fight song as he rode his bicycle home from football practice in Dayton, Ohio. Back in the era when you could actually try out for a premier college football program, Faust took his quarterback skills to South Bend in an attempt to play for Frank Leahy. He stood eighth in a line of sixteen quarterbacks trying out that day. "I saw the first seven throw the football and I realized I couldn't play there," he said.

When he left, he thought, *If I can't play there, maybe one day I could coach there.*

Faust played quarterback for the University of Dayton. Then he spent two seasons as an assistant coach at Dayton's Chaminade High School, his alma mater and the place where his dad, Gerry Faust Sr., was the head coach. He left Chaminade to become the first head coach at Archbishop Moeller High School in Cincinnati. The school didn't have a team before Faust arrived. It had a national powerhouse when he left.

In eighteen years at the all-boys school of nearly a thousand students, Faust posted a 174-17-2 record. His teams went undefeated seven times. His 1976 Crusaders squad outscored opponents 488–40. He won four national titles. He won five Ohio state championships in his last six seasons. At his direction, his players prayed the Hail Mary on the sideline before important plays.

Moeller's success made it a recruiting pipeline for Notre Dame. Sixteen of Faust's players, including All-American linebacker Bob Crable, went on to South Bend. The boy from Dayton, the one who whistled the "Victory March" and tried out at QB, never lost his love for the university. In 1977, Faust sent a letter to Fr. Edmund Joyce, Notre Dame's executive vice president, who oversaw athletics. Father Joyce wrote him back, and to this day Faust remembers the letter verbatim:

> *Coach, we're elated and excited that you would be interested in being the head football coach at the University of Notre Dame. But we're very happy with coach Dan Devine and we expect him to be here for years. But we'd also like to thank you for all the quality young men sent from Moeller High School. Not only are they great football players, but they are outstanding human beings in life.*
>
> *God bless you.*
>
> *Go Irish,*
>
> *Fr. Edmund P. Joyce*

Then, in August of 1980, Devine announced he would retire at the end of the season. This was the opening for Faust. At the time there were reasons to believe Faust could be an ideal pick to lead the Irish. He had built a nationally recognized high school dynasty. His players were good kids. He was a Catholic who attended Mass every day, and to say he wanted to be at Notre Dame would be making an enormous understatement. When he became the head coach he was moved to tears at his first practice.

There were also reasons to question Faust's ability to succeed at the college level. Faust was also a lunchroom supervisor at Moeller.

How could a lunchroom supervisor hold one of the most scrutinized jobs in both college football and the Catholic Church? How could he compete for recruits against college coaches like Bo Schembechler and Joe Paterno who had been doing it for years? How could a high school coach win at *the* University of Notre Dame?

Gene Corrigan took over as Notre Dame's athletic director in January of 1981, but he said the hiring of a high school coach gave him second thoughts about accepting the position.

"I'm a history major, and I was worried. The only high school coach who had ever made it was Paul Brown. There had never been one," Corrigan said. "That's just too much for a guy to come in and handle a job like this. This is a job where everybody in the world figures their season is good if they end up beating you. That's a lot for a guy coming from high school."

However, Faust wasn't just any high school coach. He constructed Moeller football into a specimen for others to behold. Cincinnati pro teams—football's Bengals and baseball's Reds—studied his training regimen, which included ballet sessions and all-year weight lifting. He helped raise funds for a $1.4 million high school sports complex. His team had eighteen assistant coaches, twenty-five student managers, and two-hundred-page game programs. Before he left for Notre Dame, he had won ninety of his last ninety-three games.

Things started out well in South Bend. A record 35,675 fans attended Faust's first Blue–Gold intrasquad spring football game. The Irish entered the 1981 season as the third-ranked team in the country. They opened with a 27–9 home win against Louisiana State University. With that victory Notre Dame leaped to the top spot in the polls. "People said, in some seriousness," Corrigan recalled to *Sports Illustrated*, "that we might never lose again."

The following week, Faust and his No. 1–ranked Irish headed to Ann Arbor to face the eleventh-ranked Michigan Wolverines. This is where it started to go downhill. Notre Dame lost 25–7 and then followed that with a 15–14 defeat on the road against an unranked Purdue team. Notre Dame left the Associated Press Top 20 poll for the remainder of the season. In the twelve years preceding Faust, the Irish went unranked in fifteen polls. In his first year, the Irish went unranked in eleven straight polls. The team finished 5-6, the school's first losing campaign since 1963.

In Faust's second season the Irish climbed to the ninth spot in the polls with wins against No. 10 Michigan and No. 17 Miami. Then a home loss to unranked Arizona and a tie at Oregon left the Irish unranked. In early November, Notre Dame headed to Pitt for a showdown with the No. 1 team in the country. The Irish stunned the Dan Marino–led Panthers with a 31–16 win. They were 6-1-1 with three games to play. Then they dropped three straight to Penn State, Air Force, and Southern California to finish 6-4-1.

Outsiders might view the Faust era as simply mediocre, but in the eyes of a Notre Dame fan it looked more like something out of the book of Revelation. Two seasons: no bowl games, no ranking in the postseason polls.

Coaching at Notre Dame has a unique ghost-chasing aspect, and Faust was not within reach of any of these ghosts. With the exception of Knute Rockne, the first legend, every Fighting Irish coach works in the lingering shadows of those who came before him. These are the inescapable built-in comparisons that come with the job.

Rockne went 105-12-5 in thirteen years. He won three national titles. His players included the Four Horsemen, "the Gipper" George Gipp, and Curly Lambeau. He was an innovator, introducing a shifting formation on offense and using "shock troops"—starting second-string players to surprise and wear down the opposition. While college football was regional, Rockne set up games in New York City and around the country, making the Fighting Irish a national draw. He became an iconic figure and remains embedded in the country's pop culture consciousness. A movie starring Ronald Reagan as the Gipper was made about Rockne's life.

Frank Leahy, who played for Rockne, posted six undefeated seasons at Notre Dame, including a post–World War II streak that saw the Irish peel off a 36-0-2 run from 1946 to 1949. With military veterans filling the roster, Fr. Theodore Hesburgh,* a Notre Dame luminary and the school's legendary former president, said they "had players who could beat the Chicago Bears." Leahy won four national titles and coached four Heisman Trophy winners—Angelo Bertelli, Johnny Lujack, Leon Hart, and Johnny Lattner.

Even though Ara Parseghian left the job after the 1974 season, his aura still loomed large on the campus where Faust sought success. In eleven seasons at the helm, Parseghian resurrected a down program, winning two national championships and 84 percent of his games. His worst season was an 8-3 campaign in 1972, and the Irish still finished ranked fourteenth. Devine followed Parseghian and was never quite fully embraced by all corners of the Notre Dame football universe. Devine won a national championship and coached Joe Montana, but rumors of his ouster—and possible replacement with Parseghian—started just seven games into his tenure. Devine was 5-2 at the time.

Faust's third year was highlighted by a Liberty Bowl win against Boston College and Doug Flutie. They started the season ranked fifth, and ended up in a lower-tier bowl, which they almost didn't go to, and finished 7-5.

Students began to openly mock Faust. In Bookstore Basketball, the annual, campus-wide five-on-five outdoor tournament, Faust played with four assistant coaches on The Old Men on the Block. In

---

*After serving as professor and chairman of the Department of Religion, Father Hesburgh became Notre Dame's executive vice president in 1949. He was the school president from 1952–1987.

Faust's first-round game their opponents, five engineering students called The Esophagus Constrictors, pulled off their sweatshirts to unveil green T-shirts, a good-natured dig at Faust having the Irish wear green jerseys in the previous season's win against Southern California. In the second round, Your Freudian Slip went for the public insult. The team sported football jerseys from Michigan State, Miami, Pitt, Penn State, and Air Force—the five schools that beat Notre Dame in '83.

Faust's football teams consistently blundered in big spots. In 1984, they lost 36–32 to No. 11 South Carolina. The lowlight was an offensive lineman slipping and kicking the ball out of the quarterback's hands, causing a fumble at the Gamecocks' 1-yard line. This was the third consecutive home loss for the Irish, the first time they had done that since 1956.

In their next game, the Irish were double-digit underdogs when they upended No. 7 LSU, 30–22, in Baton Rouge. Although at this point a win against a top 10 team didn't matter. The "Oust Faust" movement had already begun and continued to gain momentum.

After that LSU win, Faust and the headline quote "I'm gonna make it" landed on the cover of *Sports Illustrated*. The feature article depicted Faust as a prayerful, besieged, and dedicated coach. There were those who stood by Faust, but other alums and the devoted fans who never attended the school—the subway alums—unleashed their ill feelings in letters to the nation's premier sports magazine.

So Gerry Faust is a nice guy—he prays a lot and is an excellent recruiter—but that doesn't make him a major college football coach. The pap offered by the author in an attempt to justify Gerry's record at Notre Dame was revolting to this alumnus.

—*Charles Duryea, Hudson, N.Y.*

"Pray for me, who am so miserable." Instead of Gerry Faust uttering this prayer to Saint Jude these days, thousands of loyal Notre Dame fans are doing it. Faust says he would never stay if Notre Dame didn't want him. We don't want him!

—*Joe (Superfan) Thilman, Troy, Mich.*

"I didn't mind the fans when they were yelling or getting mad . . . You know what, they love Notre Dame and if they didn't love Notre Dame they wouldn't get upset," Faust said. "That's what makes Notre Dame so great. Its fan base."

His undying love for Notre Dame, which remains today, did not save him from the battering. By the end of his fourth season, Faust's likeness had been hanged in effigy. He had been asked to resign by *The Cincinnati Enquirer*—the newspaper that covered him at Moeller—and he failed to connect with some of his players.

The seniors actually opposed the trip to the Liberty Bowl in '83, and three team votes had to be taken to gain approval. Faust ended his use of sideline prayers because the players didn't buy into the idea that saying a Hail Mary would help the team get a first down. Quarterback Blair Kiel had led a campaign to shorten practices. Eventually they were cut down from three to two hours.

Forget that the raspy-voiced Faust loaded a roster with thirty *Parade* high school All Americans. Forget that he day-tripped to Hawaii for a coaches clinic so he could get back to work. Forget that he worked half a day, had knee surgery, and returned to the office the next day. Against the backdrop of Notre Dame lore the losses were intolerable.

After his fourth season, Faust met privately with Father Hesburgh.

"You better fire me. I'm just going to ruin this thing," Faust said to Father Hesburgh.

"Hey, we signed a five-year contract with you, and if you lose every game you're still going to be coach for this season. So I don't want to talk about it. We don't play those games. Now, if you just want to walk away, I can't control that, but you probably don't."

"I don't," Faust said.

"Well, I'm not about to fire you. We signed a five-year contract and that means five years."

End of meeting.

This was the Notre Dame way. Under the leadership of Hesburgh-Joyce every football coach had five years. Period.

"When he got here, in the big time, there's a big difference between high school and college coaching and I found that out," Father Hesburgh said.

Of Faust's 26 losses at Notre Dame, 14 were by a touchdown or less, but most of those close defeats came in Faust's first three seasons. In that final year, the losses got less competitive and the ineptitude amped up.

There was trouble with basics, such as the number of players legally allowed on the field—eleven. Against Purdue, Notre Dame revived a Boilermakers touchdown drive after being penalized for having twelve men on the field. A week later they lined up with fourteen players against Air Force. Then a month after that a timeout had to be called because sixteen men were on the field against Navy.

Indecision as to whether to punt, go for it, or kick a field goal led to John Carney rushing a wayward 59-yard field goal attempt against Air Force. The game ended with Notre Dame's fourth consecutive loss to the Falcons, a service academy.

Playing No. 1 Penn State, the first of three games against ranked opponents that would finish the 1985 season, Notre Dame had 5 turnovers in a 36–6 loss. The close of the Faust era was nigh.

While the media turned its attention toward rumored replacements, Faust focused on the last home game for the seniors against

No. 17 LSU. Down 10–7 with less than two minutes to go, the Irish drove for a potential game-winning touchdown.

Quarterback Steve Beuerlein dropped back and threw to a wide open Tim Brown in the middle of the field. Brown took his eyes off the ball to look at the open path between him and the end zone. He looked back and it was too late. The ball bounced off him and ricocheted into the arms of an LSU defender. Interception. LSU ball. Game over.

As Faust met LSU coach Bill Arnsparger at midfield for the obligatory postgame handshake, a Notre Dame assistant coach grabbed Faust's attention.

"You've got to get in the locker room."

"What's wrong?" Faust asked.

"Tim Brown's crying."

"What's he crying for?"

"Said he lost the game. Said if he makes that catch he would've scored a touchdown."

Faust headed to the locker room for a sight he would never forget. The losses didn't matter. The bumbling plays faded to the background. The "Oust Faust" chatter had never penetrated his world. This did.

Tim Brown sat slouched in the back corner of the locker room, crying profusely. Faust went over and put his arm around him.

"Timmy, what's wrong?"

"Coach, I lost the game. If I make that catch, I score."

"Timmy, you didn't lose the game. I lost the game. If I made three or four different calls, you wouldn't have had to make that catch and I would see you walk out of here, truly a Notre Dame man."

In those moments—seeing his receiver crying, hearing Brown blame himself—Faust decided to expedite the inevitable.

"Right then I decided to step down," he said.

The next day, Faust told his family his decision. He then contacted Father Hesburgh, who was attending an international nuclear disarmament meeting, and asked him not to tell Father Joyce. On Tuesday morning, Faust met with Father Joyce as he did every week.

At the start of the meeting Father Joyce slammed his hand on the table. "We win that game, we've got a winning season," he said.

"I've got to step down," Faust interrupted him.

Father Joyce got up, walked around his desk, gave Faust a hug, and said, "Coach, I was hoping you'd do this."

"Father, you let me live my dream. Notre Dame needs a new direction. We need a new coach. The players need it. The student body needs it. The school needs it. I can't thank you enough for the five years," Faust told him.

For Faust this was just the right thing to do, and doing it when he did further displayed his care for the university.

"They had to hire someone then so they wouldn't miss out on recruiting. That's why I stepped down before the season was over," Faust said.

The search committee for Notre Dame's next head coach met at a kitchen table in Granger, Indiana. The entire committee was made up of two men—Corrigan and Parseghian. The kitchen table was in Parseghian's house.

The athletic director and the two-time national-championship-winning coach put together an initial list of five men. All five were Catholic, and all five had head-coaching experience in the NFL or college. Media reports listed former Philadelphia Eagles coach Dick Vermeil, UCLA's Terry Donahue, Maryland's Bobby Ross, Virginia's George Welsh, and Lou Holtz of Minnesota.

Parseghian said it came down to Welsh and Holtz. Notre Dame officials only spoke to one man for the job.

"Lou has a lot of charisma," said Parseghian, who had followed Holtz's career and got to know him by doing color commentary for some of Holtz's games at Arkansas. "He was excellent strategically. He was abreast of any trend. He just had a lot on the ball."

While language did not exist in his contract with Minnesota, the word in public was that Holtz had a "Notre Dame clause." If Minnesota accepted a bowl bid and Holtz was offered the Notre Dame job, he could accept the post with the Fighting Irish and terminate his contract with the Big Ten school, according to Holtz's memoir.

The clause wasn't Holtz's way of waiting for the Notre Dame job to open. He had to bring improvement to Minnesota in order for it to kick in. The Gophers' last bowl appearance was six years before Holtz arrived. The team had gone 24-41-1 in that time, with a dismal 4 wins in the two seasons preceding Holtz.

In the locker room after Minnesota posted a win that would ensure a bowl invitation, Holtz reminded Gophers Athletics Director Paul Giel that accepting the invite would set the Notre Dame clause in motion.

"He always told me years before that Notre Dame was his dream job," Corrigan said.

Corrigan had known Holtz since the coach had been at William & Mary. When Corrigan was the athletic director at Virginia, Holtz was a head coach in the same conference at North Carolina State. When Faust resigned, Holtz's son Skip was already attending Notre Dame, and Corrigan's son Tim was a classmate.

Before any offer was made, Corrigan had to let Holtz know a few things about coaching at Notre Dame. First, Holtz's salary would be less than $100,000. Under the leadership of Father Hesburgh and Father Joyce, no one, including coaches, made more money than the university's provost.

He couldn't accept junior college transfers. That wasn't something Notre Dame did. "They just won't do that. It's part of who they are," Corrigan said.

There were no athletic dorms to offer recruits. Football players lived among the rest of the student body.

"Understand, this is more like William & Mary than any other place where you've worked," Corrigan told Holtz.

Then there was the admissions part of the conversation. "You're going to submit names, and Admissions is going to make a decision. You're not going to get them in based on NCAA [test] scores," Corrigan said. "The admissions people are not going to take anybody that they don't feel can graduate."

"I wanted him to understand. I didn't want him to come to me after two or three games and say, 'We've got to change this.'"

Father Hesburgh credits Father Joyce with overseeing the Athletic Department during the duo's tenure, but before any head football coach was officially hired, Father Hesburgh had to meet with him. The meeting with Holtz wasn't much different than the others.

"Look, I don't care what you know from other schools, but you come here, you're not just an athletic guy, you're an academic guy and you're dedicated to the school. We have a real tough set of rules. You read our rules?" Father Hesburgh asked.

"Yes, sir," the coach answered.

"Are you prepared to carry them out to the letter with no fudging?"

"Yes. I am."

"You're hired."

Father Hesburgh recalled, "It was that simple. But I always got that commitment from them personally before offering them the job."

At his first press conference, Holtz began to charm the Notre Dame media corps. The program had its new leader, and it was less than twenty-four hours since Faust resigned.

Thanksgiving week meant Notre Dame played its final game of the regular season, either at USC or another warm-weather spot if the

Irish had played the Trojans at home that year. On Tuesday, the day Faust announced his resignation, the players had been sent in different groups to eat Thanksgiving meals with various families in the South Bend area. When the evening news came on TV, that's when many of them heard their coach had stepped down. The next day, the team headed to Miami, but the chatter on the plane wasn't about the opponent. It was about the shake-up in the program.

"I made the mistake of not talking to the kids about it. I just went on with practice—'Come on, let's get ready for Miami,'" Faust said.

After losing its opener to Florida, Miami peeled off nine straight victories, including a 27–14 handling of No. 3 Oklahoma in Norman.* Before the Hurricanes took the field against Notre Dame, they were already headed to the Sugar Bowl and had climbed to No. 4 in the country. They couldn't understand how voters continued to rank Oklahoma ahead of them. They had an outside shot at the national championship, and they were gunning for it. Miami knew No. 1 Penn State had beaten Notre Dame by 30; they wanted to beat the Irish by more. The 'Canes were intent on a statement-making, attention-grabbing win. The Irish were 5-5 and in a bit of disarray.

Miami's second-year head coach, Jimmy Johnson, gathered his team in the Orange Bowl locker room moments before kickoff. He delivered this message: "We get a break, things go our way, let's pour it on them. Pour it on them and don't let them up. Play with class. Play with poise. Do whatever it takes."

Meanwhile, CBS's Pat O'Brien offered the report on Faust's final pregame words at Notre Dame. "It was the shortest locker room speech I've ever heard," O'Brien said. "He said, 'Let's go kick their heads off and send them to the Sugar Bowl with two losses.'"

---

*The game saw the Sooners lose their starting quarterback, Troy Aikman, to a season-ending injury. He was replaced by freshman Jamelle Holieway, who became a wishbone sensation.

This was the nationally televised showcase game on CBS that Saturday afternoon. Play-by-play man Brent Musburger opened the broadcast by turning to Ara Parseghian, the color commentator, to ask him what happened during the Faust era. An obvious question, but it came with an undertone of *How could this have happened to one of America's sports dynasties?*

"To summarize with just one word: inconsistency," Parseghian said.

Miami received the opening kickoff and set their offense to cruise control. They lined up with quarterback Vinny Testaverde, who was a year away from winning the Heisman Trophy. They chewed up the clock with long drives as they sliced through the Notre Dame defense, taking a 13–0 lead on their first three possessions. With 47 seconds left in the first quarter, the Irish had not entered Miami territory. They didn't have a first down.

On the next Notre Dame possession, quarterback Steve Beuerlein led the Irish into the Miami side of the field. Scrapes of Hurricane orange already tattooed the side of his golden helmet as he crouched under center. He dropped back and faked a handoff to sophomore fullback Frank Stams. The fullback had to immediately lay a block on blitzing safety Selwyn Brown. Beuerlein wanted to roll out but stopped in his tracks to avoid the pressure. He turned, faced upfield, set his feet, and threw the ball across his body, avoiding the sack from another Hurricane player who lunged and leaped, swinging an arm at the pass.

Beuerlein wanted to connect with Allen Pinkett, Notre Dame's most-utilized offensive threat. Some joked that Notre Dame ran the 4-P offense: Pinkett-Pinkett-Pass-Punt. This was Pinkett's final game at Notre Dame. He would leave as the school's all-time leading rusher, but he wouldn't make this catch. As Beuerlein's pass traveled toward the running back, Miami safety Bennie Blades swooped in, swallowing up the ball in his midsection and keeping stride as he headed for the end zone.

Blades had 61 yards of grass separating him from a touchdown. With no barrier between himself and 6 points, he switched the ball to his inside hand so the outside hand, the one everyone could see better, could start the celebration. For the last 30 yards Blades trotted and wagged his No. 1 finger above his helmet, though he managed to stop the finger flaunting to high-five Selwyn Brown at the 3-yard line. Then the pair galloped into the end zone together. Miami 20. Notre Dame 0.

The Blades interception return has been called the birth of Miami's swagger, the braggadocious, taunting-flaunting style that marked the 'Canes era of college football dominance. Unfortunately for Notre Dame, the interception was not even the midway point in a historic beating that would have far greater low points.

Notre Dame scored to make it 20–7. Miami answered right back with another touchdown drive. Miami's offense scored on every possession with the exception of the two that were stopped by the end of the first half and the end of the game.

With 20 seconds left in the first half, the 'Canes had a third down at their own 30-yard line. They passed and converted it for the first down. Forget football logic, which would have been to run out the clock with a 20-point halftime lead. Instead, Miami passed and risked turning the ball over in a possible momentum-shifting play. The play call and conversion made the statement *We own you. We can do anything we want today.*

"I never felt sympathy for them," freshman wide receiver Michael Irvin told the *Sun Sentinel.* "Once you got an ant down, you stomp him with a sledgehammer."

With the outcome already decided, the blowout became the main story for the broadcast.

"Johnson and the 'Canes, you would think, would go to work on the clock right now, Ara," Musburger said with Miami up 30–7 and driving.

"I imagine they'll keep it on the ground right now," Parseghian said as Testaverde completed a 14-yard pass to the Irish 20-yard line. A few plays later, Testaverde connected with Irvin to go up 37–7.

Notre Dame didn't help itself. With no defenders in sight, Irish backs and receivers dropped passes. Linemen missed cut blocks and looked like babies crawling on the ground as Miami players moved beyond them to attack the ball.

With Miami up 44–7 and less than seven minutes to play, Johnson went for and converted a fourth-down play at the Notre Dame 20.

"They try to pick up the first down and keep the massacre going," Musburger said.

"This would be a good time for Jimmy Johnson to show a little compassion," Parseghian said.

As if on a nightmarish cue, on the next play after Ara's call for mercy, Geoff Torretta, Testaverde's backup, hit Andre Brown for a touchdown. Miami led 51–7 with 6:11 to play.

A few minutes later the 'Canes only needed ten men on the field to block a Notre Dame punt. Miami recovered the ball in the end zone to cap the scoring at 58–7. Pat O'Brien reported from the Notre Dame sideline that a couple of Fighting Irish teammates were shouting and shoving each other.

Miami reveled in the 51-point victory. It was the second-most points scored against the Irish in the 878 games since Notre Dame starting playing football in 1887.

"I don't like Gerry Faust and I don't like Notre Dame. I don't like their false tradition," guard Paul O'Connor told *The Miami News*.

Parseghian's comments led to a media quarrel. *Miami Herald* sports editor Edwin Pope wrote a front-page column defending Johnson's never-let-up tactic and took umbrage at Parseghian's remarks. Pope pointed to Parseghian's Notre Dame teams running it up—beating Pitt 69–13, Duke 64–0, and Army 62–3.

In interviews then and now, Parseghian stands by his broadcast comments. He knows his teams posted huge blowout victories, but those happened with the second string playing most of the second half and with him calling basic offensive and defensive plays. He even sent Pope a letter outlining what happened when his Notre Dame teams demolished opponents.

"Very simply, that would never have happened had I been the Miami coach. We would've won, maybe 45–0. You don't tell your kids to lay down. You can't do that. But you can put in your reserves and run off tackle and run up the middle."

Back in the CBS studio in New York during the postgame broadcast, commentator Pat Haden called Jimmy Johnson "bush" league. Jim Nantz said it was obvious Notre Dame players quit during Faust's final game.

Toward the end of the broadcast, CBS aired a perfectly lame mid-'80s music montage with Faust-era highlights and miscues set to the Lite-FM sappiness of Quincy Jones's song of heartbreak "Just Once."

The game at Miami is forever an offensive sight for Notre Dame eyes. The lopsided score would not be forgotten. Those figures, 58–7, were permanently etched in the Notre Dame football psyche. This was the undeniable state of Notre Dame football. Nevertheless, Parseghian's final words on the broadcast offered hope.

"Notre Dame will rise again. From these ashes will come the winning Notre Dame team."*

---

*Parseghian had said this once before. It was after the 1973 Orange Bowl in which Notre Dame lost 40–6 to Nebraska. The following season, Parseghian led the Irish to an undefeated national championship.

CHAPTER 3

In Lou We Trust

Lou Holtz watched Miami thrash Notre Dame from Palm Springs. He was there for the weekend with his family. The short vacation at a Minnesota booster's home was planned before he took his new job.

"You just looked at it and you felt bad," Holtz said.

Holtz watched the game with his eyes on the Irish's execution. He looked for what could be corrected. He wanted to see the team's attitude.

"It is what it is. That's where I'm going. There wasn't any sighing or complaining," Holtz said. "Here's where we are and here's where we have to go."

Holtz left the West Coast and headed for South Bend. Presumably, he had far easier travels than the team he was about to inherit.

Sore, tired, hungry, and beaten, the Fighting Irish football team waited in the Miami airport because of a weather delay. Players and assistant coaches grouped themselves into different cliques. Some were loud and pitching pennies. Others took the defeat solemnly. Then members of the different groups started to have words. Faust had to step in and address the behavior before they boarded a tumultuous flight.

"The plane was pitching and dropping. I was certain that thing was going down," said Andy Heck, a freshman tight end.

As they got close to the Michiana Regional Airport, the pilot's voice came through the loudspeaker. He announced he would attempt a landing. The aircraft descended below cloud level. Out of their windows, players saw the lights of the terminal through a blizzard.

The plane closed in on the ground. At the time wheels would normally touch the runway and begin a skidding stop, the pilot pulled out, raising the plane. They couldn't land safely. They flew through another hour of turbulence to Chicago. There they waited for buses to pick them up for the snow-filled four-hour ride back to campus.

"We end up pulling into South Bend at five or six in the morning completely embarrassed and depressed," said Beuerlein, the quarterback.

Within hours the determined new coach and the team in shambles would collide in the team meeting room in the Athletic and Convocation Center—the heart of Notre Dame's athletic facilities.* They didn't know much about Holtz. Most players had heard only snippets from news reports. What was this new guy all about? Would they fit into his scheme? Still tired from the beating and the travel, they sat or slouched in the theater-style room. A backup center and future co-captain, Chuck Lanza, was in the front row with his feet resting on the raised platform from which the coach would speak.

The back doors of the room burst open. Holtz, in a trot, moved to the front. He immediately saw the nonchalance and was disconcerted; such casualness should not accompany meeting the new guy in charge. With a few feet separating him from Lanza, his eyes locked on the player. "Get your feet on the floor. Sit up straight and act like you're interested in what I'm talking about."

---

*The Athletic and Convocation Center was renamed the Joyce Athletic and Convocation Center in 1987 after Notre Dame's longtime executive vice president Fr. Edmund P. Joyce.

"With the very first words that came out of his mouth there was a very clear understanding that this was different. This is serious. 'If you don't buy into what I'm saying, it's okay. You won't be part of it.' We all got that message very clearly, very quickly," Beuerlein said.

Within the first ten seconds of meeting their new coach, the players sat up straight, took off their hats, and put their feet on the floor. The thin, glasses-wearing 5' 8" guy who spoke with a lisp addressed the lack of relationship in the room.

"I know you didn't have any choice in who you would hire. If you had a choice, I wouldn't have been hired. But you had no choice.

"But what I want you to know is I had a choice. I had a good job. I could've stayed where I was. I came here because I wanted to be with you. So I chose you even though you didn't choose me, and we're all here for the same common cause."

He told them he believed in them. He spoke about where he wanted the program to go and how they would get there as a team. It didn't put an instant end to the discord that reared itself in the Miami airport, "but it set the tempo," he said.

"More than anything the culture just automatically shifted when he came on board. He told us how to win football games," said Mark Green, a freshman flanker.

Holtz used the meeting as an hours-long seminar on who you had to be to win. He wrote "trust, love, and commitment" on a board behind him and told the team this would be the focus. He listed individual priorities on another board—God, family, school, athletics, social life. Delivering more than coachspeak bluster, the new guy in front of the room spoke with an unwavering belief that the program would be a winner, and the players, if they followed the path he put in front of them, would be winners, too.

"It was very clear to all of us: This guy knows what he's doing," Beuerlein said.

•   •   •

Coaching football wasn't Holtz's initial plan. The post-high-school future looked like a job at the mill and the ability to buy a car. That would've been just swell.

Holtz was born on January 6, 1937, toward the end of The Great Depression and nearly five years before the United States entered World War II. He was the middle child, between two sisters, born to Anne Marie and Andrew Holtz. His first home was a two-room basement apartment in Follansbee, a northern West Virginia town wedged in the sliver between Ohio and Pennsylvania. His paternal grandfather had moved there to work in a steel mill after leaving a Pennsylvania coal-mining job. The family was poor, like most in the area at the time. They had no refrigerator, no shower, and no privacy. They bathed in the sink, which was next to a bed. He had one outfit, a pair of overalls and a flannel shirt, Holtz wrote in his memoir.

The family never went without food or football, though. Holtz's introduction to the game came as he sat on his uncles' laps listening to the radio broadcasts of Notre Dame and Ohio State games. When World War II came, the Holtz men enlisted in the military. With his dad serving in the navy, Holtz's mom moved the family to East Liverpool, Ohio, to live with her parents, Louis and Carey Tychonievich, immigrants from Chernobyl in the Ukraine.

Grandpa Lou told him stories about Rockne's Irish. While hearing about the 1924 national champions and the Four Horsemen, young Lou was indoctrinated, by his grandpa, with the logic that "every good Catholic had to support Notre Dame."

In 1946, Lou's uncle Leo Holtz took him to his first college football game—the University of Illinois at the University of Pittsburgh. The Illini drubbed Pitt 33–7, and Lou became an avid Illinois fan, splitting his allegiance with the juggernaut that was the Frank Leahy–led Irish.*

---

*Ironically, Notre Dame pounded Illinois 26–6 the week after Holtz saw the Illini. The Illinois team won the Rose Bowl that year, and Notre Dame

Holtz started playing football at age nine, "an eighty-pound wonder boy who made up for his lack of size by being slow and weak," he wrote. Never the star athlete, he had a knack for knowing the responsibilities of every position on the field. His coach at East Liverpool High School, Wade Watts, picked up on this. After Holtz's junior year, Watts left East Liverpool to become the head coach at Canton McKinley High School. Before Watts departed he asked for a meeting with Holtz and his parents. Watts told the trio that Lou should go to college and become a coach. The idea of Holtz in college didn't exist before. Nobody in his family had ever gone to college. His mother was her high school valedictorian; his father left school in the third grade to get a job. That conversation served as the launching pad.

Holtz played linebacker at Kent State. During spring practice leading up to his final year of eligibility he tore cartilage in his knee, and his playing career ended. However, his coaching career began when he stayed on at Kent to help with the freshman squad.*

He went on to assistant coaching gigs at Iowa, William & Mary, and Connecticut. Then he accepted a coaching spot at the University of South Carolina. By the time he arrived in Columbia the head coach who hired him had resigned. The new coach, Paul Dietzel, fired him and on the way out of that meeting asked Holtz if he had thought about getting into another profession. Even though the money for an assistant coach was sparse and the transient lifestyle wasn't a great fit for family, Holtz and his wife, Beth, had made a pact when they were at Connecticut that Lou would stick with coaching for at least five more years. Now he had no job, two kids,

---

won the national championship, the first of four consecutive undefeated seasons for the Irish.

*By rule, freshmen were not allowed to play varsity football. The rule changed in 1972.

and a pregnant wife, and the twenty-eight-year-old Holtz made a list of 108 lifetime goals. The list included jumping out of a plane, meeting the pope, having dinner at the White House, and coaching for Notre Dame.

Two months after being let go by Dietzel, Holtz was brought back with a 27 percent pay cut. His responsibilities included overseeing the team's academics, scouting opponents, and running the scout squad. He stayed at South Carolina for two seasons. Then his big break came. A man Holtz idolized, Woody Hayes, asked him to coach defensive backs at Ohio State. This was a chance to go back home to Ohio and learn from an undisputed winner.

Hayes was a towering figure in college coaching. By the time he sought out Holtz to coach his secondary, he had already won three national championships. He was, of course, also known for a temper that could get unwieldy.*

Holtz got plenty of advice to turn down the Ohio State job.† First he accepted it. Then he turned it down. He called Hayes at the home of a recruit to let him know he wouldn't be heading to Columbus. Hayes responded with a profanity-laced tirade and then reminded Holtz that whatever it was that made him initially say yes to the job would never go away. Holtz was back in. That year, 1968, Ohio State won the national championship.

After the single season at Ohio State, Holtz claimed his first

---

*After spending twenty-eight years at the helm of Ohio State football, Hayes was fired the morning after hitting Clemson's Charlie Bauman during the 1978 Gator Bowl. Bauman had intercepted a fourth-quarter pass and been tackled out of bounds on the Ohio State sideline when Hayes got physical with the player.

†At the same time Holtz received the Buckeye tender, he considered an offer to coach at Georgia Tech under head coach Bud Carson, who would go on to design the Pittsburgh Steelers Steel Curtain defenses of the 1970s.

head-coaching job. He went back to William & Mary and led the school to the Tangerine Bowl in his second season. Then an administration change deemphasized athletics. Holtz left after his third season and became the head coach at North Carolina State. Before Holtz got to Raleigh, the Wolfpack had won a total of 9 games in the previous three seasons. With Holtz at the reins, NC State went to four consecutive bowls and averaged more than 8 wins a year.

He left Raleigh for the NFL with what he called a "so-so commitment." Holtz coached the New York Jets during Joe Namath's last year with the team. He tried to get pro players to sing a fight song. He used practice time to teach them how to line up for the national anthem. This wasn't a good fit. He went 3-10 in 1976, resigning before the last game of the season.

Holtz returned to the college game after the brief NFL stint. There was an opening with the Arkansas Razorbacks. Head coach Frank Broyles—an Arkansas legend—was stepping aside but would remain as athletic director.

Holtz wasn't the only man up for the job. The Razorbacks defensive coordinator was in the running. He had played for Broyles. He won a national championship with Arkansas. He was Jimmy Johnson.

Broyles chose Holtz over Johnson. Holtz wanted Johnson to stay. He offered him a position on the staff. Johnson declined. He went to the University of Pittsburgh to work as the defensive coordinator under Jackie Sherrill.

Four of Broyles's last five seasons were mediocre, break-even campaigns. As at NC State, Holtz was tasked with making a winner out of a down program.

In his first season in Fayetteville, Holtz took the Razorbacks, who were unranked in the preseason, to a 10-1 regular season. Armed with Monte Kiffin as the defensive coordinator, Arkansas gave up an average of 8.6 points per game. The reward: the No. 6

ranking in the country and an Orange Bowl date with heavily favored Oklahoma and the No. 2–ranked Sooners.

A few days before Christmas, Holtz suspended three players from the game after an incident that involved police being called to an Arkansas dorm and finding the players with a partially clothed female. No criminal charges were filed. Holtz's reasoning for the suspensions was that the player's violated the "door tight" rule. Holtz had established the rule with his team as a common sense guide to make the right choices and avoid the wrong ones. The suspended players—leading rusher Ben Cowins, leading receiver Donny Bobo, and backup running back Michael Forrest—accounted for about 75 percent of Arkansas's touchdowns. All three players were black. Attempting to avert the suspension, the players brought a civil rights suit in federal district court. Accusations of racism were hurled at Holtz. *The New York Times,* reacting to a claim made by the players' attorney, reviewed the racial makeup of Holtz's New York Jets roster. Holtz's appearance at a fund-raiser for North Carolina senator Jesse Helms, an anti-civil-rights Republican, was also brought into media reports. A rumored Orange Bowl boycott by Arkansas's African American players never came to fruition. "I treat everybody the same, I tell my players I'm prejudice, prejudiced to people who can block and tackle," Holtz said days before the game. "All I can say is I did what I thought was right and fair and honest."

In the legal tussle, Holtz was represented by Arkansas attorney general Bill Clinton. The court battle lasted less than a day after the players dropped the case.*

---

*The players claimed they wouldn't be able to call witnesses who had already traveled to the bowl game. The state said they knew they couldn't win the case. In Holtz's memoir *Wins, Losses, and Lessons,* he told his side of the story, which was that of a football coach being placed in the middle of the situation. The woman involved would not press charges if the university

On January 2, the underdog Razorbacks faced off against the Sooners. Earlier in the day at the Cotton Bowl, a Joe Montana–led Notre Dame team upended No. 1 Texas 38–10. Oklahoma thought they had one barrier between themselves and a national championship—a distracted Arkansas squad. It didn't work out as the oddsmakers predicted. Arkansas won 31–6. The Razorbacks' Roland Sales, an African American, set an Orange Bowl record with 205 rushing yards. Holtz was named Coach of the Year by the Football Writers Association of America. The upset cleared a path for Notre Dame to claim the national championship. It was the school's last one until Holtz led the Irish.

Holtz's national profile grew while he coached Arkansas. He won games and went to bowls, which always garners attention, and his charismatic quirks and quips added necessary elements for a media-built caricature. After the win that assured Arkansas the Orange Bowl bid against Oklahoma, Holtz was asked what he thought of fans throwing oranges on the field. "Thank God we didn't get invited to the Gator Bowl" was the response that got picked up in news wires across the country.

At the beginning of the '78 season, Holtz, along with two of his players, one of whom was Cowins, graced the cover of *Sports Illustrated*.* He ended up on *The Tonight Show* with Johnny Carson when Carson had an Oprah Winfrey–like aura and an audience of millions tuning in each night. There was Holtz doing a magic trick on Johnny's couch. Carson even put on one of those Razorback hog hats during Holtz's visit.

---

took disciplinary action, but the university was going to follow the lead of local law enforcement, which did not intend to press charges. This left Holtz to render a decision.

*In the article, Cowins addressed the suspension, saying, "I can't accept what he did but I respect it. It took a lot of courage. And I can't really say he has been unfair."

The coach had honed his quick wit and self-deprecating sense of humor as a charming defense mechanism for a kid with a lisp and glasses. He joked with a reporter that he knew three of his four children's names, but he didn't know his home address or phone number. He was driven and fiery, and in the rough, tough football world with serious figures like Hayes, Alabama's Paul "Bear" Bryant, and Penn State's Joe Paterno, Holtz delivered laughs.

Holtz won 73 percent of his games at Arkansas, but after a 6-5 mark in 1983, his seventh season there, Holtz met with Broyles. After the meeting, Holtz was no longer the Arkansas coach. Broyles said the coach was burned out. Holtz became the head coach at Minnesota four days later.

By the time Holtz arrived at Notre Dame he had spent sixteen years as a successful college coach. He had rebuilt programs. He had won big games leading lesser talent against storied programs.

"The guy is good. When he was at North Carolina State he was 2-2 against Paterno. That's all you have to know," said Beano Cook, a longtime college football authority and ESPN commentator.

Beyond the X's and O's, he came to South Bend with seasoned media savvy and had dealt with controversies. From the time in youth football when he learned everyone's position on the field to the years he spent at South Carolina scouting opponents like Alabama and LSU, he had studied the ingredients of success. The story of him at St. Aloysius grammar school processing at recess and dismissal to the "Notre Dame Victory March" is sweet, but being a fan and knowing a song is nonessential. Knowing who you are as a head coach is essential.

"You look at who's successful at Notre Dame and it's usually a college [head] coach who's been successful at other places previously. Frank Leahy at Boston College, Ara Parseghian at Northwestern, Dan Devine at Missouri, me at NC State, Arkansas, and

Minnesota. But that's because you have confidence in what you're doing and how you're doing it," Holtz said.

Holtz made some immediate changes to the uniform. He took the player names off the back of the jerseys—individualism was not part of the plan. He wanted a large ND on the helmet. He didn't know that the helmets were a reflection of the Golden Dome, the second-tallest building on campus, which is topped with an open-armed Mary, mother of Christ, for whom the school is named.*

He asked Father Joyce about branding the helmets with a nice-sized interlocking ND.

"That helmet represents Our Lady on the Dome," Father Joyce said.

"Well, have you ever thought of putting ND on the dome?" Holtz asked with a boyish smile.

"I don't think that's real funny," Father Joyce said.

Holtz would learn other on-the-job lessons unique to Notre Dame as well. Even though he was the coach, the one accountable for the wins, losses, and academics, early on he knew the program was bigger than the man. At many places coaches are given dominion over all things football. Notre Dame was different.

"If there are two things or three things at Notre Dame that are critical as a coach one is—it's not your team, not yours. It belongs to the students, the faculty, the alumni, thousands of people," Holtz said. "You're like the mascot. You've got to take care of the mascot…But it's not your team per se, you don't do what you want to do. You don't say what you want to say. You're just one part of it. It's so important to so many people that you feel that obligation."

---

*The tallest building on campus is the Basilica of the Sacred Heart.

CHAPTER 4

Waking Up the Roster

If discipline had left the Notre Dame program, it started to return with 6:00 A.M. winter conditioning.

In that first meeting Holtz told the team he believed in them, but he also said some players would prove him wrong.

"I wanted to see what price they were willing to pay," Holtz said. "I want to tell you something, 5:45 in South Bend when it's dark and snowing and it's very, very cold, you get out of bed after spending the night studying—hopefully studying—that would tell me about their commitment to winning and how soon they would prove me wrong, if they did prove me wrong. When they did show up, would they be grumbling? Complaining? Or would they just accept it?"

Weather posed the first obstacle in the workout. Bitter cold, biting winds, cloudy days, and snowstorms paint South Bend winters. The average temperature was 25 degrees in February '86. The mercury rose above 40 degrees only twice. It snowed on eighteen of the twenty-eight days. On the only day rain, snow, and fog weren't recorded, it was overcast.

At 5:30 A.M., when most players left the warmth of their dorm rooms, they traipsed along snow-covered sidewalks against 20 mph winds that made it feel like –21 degrees.

Workouts started at 6:00 A.M., not 6:01 or 6:02. So before six o'clock the players had to be lined up in their designated spots, standing an arm's length away from each other, fulfilling the expectation of military precision.

Garbage cans lined the multipurpose workout area in the Athletic and Convocation Center as the players grouped themselves by position. In sixty minutes they would go through eight stations. Some were sprints; others called for players to move side to side or back and forth on all fours. As soon as one station ended, everybody had to run to the next. If anybody walked, sauntered, or jogged, the whole group would have to go back to its previous station and run to the new one together. At some point, when they couldn't finish a drill, players doubled over and put the trash cans to use.

"The workouts were so intense that the guys who were hanging out until two or three o'clock in the morning drinking beer and eating pizza—they were puking that pizza up all over the place," said D'Juan Francisco, a freshman running back at the time.

It was still dark outside when the workouts—or "pukefest" as the players called them—finished. Starting fullback Frank Stams would head back to his dorm room to take a nap before classes. "I'd wake up and I thought I had the worst nightmare of my life," he said.

Soon the postconditioning catnaps stopped because players started oversleeping and missing their first class. A new rule was put in place. Whether or not there was a morning workout, everyone had to sign in for breakfast. It didn't matter if they ate, but they had to be at the training table to at least show they were awake.

After a couple of weeks the teamwide attitude adjustment started taking place. Staying out late became a faux pas. Players went to bed in their workout clothes to skip getting dressed once their alarms buzzed. When some of the bigger guys couldn't handle the drills, their teammates would come alongside and pull them to the finish. "You can't quit. You can't stop. You've got to go," they'd tell each other.

"We started to be more accountable," Francisco said. "You didn't want to be that guy who was out of shape that threw up, because people, your own teammates, talked about you if you were the guy who puked."

If players loathed the workouts and the interruption of how Notre Dame football life used to be, Holtz stood unfazed. All of it was calculated.

"If you think this is bad, this is what it takes to be a winner."

Sitting in class, Mark Green received a note. Grab your stuff, go to the football office, and meet with Coach Holtz.

He knew it took time for freshmen like himself to adjust to the academics. He figured he had screwed up his grades.

"Come in. Sit down," Holtz told him when he walked into the coach's office.

"Damn it. I knew I should've studied more for that test," Green said to himself.

The freshman was so distracted with his thoughts, all he knew was Holtz was telling a "little life story." Then the story ended.

"I just want you to know I just got word that your mom passed away," Holtz said.

Green stopped thinking about grades. He wept, and sadness fell on Holtz's face. Green sat and cried for ten minutes. The most important person in his life was gone.

"It's going to be all right. Don't worry about us. I want you to focus in on what's most important, and that's your family," Holtz said as he hugged Green. "Take care of what you need to take care of."

Green took the first flight he could get back to California. Every day his mother told him she loved him, and he would never hear her say it again. She taught him how to take care of himself. He knew how to cook, clean, and do his laundry because of her. She earned him the nickname "Clean Green" in high school because every night she hand-washed his practice pants, restoring them to their unblemished white state.

Green's parents never legally married, so when things soured that made it easier for Joyce Armstrong to move and take nine-year-old Mark and his two older sisters out of South Central Los Angeles and away from their father, Andrew Green.

Andy Green grew up in Vicksburg, Mississippi. He enlisted in the air force after high school, received an honorable discharge, and became a cork maker for Alcoa in Southern California. He rose to the level of foreman before taking an early retirement. That's about when Andy and Joyce stopped getting along.

To support the three children, Joyce worked as a housekeeper. The family needed food stamps. Their housing was partially paid for by the Section 8 government subsidy. They were evicted twice. One time in high school, Mark came home to find the eviction notice on the dead-bolted door. He called two buddies and emptied the place in the two hours of allotted time they had before all the family's belongings would be repossessed.

"No matter what the circumstance, she always found a way to put food on the table. We always had a roof over our head and something to eat," Green said.

By the time Mark hit junior high school, he, his mom, and his two sisters settled in a two-bedroom apartment in Riverside. The three children shared one room with bunk beds and a twin bed.

Mark flourished at Riverside Poly High School. In his sophomore year he came off the bench on a basketball team led by future NBA Hall of Famer Reggie Miller. His classmates elected him senior class president. He served on California's Black Student Union advisory board.

On the football field he became a consensus All American highlighted by *USA Today* first-team tailback honors.

By the time college coaches came calling for his son, Andy Green was dealing drugs, sometimes using them, and spending time in and out of jail. The relationship between father and son had pretty much disappeared.

When white men pulled up to an apartment building in Mark's neighborhood, it meant one of two things—"you're going to jail or you're being recruited," Green said. In his case, it was recruited. Among his visitors were Nebraska's Tom Osborne, UCLA's Terry Donahue, and USC's Ted Tollner.

Just after he knocked on the door, Gerry Faust separated himself from all the others.

"Ms. Green?" he asked Joyce when she opened the apartment door. She extended her arm to shake his hand. Faust grabbed her, hugged her, and gave her a kiss on the cheek. She shot her eyes toward Mark with a look that said, "A white man just kissed me—you're going with him." She had probably never been kissed by a white man in her life and the gesture sold her on Faust and Notre Dame. The decision was made.

Now, about a year after he chose to go to Notre Dame, Green had to say good-bye to his mother, whose death was caused by blood clots. While at home, he pondered transferring to USC or UCLA, but his sisters sat him down for a talk.

"Hey, look, Mom wanted you to be there. It was her choice as much as it was yours. You need to go back. Our mother would want you there, not here. Go back and finish what you started," they told him.

He returned to his team and the "pukefest."

On the recruiting scene, Holtz fulfilled the closer role. In the living room, he displayed a magnetism that appealed to both the parents and the football-playing teenager with superstar dreams. The man who set the scene before Holtz ever entered was Vinny Cerrato.

Cerrato was a charmer, a few years removed from his college playing days. He was young enough to relate to the players and answer the questions they would never ask the head coach or position coaches. He knew the talent needed to build a winner and he knew how to get it. He became so successful as a recruiter that schools eventually called for NCAA rule changes to limit his effectiveness.

Cerrato was born in Flushing, New York. The son of a furniture salesman and medical secretary, he grew up in Albert Lea, Minnesota, where he played football for the local high school. The 5'11" 155-pounder of Irish and Italian descent received offers to play at Iowa, Minnesota, and Nebraska. He went to Iowa State, where he played under Earle Bruce and developed a lifelong relationship with Mack Brown, who was an assistant coach. He became a graduate assistant at Minnesota after leaving the Cyclones.

When Holtz came to the Gophers from Arkansas, he kept Cerrato on the staff, though Cerrato went from coaching the receivers to serving as a gofer and "helping" coach the receivers. His duties included driving Holtz to and from the airport when the coach had speaking engagements and appearances.

After Holtz's first year at Minnesota, the recruiting coordinator spot came open. In a staff meeting, Holtz told his assistants that if they were interested in the position, they should talk to him. Cerrato didn't approach his boss. He wanted to be a running backs or receivers coach.

At the same time, Cerrato had a lot of contact with the group of Gopher backers in the Touchdown Club. When his head coach asked him to get a player a summer job in St. Louis, Cerrato lined it up in a few hours. The quick results showed Holtz something. He told Cerrato to come see him in his office.

"Why don't you be the recruiting coordinator?" Holtz asked.

Cerrato talked about his desire to be a position coach. Holtz, ever the closer with an eye for putting talent in the right spot, told

Cerrato to take the recruiting position and when those other jobs opened up he'd be first in line.

Once Cerrato took charge of recruiting, the desire to be a position coach disappeared.

Cerrato followed Holtz to Notre Dame, where he filled a unique role. He was a full-time assistant coach who had minute coaching duties. His near-sole focus was recruiting, which kept him on the road the majority of the time. To be an effective recruiter requires a tireless work ethic and the ability to tactfully gain relationships with the high school athlete and his mother, his coach, and the high school janitor, who will call when other college coaches come to visit a coveted star. Cerrato excelled in every area.

"There was no one like him," said CBS Sports Network's Tom Lemming, a pioneer of recruiting coverage dating back to the late 1970s. "He could relate to the kids better than anybody else could in the country at that time."

In the mid-to-late 1980s, if there was an outstanding recruit, schools from all across the country would take a shot at landing him on their campus. Otherwise, powerhouses Michigan, Ohio State, Florida State, Miami, and Oklahoma mainly staked out talent in their regions. Once Cerrato got to Notre Dame, he and Bill Rees of UCLA were the only true national recruiters. They set out to build pipelines all over the nation.

On a typical Sunday, the Notre Dame coaching staff meeting ended around noon. Cerrato would embed himself in his office, put the early NFL game on mute on his TV, and start dialing for talent. He started going down his list of the Fighting Irish's top 90 prospects. He took a break for dinner and then went back to calling until 11:00 P.M. During each call he was jotting down notes. He never had a short conversation. No matter who picked up the phone, Cerrato got the person talking and culled more and more information on the recruit.

"I had pretty good connections because I would make a point to get to know everybody and I would get to know who was important in the kid's decision making," Cerrato said. "I knew everybody in the family. I knew everything about the kid."

He repeated the calling process Monday, and by Tuesday night he would have reached all ninety. It became a weekly pattern, and soon the players and their families expected the phone to ring and to hear Cerrato on the other end. "The kid would say, 'Coach I was waiting for you to call at one, you normally call me at one, it's three o'clock.'"

While he flew throughout the country, Cerrato used nearly every layover moment to make calls to recruits and coaches. He had eyes and ears on the ground even when he wasn't there. He was on a first-name basis with the high school secretaries, the gatekeepers of the comings and goings.

During the football season, he told the Notre Dame assistant coaches not to worry about recruiting; he'd handle it. Once it was time for them to hit the road in the off-season, he handed them dossiers on their prospects and told them how many players they needed to sign from their assigned regions.

He used a clunky first-generation cell phone to call recruits from the sidelines of games. He would hold the phone—which was about the size of a box of frozen waffles—up to the crowd during the kickoff of a Notre Dame home game, putting the recruit right there.

"The kids would eat it up," Lemming said.

Being an Independent, the Irish didn't compete for a conference championship; they played for the national title. To do so they needed to recruit the same type of talent found on the rosters of Florida State and Miami, two programs that had become perennial powers in recent years.

"What do those teams have that we don't have? That's speed. We've got to go get speed. We needed to get speed," Cerrato said.

Speed had always been a necessity in football, but by the mid-1980s it had changed the game. Heavy-footed, big, mean guys with baby fat were once the perfect fit to play linebacker or lineman, but that had changed. Now, tough guys with speed typically reserved for running backs and receivers were sought for those roles.

"We never wanted to recruit a fat kid because a fat kid is always going to be worried about losing weight, and he could never reach his strength potential because he would always be trying to diet... We wanted the leaner guy that we could build up into what we wanted him to be, so we always looked for a tight end to be the offensive tackle," Cerrato said. "We would take as many option quarterbacks as we could get because they could play different positions."

Pat Terrell ran the option for Lakewood High School in St. Petersburg, Florida. Notre Dame didn't make his initial top 10 list of college choices. Even though he didn't know the school's colors, Minnesota made the list because of Lou Holtz.

"Quite frankly, I just liked the guy, and in Florida you don't hear a lot about the Golden Gophers," Terrell said.

Terrell felt at home with the coaching staff when he visited Minnesota. The only snag came when Holtz took the Notre Dame job. Terrell looked at the South Bend campus, but his college choice remained unclear. He laughed when his home-state Hurricanes spanked Notre Dame. His buddies couldn't believe it when he started considering the Irish, especially when he could stay close to home and play for Florida, Florida State, or Miami.

Turns out Terrell's dad, Grady, put Notre Dame at the top of the list, and he *kind of* let Pat make his own decision.

Grady Terrell grew up in Millington, Tennessee, and attended Father Bertrand Catholic High School. His class valedictorian, Frank

Yates, an African American, went to Notre Dame, and when he graduated Millington threw a parade for him.

"He didn't win the Heisman. He just graduated from the University of Notre Dame," Pat said. "That vision stuck in my dad's head for his whole entire life."

As national signing day in February '86 drew close, Grady sat down with Pat and went over some numbers.

"You're looking at this school. That's a good school. What's the tuition?" Grady asked.

"I don't know; it's about $4,000 a year," Pat answered.

Grady, who ran his own oil company, took out a pad and wrote an equation: $\$4,000 \times 4 = \$16,000$. He put the pen down and shook Pat's hand.

"Son, I'm proud of you."

"What do you mean?"

"You've worked hard; you've stayed out of trouble. You've made your mom and me very proud, and because of that you've earned yourself $16,000 worth of education." A silent pause followed. "Who else you looking at? Notre Dame?"

"Yeah."

"How much is Notre Dame?"

"Around $15,000."

Grady wrote the equation with Notre Dame's numbers.

"Now, it's your decision, but you can get a $60,000 education or you can get a $16,000 education. There's a value. I know what kind of value you're bringing the university, but what kind of value are you getting back out of it?"

Pat decided to join Holtz's first recruiting class at Notre Dame.

Dean Brown enjoyed the lively party scene and female hosts during his visits to Big Ten Conference schools. The best visit came at Ohio

State. For an Ohio football player like Brown, Ohio State was Mecca. The lineman flew on a private jet to the campus. He ate dinner with Archie Griffin, the Buckeye hero and college football's only two-time Heisman Trophy winner.

His recruiting visit to Notre Dame had been a dud. The hyped-up party he went to amounted to a group of guys standing around a trash can drinking beers in the Fisher Hall dormitory. The evening's main event was bowling. Brown told his mother he would never go to Notre Dame.

Nevertheless, a few things kept drawing Brown to the Fighting Irish. The first letter of interest he received was from Notre Dame. While the social scene turned Brown away, the former players he met had found success after football.

His final conversation with a Faust assistant shocked him. "I probably will not be your recruiter after today, but that does not change what I really believe about Notre Dame. You will be a great fit there, and it will probably be the best move you can make," the coach said.

As Brown listened his thoughts drifted. "This guy is getting fired. I was used to people getting bad-mouthed, and he would not do it. This guy is still maintaining his love of the school."

That conversation made Brown decide to don the gold and blue.

"When I look back on the way I grew up, I don't see myself as somebody who was groomed to be a Notre Dame graduate," Brown said.

The personality of the 6' 3", near-300-pounder belied the life he had lived. On campus, his nickname became Big Happy. He liked to sing Luther Vandross, and the cartoon *Fat Albert* ranked as his favorite TV show. In a questionnaire, he listed flying a kite with a jug of Kool-Aid by his side as one of his hobbies.

He was born to a twenty-one-year-old mother. His dad left when Dean was about four years old, just before his mom had the stroke.

He remembers the yellow trash can in the bathroom. That's what he grabbed for his mother when she lay on the couch, spitting up blood. He remembers climbing onto a kitchen chair to pull the phone off the wall and dial his grandmother. The next thing he remembers is the ambulance coming to get her. The stroke left her with a permanent limp and unable to work for eight years.

Neighborhood kids ridiculed him when he didn't have the money to buy a treat from the ice cream truck. He asked his mother for money. She said, "No."

"*Man, she has some money somewhere,*" Brown thought.

He went into her purse and found sixty-three cents. That was it. There was no savings account at the local bank. That was it until next month's assistance check came in the mail.

Brown started hustling food stamps so he could have the stuff a ten-year-old wanted and not be a burden to his mom. He collected people's food stamps, and for every dollar he bought twenty-five cents' worth of candy. He gave the seventy-five cents back to the original food stamp recipient, who used the cash to buy liquor. Brown then sold the candy at a marked-up price to the kids at school. Now he could buy himself an ice cream cone.

Only luck can explain how he avoided being shot. At the Jackson Park Homes in Canton, where he lived, Brown ducked down to put his baby cousin to bed in a crib. Gunshots sprayed out in the public housing development. One bullet crashed through the window, hitting the wall behind where Brown had been standing.

At McKinley Senior High School, Brown focused on school and sports. He set school records in the discus and shot put and teamed with Michigan State–bound linebacker Percy Snow on the football field.

He believes God pointed him toward Notre Dame. "I was probably the most privileged guy to be on that team," Brown said. "I consider myself the least of every guy on that team. Not that I'm lower than them, but I was probably the guy that benefited the most."

With a reduced timeline for recruiting that first year, Notre Dame would rely heavily on the Chicago Catholic schools, which had been a historic pipeline of talent for the Irish.

On Cerrato's first day at Notre Dame, he and Holtz road-tripped to Chicago. Cerrato, who continued his role as driver, thought he had good directions, but driving alongside Lake Michigan it was clear they were going to be late to meet John Foley, the *USA Today* Defensive Player of the Year, at St. Rita's.

"Just take your time now. It's all right, you just lost the best player in the country," Cerrato recalled the voice from the passenger seat.

The young assistant took to speeding down city streets.

"Slow down. It's over," Holtz said.

They made the meeting with Foley. They would meet with him again at his home later that night where Foley would commit to the Irish, but first Cerrato and Holtz had to go to St. Laurence. Holtz saw potential in four of the five recruits they were scheduled to meet. Jeff Pearson and Paul Glonek were All-American linemen. Mike Harazin graded on the next tier. Tim Grunhard, another lineman, didn't even make the All-Area team, but the most perplexing recruit was Stan Smagala.

Here was a 5' 10" 160-something-pound running back who was a backup until his senior year. Only recently had he started to beat his dad in the forty-yard dash, and his dad was the most noteworthy thing about Smagala.* The only scholarship offer Smagala had re-

---

*Stanley Sr. had become a forty-two-year-old running back for Moraine Valley Community College. *People* magazine even wrote an article about the insurance salesman turned touchdown scorer in the October 28, 1985, issue.

ceived came from Notre Dame.* Faust had offered it to him, but Holtz made it clear that he didn't think Smagala had the skills to play for the Irish.

"What he told my family and me is 'Gerry Faust offered you the scholarship. I don't want to honor it, but I have to honor it.' He said he had a responsibility to Notre Dame to honor it," Smagala said.

Smagala's mother cried. Stan was disappointed, but he understood Holtz's perspective. "I was obviously a white running back," Smagala said. "I started my senior year in high school, but was injured quite a bit. Didn't have too much film on me, just never thought I would even step on the field at Notre Dame."

Smagala got the scholarship offer when he attended the Notre Dame football camp the summer before his senior season. On the first day, coaches put campers through an agility test, timed their forty-yard dash, and measured their vertical leap. That night, coaches pulled Smagala aside to videotape him doing more agility tests. The next day he was told Faust wanted to see him that evening. During the meeting, Faust offered the scholarship.

"You know what? I still had a scholarship to Notre Dame and I took it," Smagala said.

He ended up being one of ten players from the Chicago area in Holtz's first recruiting class. Foley and the St. Laurence five show the capricious nature of predicting a "can't miss" future in recruiting. Foley was injured at the end of his sophomore year and never played again. Of the St. Laurence crew, Smagala and Grunhard became three-year starters. Glonek was never admitted. Pearson transferred to Michigan State, and Harazin never played due to health issues.

In total, twenty-one players signed to play for Notre Dame that February. When the freshmen first reported to training camp in the

---

*When Faust later landed at Akron he offered Smagala a scholarship there.

summer, Holtz told them they were the worst recruiting class he had ever assembled in his entire history of coaching. Along with the Windy City Catholic schoolers, the group included Brown, Terrell, Anthony Johnson, Michael Stonebreaker, Jeff Alm, Braxston Banks, Bryan Flannery, and Rod West.

One other recruit never heard Holtz disparage the class. The prize of the litter, a quarterback who came with controversy, wasn't allowed to be there, and it was questionable if he would stay at Notre Dame.

CHAPTER 5

The Quarterback

Tony Rice scored 12 points and grabbed 6 rebounds for Woodruff High School in a win against the Palmetto High Mustangs. The legend of the freshman guard wearing number 24 on the varsity squad had been building for years. At nine years old the teenagers at the neighborhood park plucked Rice away from his friends so the youngster could play hoops with the big kids. In eighth grade he ran varsity track. When he began starting for the Woodruff Wolverines basketball team, he had no idea a convention happening at the same time on the opposite coast would end up coloring his college experience.

More than one hundred college presidents descended on the seventy-seventh NCAA Convention in January 1983. Never before had such a large group of presidents attended the event. They took charge of the gathering normally run by athletic directors and top administrators, asserting themselves in the policymaking and governance of college athletics. The presidents addressed threats to college sports' image and vitality against a backdrop of court fights, academic improprieties, and illiterate athletes.

When the convention came to order, the NCAA found itself ensnared in a legal battle that would eventually be heard by the U.S. Supreme Court. Led by the University of Oklahoma and the University of Georgia, schools challenged the NCAA's authority over football TV broadcast rights. The schools wanted to negotiate their own TV deals and claimed the NCAA violated federal antitrust laws by handling contracts—including determining what games aired in what regions.

The lack of care for academics had become increasingly apparent with nearly two dozen schools on probation and about three dozen more under investigation in the winter of '83. A *Sports Illustrated* cover from a few years before the convention called it "The Student-Athlete Hoax." The opening of the accompanying article aggregated the reprehensible acts committed to keep athletes eligible while tossing learning aside. Some instances included:

- Twenty-eight University of Southern California athletes, including nineteen football players, enrolled in—but never attended—Speech Communications 380, a course reserved for members of the debate team.
- The University of New Mexico's head basketball coach was caught on an Albuquerque Police Department wiretap arranging false academic credits for a junior college transfer.
- The University of Oregon football team and men's basketball program were put on probation in 1981 for falsifying transcripts and giving athletes credits for classes they never attended from 1977 to 1979.

Not long before the stewards of college athletics met in San Diego, Billy Don Jackson had recently been released from a jail cell thirty-five miles north of Los Angeles. He was not the only illiterate former college athlete, but he had become the galvanizing figure for everything that can go wrong when everyone vouches for an athlete and ignores the obligation to provide an education.

Alabama's Paul "Bear" Bryant had gone to Sherman, Texas, to recruit Jackson. Texas and Oklahoma wanted him. He went to

UCLA. He became a three-year starter for the Bruins before being suspended from the team and then dropping out of school. Jackson pleaded no contest to voluntary manslaughter in the stabbing death of a drug dealer. At sentencing the judge referred to Jackson as a "functional illiterate." A high school graduate with three years at UCLA and he couldn't read.

While academics drew some focus of the 132 amendments to the NCAA bylaws, reining in the ballooning expansion of football and men's basketball did not. A measure to cut back the number of Division I basketball programs by up to forty-five schools failed. This gave more colleges a shot at exposure and the pie of money delivered through the burgeoning postseason NCAA Tournament. Delegates at the convention voted to increase the size of football coaching staffs by adding a ninth full-time assistant. A new football game—the Kickoff Classic—gained approval. Two high-profile programs would open the season in Giants Stadium and receive $550,000 each from the New Jersey Sports and Exposition Authority.

It had been five years since the NCAA adopted any new academic standards. Twelve amendments pushed for strengthened requirements. One amendment, Proposal 48, outlined new standards for freshman eligibility. Athletes would have to graduate from high school with a 2.0 grade point average in a core curriculum that included three years of English and two years of math, social science, and physical science. These athletes would also have to score a combined 700 on the Scholastic Aptitude Test (SAT) or a 15 on the American College Testing (ACT) exam.

Cliff Sjogren, admissions director for the University of Michigan who drafted the amendment, called for a higher grade point average to nullify lower standardized test scores, but the "President's Council of the NCAA chose to drop the 2.5 (grade point average) standard with the test exemption because of their fear of grade fixing," Sjogren wrote in a *New York Times* editorial.

Delegates adopted Prop 48 in the face of controversy and criticism, which called the measure racist because of cultural bias in standardized tests.

"They used literacy tests to deny us the right to vote. Then they want to use standardized tests because white boys are inferior athletes to blacks," said civil rights leader Jesse Jackson while speaking at Southern University in the days following the adoption of Prop 48.

Gerald Gurney, an academic adviser in the Iowa State Athletics Department, concluded that standardized tests were not a good indicator for minorities' academic success. In a sampling of freshman athletes at Iowa State, Gurney found that 95 percent read below a tenth-grade reading level and 10 percent were functionally illiterate. He also discovered all of the athletes were of average or above-average intelligence and had been failed by their high school education.

Prop 48 did offer a second chance. Athletes could enroll in school on a full scholarship for their freshman year. They were prohibited from team activities for the entire year and forfeited a year of eligibility. If they made the grades, they could join the team as a sophomore.

While the proposal and the controversy played out, Tony Rice was months away from becoming the Woodruff quarterback and leading the school to back-to-back state titles while posting a 35-3 record as a starter. Prop 48 first took effect in the 1986–87 academic year—his freshman year of college.

Clemson head coach Danny Ford visited Rice's house so often, he sat on the couch with his feet on the coffee table waiting for the star to come through the door. It never thrilled Mary Rice, Tony's grandmother and the woman who raised him, to come into her home and see the coach sitting comfortably and casually in the living room.

"If Danny Ford didn't come to our school every Thursday, he'd send players," said Rodney Rice, Tony's half brother.*

From his days as an assistant at South Carolina and the head coach of North Carolina State, Holtz maintained good relationships with the high school coaches in the area. He and Cerrato knew of Rice through Rickey Foggie, Minnesota's starting quarterback, whom they plucked out of the Palmetto State.

Cerrato never saw Rice play football. He watched his footwork and quickness on the basketball court. "He was a phenomenal basketball player," Cerrato said.

He knew Rice's football coach, Willie Varner, wanted the quarterback to go to Notre Dame. If Rice had an hour to meet with recruiters, Varner set it up that Cerrato had fifty-five minutes with him. Cerrato also backed away a Clemson recruiter, quarterback Randy Anderson, who came to Rice's doorstep.

"Tony, you know they want you to come down and visit next weekend," Anderson said.

"Why's he want to do that?" Cerrato interrupted and went into his pitch for the Fighting Irish. By the time Cerrato finished he had Anderson convinced.

"Man, Tony, you need to go to Notre Dame," the Clemson product said.

The pressure for Rice to stay in state was fierce. If it wasn't Clemson, he could go to South Carolina. To the local football zealots, who were plentiful, those schools were the only possible destinations for Rice. However, South Carolina wanted Rice to play defensive back because Todd Ellis had been groomed as the starting quarterback.

A few weeks before signing day, Rice announced he would

---

*Rodney and Tony had different fathers, but they refer to each other only as brothers, not half brothers.

leave the state of South Carolina and choose between North Carolina and Notre Dame. Clemson alums and supporters told him he owed the Tigers and should still go there. Others said he was letting them down personally and letting down the state. The hate mail flooded in. Anonymous letters called him nigger and said he would never get a college degree. One unsigned letter accused Notre Dame of offering Rice a job, money, and (the writer obviously not knowing his grandmother raised him) a trip for his parents. "The only thing Notre Dame promised me was a good education," he told the media.

Holtz and Cerrato flew to make the crucial home visit to Rice, but the airline canceled their connection out of Atlanta. They took to the road for the nearly two-hundred-mile drive. Cerrato drove, as usual, and Holtz, with his customary Diet Coke and pretzels, rode shotgun.

Holtz took his shoes off when he entered the three-bedroom home in the Kelly Acres public housing development where Rice lived with his grandmother, half brother, and two cousins.

"He was very, very respectful," Rodney Rice said of Holtz.

During the visit Holtz pulled out his magic, literally. He did the trick where you cut the rope and restore it to its whole form for Rice's grandmother. She loved it.

"You're going to follow that little man," she told Tony after shutting the door behind Holtz and Cerrato.

"That was the best decision my grandmother could've made for anyone," Rice said.

Holtz liked Rice. He liked that when he walked through the Woodruff High halls everyone loved Tony Rice.

"He's a pretty good student. He's got good grades. But I don't know his test scores," Holtz said years later. "The test scores come out and we can't get him in. He'd already told all these other schools he knew where he wanted to go to school."

Rice scored a 690 on the SAT, ten points below the standard set by Prop 48. With a late start on recruiting and this being his first time dealing with the admissions office, Holtz had no idea how big an issue this would become. The coach had to meet with Father Joyce.

"You will not do that again," Father Joyce told him, but the university would admit Rice and take the criticism that followed.*

Before Rice rode a Greyhound bus for two days to start his freshman year in South Bend, editorials in *The Observer,* the student newspaper, argued that he didn't belong on campus.

Rice didn't understand the judgments leveled against him from people he never met. "I haven't said a word to anyone," Rice said. "I'd rather go home. These people don't know me from Adam."

Years later Rice admitted those feelings, but to nearly every soul on campus he flashed his wide smile and maintained his happy-go-lucky, nothing-gets-me-down exterior.

He had tutors to help him during his freshman year, but he had no contact with the football team. Prop 48 kept him away from all practices, meetings, workouts, and games. He volunteered at a local hospital as a candy striper. He lifted weights on his own. He wasn't allowed to play full-contact intramural football, so he threw to dorm mates on the quad.

Rice walked into a packed Stepan Center for the Michigan pep rally. The eve of the Holtz era had come. A shirtless drum line pounded away as a coed in bunny ears held some of their percussion instruments. Team captain Mike Kovaleski addressed the crowd wearing faded blue jeans and a blue button-down shirt. Dean Brown provided the beat-box sound to the rap song delivered by wide

---

*Rice, John Foley, and basketball player Keith Robinson enrolled in Notre Dame that year and are the only Prop 48 qualifiers the Irish ever admitted. All three graduated with degrees from the university.

receiver Alvin Miller, who wore kelly green pants and a navy blue sweater with kelly green trim that matched the pants. Holtz, in a jacket, tie, and dress slacks, caused an uproar with his brief words that included talk about bringing a national championship to Notre Dame.

Rice, like any other student, watched all of it from the crowd, where a child recognized him. Rice shook his hand, and the boy's father pulled his son away.

"You don't want to shake his hand. He's dumb," the father said. "You don't want to be like him."

Rice smiled and said, "Take care," as they walked away. The stigma of Prop 48 further isolated the nineteen-year-old Baptist with a thick southern accent.

The negativity took its toll. He called his grandmother, asking to come home.

"No. We don't have any money to send you home. You stay there. You started something. Finish it," Mary Rice told her grandson.

The day after the pep rally, a disputed incompletion to Joel Williams, which would have resulted in a game-winning touchdown, and a John Carney missed field goal in the closing moments enabled No. 3 Michigan to stave off the Irish, 24–23, in Holtz's first game. After the game, Rice's roommate, Dean Brown, walked across campus slightly bewildered by the student body's enthusiasm at a loss. People kept telling him, "Great game," as he made his way back to Dillon Hall. Eventually, he understood the excitement and started to feel it. The team was last seen losing by 51 points. On this day, they came within 1 point of beating the No. 3 team in the country.

He opened his dorm room and saw Rice sitting in silence at his desk. Brown put the brakes on the fervor and downplayed the game. "Reality hit me. It was very difficult for him," Brown said.

Rice relied on Brown. He vented to him. He showed him the hate mail that continued to come from South Carolina. "He hardly ever talked about football," Rice said, appreciating that he didn't have to hear about what he was missing.

During the basketball season Rice went to watch the Irish play the No. 1–ranked North Carolina Tar Heels. Notre Dame pulled out a come-from-behind upset, but Rice couldn't escape the Prop 48 scarlet letter as he walked in the arena's concourse.

"Hey, little dummy. Why aren't you back in your room studying?" a fan shouted at him.

Rice had had enough. The next day he sat crying in the office of George Stewart, one of the assistant football coaches. "It crushed him for someone to say that to him," Stewart said. "It wasn't easy for Tony."

Holtz knew it would be difficult for Rice to be separated from the football team and the supportive community that went with it. "I was surprised he stayed."

CHAPTER 6

Readying for the Rise

George Stewart walked into the maintenance shop in the Athletic and Convocation Center and handed Laurie Wenger a piece of paper.

Stewart was acting on the direction of Holtz, who wanted a sign up in the locker room tunnel. The players would tap it as they headed to the field.

Wenger looked at the paper and the five words PLAY LIKE A CHAMPION TODAY. The South Bend native's job was to paint signs for functions. Some routine assignments included painting game balls and signs for Junior Parents Weekend. This project took her about a week to complete. Her co-workers cut a three-foot by four-foot piece of wood. Wenger primed it and then painted it in a yellow-gold. She let the color dry and then used blue paint to brush on the phrase in all capital letters.*

Notre Dame lore has it that shortly after Holtz became the head coach he went through books on Fighting Irish football history and found a photo of the sign. However, nobody, including former coaches, remembered it being posted anywhere.†

---

*The font, later trademarked by Wenger, is called Laurie.

†While the phrase is associated with Notre Dame, the University of Oklahoma has used PLAY LIKE A CHAMPION TODAY signs since the Bud

Regardless of where the photo came from, the Notre Dame players who left the locker room to take on No. 3 Michigan in '86 were the first to touch the sign. The 24–23 loss to the Wolverines was so impressive, the 0-1 Irish went from unranked to the No. 20 spot in the Associated Press poll.

The following week Notre Dame played Michigan State, and Spartans defensive back Todd Krumm played spoiler. In the 20–15 Irish loss, Krumm had an interception return for a touchdown and grabbed another at the Michigan State 20-yard line with 1:26 left to play.

After throttling Purdue 41–9, Notre Dame played No. 2 Alabama at Legion Field in Birmingham. Before 75,000 fans in 90-degree October heat, the chasm of speed between the Crimson Tide and the Irish showed. Alabama players galloped away from the Irish on a punt return for a touchdown and a scoring seam route from Mike Shula to Albert Bell. Linebacker Cornelius Bennett put his helmet under Steve Beuerlein's chin in a fumble-causing sack, hitting him before Beuerlein could set his feet on a rollout. The 28–10 Tide victory was the first time Alabama beat Notre Dame.

Holtz saw what everybody else saw in Alabama, and he approached his recruiting coordinator after the game.

"I'm sitting on the bus and Coach comes in, sits down next to me, and says, 'We have to get talent like everybody else,'" Cerrato said.

The Alabama game would be the only time Holtz's team would be outclassed that season.

"We went back to fundamentals," Holtz said. "In the kicking game we decided I was going to put people on the field who cared about how well we did. Kids like Tom Galloway, Peter Graham, my

Wilkinson era. Exactly when Wilkinson started using it is unknown, but he coached the Sooners from 1947 to 1963.

son Skip—who probably didn't earn it, but I felt like, knowing him, he would have the attitude I wanted. I just took a bunch of guys like that."

The reconfigured special teams blocked the way for Tim Brown's kickoff return for a touchdown in the 31–3 victory against Air Force. The Irish put together a three-game win streak heading into a home game against Joe Paterno and No. 3 Penn State.

The highly ranked, established power and the hopefully resurgent college football dynasty combined for all the trimmings of a big-time game, including the attendance of the country's vice president, George H. W. Bush.

Late in the fourth quarter Notre Dame still had a chance to win despite some miscues. A penalty nullified a 50-yard return by Steve Lawrence, and the Irish had lost 2 fumbles. A clipping penalty negated a 97-yard kickoff return for a touchdown by Brown, who tallied 140 all-purpose yards running, receiving, and returning the ball.

Down 24–19 with 2:29 on the clock, Beuerlein started a drive from the Notre Dame 20-yard line. He took a minute off the clock while leading the Irish to the Penn State 6 and surpassing the 300-yard passing mark on the day. With 52 seconds left, a third-down pass slipped off the fingers of tight end Joel Williams, and Penn State held on for the win.*

For the flock of Irish fans, the heartbreak of the loss felt better than the seemingly predetermined outcomes of recent history. The previous November, Notre Dame didn't come within 30 points of Penn State; on this day they were 18 feet from victory. The head coach didn't see it the same way. Notre Dame's athletic director, Gene Corrigan, looked at a depressed Holtz after the game.

---

*Penn State went on to win the national championship, defeating Miami in the Fiesta Bowl.

"You've got them playing, man. They just don't know how to win yet," Corrigan told him.

The week after Penn State, the Irish played at No. 8 LSU. A failed 2-point conversion with less than four minutes to play left the Irish down 21–19. On the ensuing drive the defense forced the Tigers into two third-and-longs. On both plays LSU quarterback Tommy Hodson eluded the rush and converted for a first down, first with a scramble and then with a long completion. Notre Dame never got the ball back.

The LSU loss meant a second consecutive losing season for the Fighting Irish, a streak matched only by the 1887 and 1888 seasons, the school's first two years of football. Five of the 6 defeats in 1986 came by a total of 14 points, less than a field goal per loss. Add the 18-point Alabama loss and the average margin of defeat in Holtz's first season was less than a touchdown, compared to the 17-plus points averaged in the Irish's 6 losses the year before.

The season finale at USC would close Beuerlein's college career. When Holtz took over, Beuerlein figured his college playing days had ended. The quarterback was coming off an interception-plagued junior season, and Holtz preferred quarterbacks who could run, which was not a Beuerlein specialty.

The first time Holtz met with Beuerlein, he told the quarterback he'd be the starter.

"I love your leadership. You've got all the things we're looking for," Holtz said. "You're going to be the guy, and we're going to throw the ball, and the reason we're going to throw the ball is because that's what you do, Steve, and you are not going to throw interceptions.

"Beuerlein, you will not throw more than six interceptions the entire season. I know this because it just won't happen."

"Coach, this is unbelievable. I can't believe all these good things. But how do you know I'm not going to throw more than six interceptions?"

"Well, if you need to know, as soon as you throw number six your ass is on the bench behind me."

Going into USC, Beuerlein had become a steady passer. He had gone from a projected undrafted free agent to an early-round NFL pick. He had also already thrown 6 interceptions when Holtz met with him the night before the game.

"If you throw an interception tomorrow, I'm going to take you out," Holtz told him. "I've already given you the benefit of the doubt here. I've told you, you would not throw more than six, and you've thrown six."

In the second quarter, Beuerlein threw an interception to Louis Brock Jr., son of the Hall of Fame baseball player, who returned it 58 yards for a touchdown and a 10–6 USC lead. Beuerlein went to the bench.

Beuerlein, who attended nearby Servite High School in Anaheim, couldn't believe this was how his time at Notre Dame would end. He already had tear-filled eyes when Holtz came out of nowhere and put his face in front of Beuerlein.

"Are you ready to play some football, son?"

"Yes sir. You will not regret it."

"Get your butt back out there and go win us the football game."*

The Irish had trailed by as many as 18 points in the game, and with 12 minutes to play the Trojans led 37–20. On a rollout, Beuerlein threw a 42-yard bomb to Milt Jackson in the corner of the end zone. USC drove to the Notre Dame 5-yard line, but instead of kicking a field goal to go up 40–27, the Trojans went for the first down. The Irish stuffed quarterback Rodney Peete, who argued the

---

*Beuerlein and Holtz joke with each other about the benching and reinsertion into the game because when Holtz tells the story he says Beuerlein begged him to go back in. Beuerlein, who remains friends with the coach, says that's not the way it happened.

call and got a 15-yard unsportsmanlike conduct penalty, which gave Notre Dame the ball at the 20-yard line. Beuerlein responded with a 49-yard pass play to Tim Brown. He eventually hit Braxston Banks for the touchdown and then Andy Heck for the 2-point conversion. USC 37, Notre Dame 35.

The Irish forced a USC punt, which Brown returned 56 yards to the Trojan 16-yard line. With 2 seconds left John Carney capped the 38–37 historic comeback win with a 19-yard field goal.* The game became a turning point for the new era of Notre Dame football.

"That's when everybody really believed," Corrigan said.

Sports Illustrated's college football preview in 1987 featured Brown on the cover with the headlines NOTRE DAME'S MR. T and TIM BROWN: BEST PLAYER IN THE LAND.

The No. 16 Irish opened the season with a decisive 26–7 win in the Big House in Ann Arbor against No. 9 Michigan. The Irish forced 7 turnovers and gave Wolverines head coach Bo Schembechler his first home-opening loss since he took over the program in 1969. Senior Terry Andrysiak, who won the starting job at quarterback, connected on 11 of 15 passes, including a touchdown score to Brown.

In a night game on ESPN against Michigan State, Brown returned back-to-back Spartan punts for touchdowns. The plays happened so close together, Brown was still out of breath when he took the field for the second return. He told special teams coach George Stewart to go for the block because he was gassed. With everyone charging the punter and no one blocking, Brown caught the ball and wanted to get out of bounds, but as he ran toward the sideline a

---

*The field goal aired on a delay because CBS, which broadcast the game, was still in a commercial break when Carney made the kick.

Michigan State defender forced him to cut upfield. Brown turned inside and was gone. Even though Heisman Trophy voters wouldn't cast ballots for months, Brown won the award that night.

Holtz wouldn't place the Irish in the top 15 of the coaches poll, but 3-0 Notre Dame crept up to No. 4 in the AP rankings as the team headed to Pittsburgh. The Panthers jumped all over the Irish. Pitt was leading 27–0 late in the first half when Andrysiak broke his collarbone. Holtz had to turn to Tony Rice. He offered some quick last-moment coaching to his second-string quarterback.

"If Tim Brown is covered with three guys on him, throw him the ball. Do what you did in high school."

Coach, I haven't played high school in two years, Rice thought as his mind raced. He had to find his mouthpiece. His chinstrap needed tightening. Holtz continued, now reminding Rice of the running hole numbers that corresponded to the play calls.

"You know your numbers—two, four, six, eight is to the right. The odd is the left. Run the ball. Go out and have fun."

Rice, in his thick Geechee accent, called the play and broke the huddle. He walked up to the line of scrimmage, crouched down behind a lineman, and heard a voice.

"Tony, could you please move over," said the calm, direct tone of fullback Anthony Johnson.

Rice had lined up under the left guard, not the center. "I was scared," he said.

After the preplay blunder Rice took over the game, rallying the Irish in the second half. Notre Dame lost 30–22, but the first-year quarterback's talent had become evident.

"You saw an instant spark in the offense," said Tom Lemming. "Everybody in the press box started talking about him."

After stumbling at Pitt, Notre Dame peeled off 5 straight victories with Rice under center. The Irish trounced Alabama 37–6 to go 8-1. Seventh-ranked Notre Dame played unranked Penn State on a cold November day in State College. Winds gusted up to 25 miles per hour, and the wind-chill factor ranged between −8 and −20 degrees.

"It's the coldest I've ever been in my life. I mean it was miserable," Holtz said.

Penn State's Blair Thomas rushed for 214 yards, and the Nittany Lions limited Brown. Rice scored 2 touchdowns and led a twelve-play, 62-yard scoring drive to pull the Irish within 1 point, 21–20. With 31 seconds left, Holtz played for the win and went for the 2-point conversion.* The play broke down. Rice ran into Penn State tacklers.

The Irish fell to 8-2, but they earned an invitation to the Cotton Bowl before the regular-season finale at Miami. It was the first meeting between the schools since the 58–7 dismantling ended the Faust era. The media coverage honed in on the revenge factor and the opportunity for Notre Dame to derail the No. 2–ranked, undefeated Hurricanes' national championship hopes.

While parties on both sides said typical things about focusing on the present game and not the past, the head coaches, a pair of motivational masters, took their veiled and not-so-veiled swings.

Jimmy Johnson, the Miami head coach, answered questions about running up the score. "Maybe when the score gets to a certain point," Johnson told the media, "maybe the opposing coach should give you a list of plays you can run and those you can't."

He and Holtz traded lines in the newspaper. Johnson said the Hurricanes hadn't played well in recent weeks. Holtz said he expected to see the best of the 'Canes after they had spent weeks playing soft opponents.

"I don't think Miami wants to say, 'Hey we're afraid of Timmy Brown.' That's not Miami's nature. Miami's not afraid of the FBI,

---

*College football started using overtime in 1996.

the police, or the opposition … They intimidate people," Holtz told the media, and, intended or not, threw a jab at the Hurricane-filled police blotter.

In the game, Miami bottled up Brown, holding him to 95 all-purpose yards, his lowest output since the season opener against Michigan. Uncharacteristically, Holtz called nearly thirty pass plays, and Miami had 6 sacks. Rice completed 7 of 19 attempts for 84 yards and an interception.

The Hurricanes held Notre Dame to 169 yards of offense while gaining 417 yards, including 204 yards on 50 rushes. Notre Dame never moved the ball past the Miami 26-yard line in the 24–0 loss.

"They play with no class, but they're a bunch of guys who know how to play," Brown said after the game.

Brown picked up the Heisman Trophy. Miami went on to win the national title.

The Irish had their names on the back of their jerseys when they played in the school's first major bowl appearance in seven years. Notre Dame faced Southwestern Conference champ Texas A&M in the Cotton Bowl.

The Irish came out throwing, with Andrysiak making his first start since breaking his collarbone at Pitt. In the first 26 minutes, the Irish built a 10–3 lead and had passed for 50 yards more than their full-game average. Looking to go up two scores before halftime, Notre Dame had the ball at the Aggies 18-yard line. Andrysiak zipped the ball to the corner of the end zone, but A&M defensive back Alex Morris made a one-handed interception before falling out of bounds and getting up to celebrate with the cabbage patch dance.

"Then all hell breaks loose," Holtz said.

The Aggies drove 80 yards to tie the game. On the next Irish play, Braxston Banks fumbled what could have easily been called an incomplete pass. The Aggies drove 23 yards for the score, the 2-point conversion, and the 18–10 halftime lead. Notre Dame never recovered. Brown, who was playing in front of hometown fans for the first time since high school, left the 35–10 loss after picking up a 15-yard unsportsmanlike conduct penalty. Referees flagged the All American when he tried to retrieve his hand towel, which was stripped from his waist by a Texas A&M player on a kick return.

Holtz saw the dud coming. The practices were flat. "They were looking at the bowl game as a reward rather than an opportunity to elevate the caliber of season you had. They thought I worked them too hard. It just wasn't the way it needed to be," Holtz said.

Holtz wore the loss to the postgame press conference.

"Lou Holtz looked like an 85-year-old man, a beaten down 85-year-old man," said Lou Somogyi, editor of *Blue and Gold Illustrated*.

"I've never been that miserable. That upset," Holtz said.

In the locker room one player cried. Freshman Chris Zorich didn't play a snap. He was a practice squad player, but he sat with tears streaming down his face. "I truly felt I let my team down even though I was a practice dummy," Zorich said. "I didn't do my job [preparing the team] and I felt bad about it, and we got the crap beat out of us."

With a fierce tone, Holtz commanded his players to soak in the beating. "I want you to remember how this feels because we're never going to feel like this again," he said.

The program went from a revival to three straight losses with two noncompetitive games against top opponents. The entire starting offensive line would be gone by next season. John Foley, the *USA Today* Defensive Player of the Year from Holtz's first recruiting class, was injured in the game and would never play another down of football. Tony Rice showed great athleticism, but could he be the guy at quarterback?

Dick Rosenthal, who had become Notre Dame's athletic director shortly before the season started, sat in a small Cotton Bowl

Stadium coach's office with Holtz. Silence filled two minutes.* Holtz looked up and offered thirty seconds of should'ves and could'ves.

Then he spent the next twenty minutes going into detail, telling Rosenthal exactly what needed to happen and how it was going to happen to ensure Notre Dame would be a winner next season. Before he left the meeting, Holtz asked Rosenthal to schedule meetings with all his assistant coaches starting at 6:00 A.M. the following day.

If the comeback against USC in Holtz's first year had the Irish faithful believing, the Cotton Bowl had the coaches and players believing they never wanted this losing feeling again.

---

*Gene Corrigan became the commissioner of the Atlantic Coast Conference, opening the position.

CHAPTER 7

Demanding Perfection

The 1988 season began the day after the Cotton Bowl. Holtz boarded a plane for Japan and had sixteen hours to think about a 25-point wound that hadn't scabbed yet.

He went through the roster asking himself three questions about every player: Could I trust him? Was he committed to excellence? Did he care about his teammates and Notre Dame's future?

Texas A&M coach Jackie Sherrill sat on the same flight because he and Holtz would oppose each other again as coaches in the Japan Bowl. Holtz spoke to Sherrill about Joe Moore, who had been Sherrill's offensive line coach at Pitt. For a while, Frank Fuhrer, a friend of Holtz's and a Pittsburgh beer distributor, praised Moore when he spoke to to the Notre Dame coach.

Holtz's veer option offense predicated itself on controlling the line of scrimmage. Success in Holtz's system wasn't razzle-dazzle or surprise, it was imposing one's will on an opponent who already knew what plays were coming. In football, there are few things more emasculating than having the ball run at will on your defense. Moore built offensive lines that provided the blocking to do that.

In a 1983 profile, Tom Wheatley of *The Pittsburgh Press* described Moore as "a man among men in a man's game. He has a leathery face, leathery ears and even leathery-looking hair. Above all, there is that matchless leathery voice." Its timbre came from cigarettes; one constantly hung from Moore's lips.

Under Moore, Pitt became an All-American offensive line factory. From 1980 through 1984, every first-string Pitt lineman went on to start in the pros. Three of the NFL's 1980s All-Decade linemen—Russ Grimm, Jimbo Covert, and Bill Fralic—learned from Moore's tutelage. In 1984, to quantify Moore's offensive line success, people at Pitt created the pancake statistic, denoting an offensive player flattening a defender on a block.

Mark Stepnoski, a 1990s NFL All-Decade team center, went to Pitt because of Moore. He played one season before Moore was fired as part of a head-coaching change. Like most Moore descendants, Stepnoski remains forever loyal to the coach.

"It's one thing to work hard; almost everybody does that. It's different to maximize that time on something that will help you be productive. That was the big thing with him. We were doing drills that professional teams were doing," Stepnoski said. "He was very demanding, but he was fair. You knew he was always on your side even if he was hard on you."

Holtz hired him. Moore had spent the previous two seasons at Temple. At Notre Dame, his initial role was to coach tight ends and tackles.

"Joe Moore was a piece of work. You want to talk about two guys. I was so fundamental and he was so common sense," Holtz said. "But we made a great team."

Holtz made another critical staff change. Foge Fazio, the former Pitt head coach, who had served as Notre Dame's defensive coordinator for two years, moved on to become an assistant with the Atlanta Falcons.

Irish linebackers coach Barry Alvarez had a shot at the opening, but no guarantee. Alvarez had spent eight years as the linebackers coach for Hayden Fry at Iowa. The man above Alvarez on the

Hawkeye table of organization, defensive coordinator Bill Brashier, was Fry's childhood friend, and he wasn't leaving Iowa City. In '87, Alvarez made the lateral move to Notre Dame because it put him on a quicker pathway to become a coordinator and then a head coach.

Even after working with him for a year, Holtz interviewed Alvarez three different times for the coordinator post.

"I promise you my guys are going to be physical. We're going to be sound," Alvarez told him. "We will whack you."

Holtz prayed about the decision.

"You know when you're getting Foge Fazio you've got a high profile defensive coordinator—*the guru.* Barry Alvarez. 'Who's that?' But...it felt like the right thing to do," Holtz said.

Notre Dame's new defensive coordinator grew up in a tiny place called Langeloth. It came into existence to support one of Western Pennsylvania's many coal-mining companies. Even today Langeloth has a population of about 700 people. In high school, Alvarez starred as a linebacker. He played at Nebraska for legendary coach Bob Devaney. Alvarez led the '67 Cornhuskers in tackles. Nebraska went 25-7 and played in both the Sugar and Orange bowls during his three varsity seasons. After college, he coached high school ball in the Cornhusker State and Iowa before joining Fry's staff. He was a coach on Hawkeye teams that went to six bowl games, including two Rose Bowls. Alvarez experienced winning. He had the successful credentials, and now he had the opportunity to shape an entire defense.

Holtz retooled the coaching staff when he returned to the States, but on that flight to Japan he couldn't shake the image of Zorich crying in the Cotton Bowl locker room.

"He didn't even play," Holtz said. "I decided then that we were going to put people out on that field who really wanted to play. I came back and that was the whole thing. The attitude was going to be right."

He scheduled a meeting to speak to the team at the end of winter conditioning. Holtz stood before them, a one-man demand for perfection. As he had done the first time he met with the team, he mapped out the necessary elements for achievement.

"We are going to practice strict loyalty to one another. We are going to be loyal to the University of Notre Dame, the administration, coaches, and teammates," he said. "We cannot be a good, close-knit football team without showing respect and concern for one another."

Holtz put a ban on negative comments from players and coaches.

As with any leader looking to accomplish anything, these were directives, but at the same time Holtz's choice of language grouped everyone—including himself—together in this endeavor. Team togetherness functioned as a prerequisite in playing for a purpose beyond one's self.

"When we do what is right, we bring glory and honor to Notre Dame. When we win in football, we help this university," he told them.

Holtz found great inspiration in the school's history and the unfaltering determination of the twenty-eight-year-old French priest Fr. Edward Sorin, who founded it in 1842 to honor Mary, the Blessed Virgin Mother of Christ. In 1879, a fire consumed the main building, which housed nearly everything at the university. Sorin stood undaunted. "I came here as a young man and dreamed of building a great university in honor of Our Lady," he said. "But I built it too small, and she had to burn it to the ground to make the point. So, tomorrow, as soon as the bricks cool, we will rebuild it, bigger and better than ever."

Since childhood, Holtz had a strong spiritual relationship with Mary. He remembers singing songs and placing flowers on her pale-blue-robed statue back at St. Aloysius. He loved the month of May, which Catholic grammar schools, like the one he attended, devoted to her.

He spoke to the team about Mary and the school's "special mystique." He wasn't talking about the Four Horsemen or other sporting lore. Holtz believed in the spirit of Notre Dame.

He reiterated the team prohibition on in-season alcohol consumption. "Our coaches will frequent the favorite hangouts. If you can't control yourself or exercise self-discipline, you aren't going to be successful anyway."

Practices would have the same rigor, and they would need to yield greater improvement than the previous year.

Holtz credited the athletic directors, Corrigan and Rosenthal, with expressing to him the ideal that the team belonged to students, the alumni, and the fans. He embraced that and forwarded it to the players, telling them they should feel a sense of obligation to the legions of Irish fans.

He expressed his thoughts about the upcoming season and the future. This was not the quick-witted, jovial Holtz who worked the media and produced chuckles at luncheons.

I'm here to win football games for the University of Notre Dame. Not some of our games, and not most of our games; I'm here to win all of our games. Every doggone one of them. We aren't here to come close. We are here to win every single football game we ever play at the University of Notre Dame from this point forward...

I don't ever expect to lose another football game as long as I'm at Notre Dame, and I sure don't expect to lose one this year...

We're going to write another chapter in Notre Dame football history. We're going to seek perfection in football

in the same manner as the University seeks perfection in
every facet of the school ...

We are not asking for perfection—we are going to demand it. Please don't expect us to lower our standards to
satisfy people who are looking for mediocrity, because this
won't happen.

Toward the close he spoke about the team's identity. "It is going
to be tough. It is going to be physical. It is going to be relentless," he
said. "It's going to be one that performs best when it faces adversity.
We will look adversity in the eye and we will turn it into success."

After the meeting, he sent every player a letter highlighting
points he wanted the team to retain.

"That was from the heart, and we had that whole attitude
through the season," Holtz said.

The Gipper and Knute Rockne returned to the Notre Dame campus in the winter of '88.

The coach came in the form of a twenty-two-cent postage
stamp. George Gipp came via President Ronald Reagan, who por-
trayed the All-American halfback in the 1940 movie *Knute Rockne—All
American*.

Michael J. Feld, a Notre Dame Class of '56 graduate who worked
in congressional relations, started a campaign to make the stamp a
reality. According to *The Washington Post*, in January of '86, Feld
wrote 350 letters in longhand to university officials, alumni, members of Congress, and members of the Reagan administration. He
asked for their support in lobbying the postmaster general. Six
months into his letter writing, Feld sent a note to Reagan: "Turn-
about is fair play, Mr. President. It's time for 'the Gipper' to win one
for Rockne." About a year later, the postmaster general announced a
commemorative stamp to honor Rockne.

Rockne built Notre Dame football into a national sports entity. He won three consensus national titles and had five undefeated seasons. His .881 winning percentage remains the highest among any major college or pro coach with at least ten years' experience. In 1931, at age forty-three, he died in a plane crash in Bazaar, Kansas. The Columbia Broadcasting System aired a radio broadcast of his funeral from coast to coast. A crowd of 10,000 mourners paid their respects, gathering in Chicago as Rockne's body transferred from one train to another making its way to South Bend for interment.

Reagan's stamp unveiling came five days after Rockne would have turned one hundred years old. The stamp depicted a smiling, balding Rockne in a gray sweatshirt standing on a football field, clutching a pigskin.

A sign behind the podium at the basketball arena in the newly renamed Joyce Athletic and Convocation Center read NOTRE DAME WELCOMES "THE GIPPER." The words "President Ronald Reagan" stood in smaller letters on the same sign.

"He's going home. In his heart, that's where he thinks he went to school," Pat Buchanan, the conservative commentator and one-time White House communications director for the Reagan administration, told *The New York Times*.

Even though Reagan went to Eureka College in Illinois, his role as George Gipp and the myth that went with the Gipper story endured throughout his political life. Reagan delivered the commencement address at Notre Dame in 1981 and now, in the final year of his presidency, he returned, reliving the silver screen moment and beginning his farewell to the country.

Before the capacity crowd of 11,000 students, school officials, and locals, Reagan delivered Gipp's famous deathbed lines. More than recreating the script, the words spoke to his presidential legacy.

"Some time when the team is up against it and the breaks are beating the boys, tell them to go out there and win just one for the Gipper."

The applause stopped Reagan, which some observers said gave him time to get hold of his emotions before finishing.

"I don't know where I'll be then, but I'll know about it, and I'll be happy."

The president finished up by launching a pass into the crowd. Tim Brown, the Heisman Trophy winner, caught the pass, making his last reception on campus.

Holtz flirted with the idea of moving Andy Heck from tight end to tackle. Joe Moore was a bit more Joe Moore about it.

"You know, you're not a very good tight end, Andy," Moore told him, immediately grabbing Heck's attention. "Would you like to play in the NFL?"

"Yeah, that's what I want to do," Heck said.

"Well, you ought to come with me, then. You ought to switch over to the offensive line."

Heck had played tight end for the Irish since his freshman year. He studied film of Mark Bavaro, a former Notre Dame tight end, who had become a defender-carrying Pro Bowl selection for the New York Giants. In the comeback win against USC in '86, Heck caught a touchdown pass and a 2-point conversion. In '87, he was the only player other than Tim Brown to make a touchdown grab.

Heck's average-to-slow speed at tight end equaled quickness at tackle. Plus, the Irish signed a tight end out of Florida, Derek Brown, the *Parade* magazine Player of the Year. After the conversation with Moore, Heck went to equipment manager Eugene O'Neill and turned in his number 88 jersey for number 66. He attended Moore's position meetings, but Heck had between 235 and 245 pounds on his 6'7" frame. To push people around in the trenches he needed to put on weight.

Heck asked the team doctors the best way to gain. They told him to eat as many meals as he could, and they developed a 1,000-calorie shake for him. The drink combined a cup of powdered milk, a cup of Tang, and a cup of vanilla pudding mixed with a banana. Heck crammed down peanut-butter-and-jelly sandwiches. He became a regular at Shoney's. Like a character from the 1950s nostalgia scene Heck loved, he would get in his black '51 Pontiac Chieftain four-door sedan and drive to Bonnie Doon to order malts.* He noshed on snacks in the Oak Room, an on-campus spot open after the dining halls closed. Each night, he set his alarm clock for 1:30 A.M. He would wake and drive to Bob's Big Boy to ingest his fifth full meal of the day.

"It got to the point where I got sick of eating," Heck told the *Chicago Tribune*.

Heck had never played tackle before, but the move—in his final year of eligibility—fulfilled two Holtz philosophies: put the best players on the field and be fast. Holtz's assistant coaches praised his ability to find the right spot to get the most out of an athlete.

Pat Terrell had already moved from quarterback to split end. Now, going into his junior year, Terrell moved to free safety. D'Juan Francisco moved from running back to cornerback. Zorich had already moved from linebacker to nose tackle, and Frank Stams, who started at fullback earlier in his college career, lined up at rush end on the defensive side of the ball.

"It's not complicated. The first thing you do is you look for players that like the game. They're good with their teammates. They like to compete, but their speed is a liability. They never can be real great. They have all the other qualities you want in a player. But they just aren't fast enough at that position," Holtz said. "Now, where

---

*After a twelve-year NFL playing career and nearly a decade into coaching at that same level, Heck still has the Chieftain.

would that speed be an asset? All of a sudden, he's slow for a fullback, but he's very fast for a defensive end. He's got mediocre speed at tight end, but boy, what great quickness he has at tackle. Not fast enough as a linebacker, but boy, how good would he be at middle guard.

"So that's all you do. It isn't like all of sudden you're making him into a player. He was a player before. He wasn't a great player, but it was because of his speed. It wasn't anything else."

At first, Holtz had no idea what it meant when players came up to him during spring practice asking to leave early because they had a Bookstore Basketball game.

On other campuses it's spring when the mercury rises and the sun comes out. Those things could happen in South Bend, but the Bookstore Basketball Tournament meant spring had arrived at Notre Dame. The world's largest five-on-five outdoor tournament started in 1972 with fifty-three teams. By the time Holtz came to campus, more than six hundred teams signed up for the single-elimination tournament. Hundreds of people lined the perimeter of asphalt courts to watch games in the round of 128. Crowds grew even larger as teams dwindled, and being a *player* in Bookstore brought campus-wide recognition.

When Holtz found out what a big deal it was, he visited the student commissioners running the tournament. He asked them to schedule football players' games late in the day, and sometimes he even adjusted practice to accommodate the tournament. "If I knew . . . three players were leaving, I got our hard work done while they were there," Holtz said.

Holtz eventually laced up his sneakers and played in the tournament. Playing basketball among the student body added to Holtz's beloved-figure status. The coach in the sport's most scrutinized job was tangible, accessible. If anyone sent him a letter, he responded with a note, and this process repeated itself thousands of times.

When students camped out to buy season football tickets, Holtz brought them doughnuts in the morning. He stopped by their tents at night, pizza in hand, and played hearts with them. He visited the dormitories and answered questions about the team.

"I loved Lewis Hall—the ladies' dorm that knew more about football," Holtz said. "It was their team. That was my attitude."

He also loaded his Bookstore team with ringers. In '88, on the same day as the Blue-Gold intrasquad scrimmage and the dedication of the Loftus Center, a new athletic training facility, Holtz teamed with Tony Rice and quarterback Kent Graham in a semifinals game against a team led by Ricky Watters.

Watters was a freshman and a member of the '87 recruiting class. Cerrato had fulfilled Holtz's mandate from the bus conversation after the Alabama loss. The '87 class was the first of four consecutive No. 1 recruiting classes put together by Cerrato and the Holtz staff. No other school has ever matched that streak. Along with Watters, the class also included Zorich, Graham, Todd Lyght, Tony Brooks, Tim Ryan, Mike Heldt, George Williams, Scott Kowalkowski, Donn Grimm, Ryan Mihalko, and Andre Jones among its thirty signees.

"Their attitude was we didn't come here just to play for Notre Dame. We came here to win a national championship for Notre Dame. It was that simple. It didn't stop for those guys with 'Wow, I'm here and I get to run out of that tunnel with a golden helmet on.' It was more 'Yeah, I came here to be a champion,'" said Pat Terrell, who was a year ahead of them.

Upperclassmen fed off the temperament, and at the same time they worked to channel the young moxie toward team success. The former high school superstars had to adjust to Notre Dame. The confident attitude had to meld into a team-first focus.

"He was almost magical," Tony Brooks said of Holtz. "You had to take all that talent and all those egos and make sure they buy into the game plan every week."

When the coach first met with a freshman class he did two things. He had them write a letter of thanks to their parents. Some thought a phone call would suffice, but Holtz handed out paper and pencils.

"No, you're going to write them, because if you call them it's over. If you write them, they're going to read it thirty times," he said.

If an ego adjustment was needed, the second item addressed it bluntly.

"You came here to become us. We didn't bring you here to become you. I don't care how you wore your socks. I don't care how you did things. You will become us," he said.

These college rookies had to learn to take coaching. Their elite athleticism enabled them to skip parts of that in the lower ranks. With the Irish, they had to adjust from being the focus to being a role player. They would play on special teams and on the scout squad.

Holtz relied on upperclassmen to help the freshmen get acclimated. The coach paired newcomers with a big brother on the team.

"The minute you work them hard and you get all over them they're going to be down and they're going to be bitching and the senior, who is a big brother, is going to say, 'Hey, it's in your best interest to learn now. Hey, I've been there. Trust me.'"

When spring practice came the '87 recruiting class had experienced a full season. They were ready to move up the depth chart, nudging upperclassmen out of the way. Their competitive fire blended with senior leaders, who had been beaten down by two losing seasons and left hungry to win.

"It was kind of a perfect mix of new talent versus the folks that led the way with the work ethic and how you get things done," Tim Ryan said. "Even the guys [upperclassmen] that weren't starters, they were of the type of character that brings a team around."

The Blue-Gold Game, on a 50-degree late-April day with winds gusting up to 25 miles per hour, concluded spring practice.

Michigan assistant coach Lloyd Carr scouted the game as 15,699 fans watched inside Notre Dame Stadium. The Gold team won 27–9 with Tony Brooks's 68 yards rushing and a touchdown and Ricky Watters's rushing and receiving scores. Blue team inside linebackers Wes Pritchett and Michael Stonebreaker combined for 23 tackles. Irish quarterbacks completed 12 of 41 passes with 5 interceptions. The signal callers likely to play in the fall, Rice and Graham, threw 4 of the picks.

A couple of hours later, "Lou's 2 QBs and 2 Blind Men" lost to Watters's "Adworks All-Stars" 21–16 in the Bookstore semifinal.

Tony Rice had won the starting quarterback job in spring practice. Ten days before the team reported for preseason camp, on the Friday summer classes ended, Mitch Henck of WSBT, South Bend's CBS affiliate, reported that Rice would be academically ineligible for the season.

Holtz heard the news in Vail, Colorado, where he and his wife spent two days golfing with the Rosenthals. Rice found out in the Greenville-Spartanburg Jetport when a friend told him about the report as he arrived in South Carolina for a few days at home. Rice didn't believe him, but then he grabbed a newspaper and read the rumor.

Rice needed a 2.0 grade point average to play at Notre Dame. The news report shocked Rice because he knew he had made the grades. "What people say doesn't bother me," Rice told *The Spartanburg Herald-Journal*. "You know where you stand, so it shouldn't bother you. You can't always listen to what you hear."

The grades did not become official until the registrar's office certified them on Monday, which gave the rumors a weekend to swirl. Rice wasn't the only Irish player to attend summer classes, but the quarterback with the Prop 48 scarlet letter drew the most attention. The *Chicago Tribune* reported the subjects he studied: sociology, computer science, and art. His girlfriend told a reporter his grades: A, A–, and B.

On Monday, the certified grades vindicated Rice. The TV station apologized to Rice and the university in all four of its newscasts. Henck never revealed his source, but he immediately resigned.*

August heat welcomed the team to its two-a-day practices. During the workouts temperatures ranged from the mid-80s to near 100 degrees.

Chuck Heater, the new secondary coach, focused on technique until the players got it right. Each player's knees had to bend properly in a defensive stance before the unit progressed to its next drill.

"We trusted the coaches," said safety George Streeter. "We had no regard for our bodies."

Heater told the group when it was playtime and when it was time to turn it up, and this was a time to turn it up and get meticulous about fundamentals.

"We were trying to give that to him, and we just didn't drink enough water in the process," Streeter said.

Almost the entire secondary spent time in the infirmary. Streeter, D'Juan Francisco, Corny Southall, and Stan Smagala all spent nights at the on-campus health care center.

Players left these practices bruised and exhausted, and all the news they heard about their upcoming season was how they were a year away from competing for a national championship. It was a logical sports analysis. The first No. 1 recruiting class would be juniors a year later, and Cerrato and Co. had reeled in another No. 1 class to provide depth.

Privately, the seniors grew intolerant of the predictions. This

---

*Henck now has a Wisconsin lounge act, singing Sinatra and performing stand-up comedy. He is also a radio talk show host in the Dairy State.

group had been through losing seasons with Faust and Holtz and wanted nothing to do with the "they're a year away" conversations.

A punt's length off campus, in their summer housing at the Turtle Creek Apartments, they had numerous conversations about the season.

"Hey, enough of this talk that we're building for a year down the road after we would be gone. Why not now? Let's do the work. Let's come together. Let's win a national championship," said Heck, who, along with running back Mark Green and linebacker Ned Bolcar, had been named a team captain.

Toward the end of August, Holtz picked up a team flaw watching films of practice. About two weeks before the Irish hosted Michigan, Holtz stood at practice and noticed the mistake in a live-action scrimmage.

No one finished plays. Holtz and the other coaches didn't blow a whistle to stop the play, yet the players stopped on their own. Unacceptable.

"The snap of the ball starts a play. The whistle stops it. You didn't hear a whistle, you look to hit somebody," Holtz said.

The offense and defense lined up for the next play. The coaches put their whistles in their pockets. Something sort of resembling football ensued. Players chased each other up the sidelines and all over the field. Three consecutive plays lasted about two minutes each before a whistle sounded.

"It was mayhem. I mean everybody is piling on one another. They're cheap-shotting one another. It was like a free-for-all and I just stood there," Holtz said.

They learned to play through the whistle in what became an identity-cementing practice.

"It was a knock-down, drag-out thing. That's where we really took off," said sophomore linebacker Scott Kowalkowski.

CHAPTER 8

New-School Athlete, Old-School Football,
and the Kicker

The Fighting Irish prepared to host the No. 9 Michigan Wolverines, and the head coach worked the phones, trying to find a place to hold team Mass.

Typically, a dormitory hosted the private service. Most times the team gathered in Pangborn Hall because the team chaplain, Fr. James Riehle, resided there, but the pregame spiritual gathering also rotated to other dorms such as Fisher or Dillon.

Days before the season opener, the spot in Pangborn had been reserved for a big-time alum to host a private Mass. Holtz called the priest in charge of the Basilica of the Sacred Heart, the church next to the university's Golden Dome administration building.

"Could we have Mass in Our Lady's chapel?"

"No," replied Fr. Daniel Jenky.

A lot of people came through the church on game day, and Jenky did not want to close it for a private service.

Holtz pleaded with him.

"You do not allow them back to the altar anyway," Holtz said. "They aren't going to bother us. We'll have our Mass. It won't be longer than a half hour and we'll leave."

Father Jenky consented just for this one time.

Holtz had changed the game-day Mass schedule to build team togetherness. Before his tenure, the team went to Mass, ate a meal, dispersed, and met up again at the stadium. With Holtz, they went to Mass and proceeded to the stadium, sticking together through game time.

While the team had its fair share of non-Catholics, all the players knew about team Mass from the recruiting process. Holtz said sometimes it was hard to get a Catholic school player into Notre Dame because the admissions office was reluctant to admit a football player and not admit a higher-ranked classmate from the player's school.

"I was also told I would have nothing to do with admissions and I honored that," Holtz said. "I had a couple players well over 1200 [on their SATs] that ended up at Michigan, starting against us, because they were turned down."

At Mass, Holtz watched the camaraderie at the sign of peace. Typically, Catholics take about a minute to hug and kiss their relatives and shake the hands of those near them. The team took nearly five minutes and embraced each other with hugs, handshakes, and pats on the back.

Fellas, we've got to kick off soon, Holtz thought to himself.

Holtz enjoyed the Mass at the basilica so much he appealed to Father Jenky to host it again. Holtz got his way. Soon it became tradition, and students, alumni, and fans lined the pathway from the church to Notre Dame Stadium, cheering encouragement and seeking autographs.

On that first night, Tony Rice left Sacred Heart and put on his earphones. The quarterback is always the marquee man, but at this point the take on Rice painted him as "an athlete," not a headliner and definitely not a passer. Nobody questioned whether the nation's elite quarterbacks—USC's Rodney Peete, Miami's Steve Walsh, and UCLA's Troy Aikman—would get pulled from a game, but some media reports predicted backups Kent Graham or Steve Belles would see game action if Rice faltered. Rice listened to his Walkman. He had his own pregame tradition, playing a cassette of "Breakout" by Swing Out Sister. The Fighting Irish quarterback envisioned himself striding into big plays as the adult contemporary pop song filled his ears.

Rice's first season-opening start would be a meeting between the two best schools in college football history. With seven more seasons than the Fighting Irish, Michigan ranked first in wins with 684. Notre Dame held second place with 659. The Irish had the top all-time winning percentage of .754. The Wolverines were second at .741.

The 1988 edition would be the twentieth game between the two schools, with Michigan holding a 13–6 advantage.

Notre Dame's first football game, on November 23, 1887, ended in an 8–0 loss to Michigan in South Bend. The Wolverines won the first eight games of the series until Notre Dame posted an 11–3 road win in 1909. The schools split games in 1942 and '43. The rivalry picked up again in 1978, with the schools taking 4 wins apiece leading up to '88.

In '87, the Irish forced 7 turnovers and scored a convincing 26–7 win in Ann Arbor. The other recent Irish triumphs had been thrillers. In 1979, with 1 second on the clock, Bob Crable blocked a 42-yard field goal to secure a 12–10 win. In 1980, Harry Oliver kicked a 51-yard field goal as time ran out to give Notre Dame a 29–27 victory. In '82, the Irish won 23–17. Michigan had one narrow win, the 24–23 outcome in Holtz's first game. Other than that, the Wolverines' post–World War II wins against the Irish had been by a near-two-touchdown average.

Bo Schembechler manned the sidelines for Michigan. The school had had other fabled coaches, Fielding Yost and Fritz Crisler, but that was when you could get a gallon of gas for fifteen cents and a loaf of bread for thirteen. In the color television era, Bo Schembechler was Michigan football.

In college at Miami of Ohio, Schembechler first played under Sid Gillman, who established the progenitor of Bill Walsh's West Coast offense, and then Woody Hayes became his coach. Schembechler went on to serve two stints as an assistant coach for Hayes at Ohio State. When Schembechler took over the Michigan program in 1969, the Wolverines had been unranked in ten of the last twelve final AP polls. In his first season, Schembechler led the Wolverines to the Rose Bowl and, possibly more important to Maize-and-Blue fans, he beat archrival, No. 1–ranked Ohio State and Hayes. In his coaching career, Schembechler reversed the unranked trend. In twenty-one total seasons Bo's Michigan teams finished the season unranked just twice.

"Schembechler was the epitome of blazing intensity. He paced the sideline, waving his arms and sometimes smashing headsets when angered by referees," Richard Goldstein wrote in *The New York Times.*

Holtz had been friends with Schembechler since 1962. The Holtzes and the Schembechlers met on their honeymoons—a coaches clinic hosted by William & Mary.

In 1970, Schembechler missed coaching the Rose Bowl because he had a heart attack before the game. In late 1987, he had open-heart surgery for the second time. He missed Michigan's Hall of Fame Bowl win against Alabama. At that time, his coaching career could have ended. It didn't, and he brought another highly rated Wolverines squad into the season.

While the Associated Press ranked Michigan ninth, the *Sporting News* put All-American defensive tackle Mark Messner on the cover and the Wolverines in the No. 1 spot. The publication also rated the Michigan offensive line as the best in the country.

Even though they lost Jumbo Elliott, whom the New York Giants took in the second round of the NFL Draft, Michigan returned an offensive line core that had collectively started ninety-four games.

Plus, they were huge. Three players ranged between 280 and 287 pounds. Greg Skrepenak didn't factor into the starting experience, but he stood 6'7" and weighed 322 pounds. The line's runt, All-American center John Vitale, weighed 273 pounds.

In comparison, the Irish starting offensive line combined for five total starts, all from junior guard Tim Grunhard. Experience versus inexperience became a media storyline, and Schembechler enjoyed his vantage point.

"I would certainly rather be in our situation with the line than what Notre Dame has," he told reporters. "Experience can be very important, and we have more players on the line who have played than they have."

"We want them to rely on their young offensive line to knock us out of there," Schembechler also said in the lead up to the game.

The Irish's quiet, mild-mannered offensive tackle Andy Heck showed a comedic side at the South Bend/Mishawaka Area Chamber of Commerce kickoff luncheon. "I'm getting sick and tired of hearing people say, 'I just don't know how the offensive line is going to be.' Coach Moore always tells us that the coaches can't win games for us, but they can teach us how to be winners. He says, 'The winners in life get the best of everything—the best jobs, the best salaries, the best-looking girls.' I just want people to know that everyone on the offensive line has a great-looking girlfriend."

To the media, Holtz handled his concerns about the offensive line with his tongue-in-cheek approach. "I made the comment that our tailbacks need the same personality traits the kamikaze pilots needed because you know you're going to get blown up," Holtz said with a laugh. "It's just suicidal. That wasn't said in jest."

The whole speech about writing another chapter in the history of Notre Dame football had no place when Holtz spoke to reporters. He told his players not to believe what they read, just listen to what he told them. His media style functioned as another part of his game strategy. It was a combination of wit and charm, and if the opponent was provided anything, it would be false confidence.

Holtz downgraded any hype about Notre Dame's preseason rankings. The *Sporting News* said the Irish had the best backfield in the nation. The team was ranked fifth in both *Inside Sports* and *College & Pro Football Weekly*, eleventh in *Sports Illustrated*, twelfth by United Press International and *Lindy's*, thirteenth by the Associated Press, fifteenth by the *Sporting News*, seventeenth by *Street & Smith* and twentieth by *Sport*. Holtz figured they didn't know what to make of the team, and he chalked it all up to desire for newsstand sales.

"There are so many Notre Dame fans around that the minute they see you're in the top 20, they get enthused and they want to buy that magazine to read about you," he told the press.

Regarding the best team in the country, most publications concurred with the AP and UPI polls. For the first time in school history Florida State held the preseason No. 1 spot. Bobby Bowden's team also believed the ranking. They even recorded a song about it. A few years earlier, in 1985, the Chicago Bears had performed "The Super Bowl Shuffle," an iconic tune that charted on the Billboard 100. "The Super Bowl Shuffle" was quirky and unique, and the Bears backed it up by winning the Super Bowl, but it inspired unfortunate spin-offs made worse by lame teams trying to capture the pop-culture MTV vibe. "The Seminole Rap," with its synthesizers and computer percussion sound, epitomized electronic '80s music. The video features awkward lyric spitting from quarterbacks Chip Ferguson and Peter Tom Willis and the hip gyrations of All-American cornerback Deion Sanders, but the 'Noles were No. 1, and "The Seminole Rap" received radio play in Tallahassee—for about a week.

Florida State played No. 6 Miami to open the season on the Saturday night of Labor Day weekend. The Hurricanes, the defending national champs, dismantled the Seminoles 31–0. The 'Canes had seen their cross-state rival's music video as a sign of disrespect. Miami outgained Florida State by 208 yards. Running back Cleveland Gary went in for a score with Sanders grabbing and tugging at his waist like a child trying to tackle a grown-up. Steve Walsh, the Miami signal caller, threw for 228 yards and 2 touchdowns. He went unsacked and controlled the game, changing the play at the line of scrimmage on multiple occasions.

Miami replaced Florida State as the No. 1 team in the next Associated Press poll. The 'Canes had the following week off to watch Notre Dame–Michigan, two of their future opponents.

Holtz teased his team about Michigan. Each day as they stretched before preseason two-a-day practices, he told them he spoke to Schembechler and asked the Michigan coach if he had given his team the day off. Then he supplied the answer.

"No. We've got a tough game against Miami the second week. We can't afford to take a day with Miami on the horizon. The only thing these guys have to worry about is Miami. We'll start on Notre Dame maybe the Wednesday of that week," Holtz told the Irish, joking and needling at the same time.

Holtz had a 1-3 record against Schembechler, a win and a loss with Notre Dame and 2 blowout losses with Minnesota.

Schembechler knew a Holtz Notre Dame team would be different than the Golden Gophers Michigan dropped by a combined score of 79–14. When Holtz took the job, Schembechler spoke to his team about the Fighting Irish they should expect to face. "Men, you guys are not going to believe it. He's done wonders at Minnesota with a bunch of ham and eggers. He's got a bunch of athletes now. We've got to buckle it down because it is going to be a bitch."

Beyond the offensive line, Holtz had other concerns heading into the season opener. The lack of overall experience showed, with nine players making their first start and two others making their second. The offense remained a mystery. The unit hadn't moved the ball well in practice. Maybe the defense was great, but if the defense was average, that meant the offense was weak.

Holtz went into the game with a young coaching staff. Six of the nine coaches were under thirty-six years old. Barry Alvarez put together a new defensive staff, and for the first time since before the Rockne era, no coach had graduated from Notre Dame.

Barry Alvarez stood on the sideline watching warm-ups on the 72-degree South Bend night. The defense had been strong in practice, but the forty-one-year-old coaching his first game as a coordinator wondered how his unit would play. Then he saw something he would never forget.

"You could see sparks coming off those helmets in pregame. There was like an aura around those helmets," Alvarez said.

He looked over at defensive line coach John Palermo. "I'm telling you, they'll play better than you've ever seen them play," Alvarez said. "When the lights come on and they paint those helmets gold, those cats play different."

CBS televised the game nationally in primetime. For both teams, it would be a barometer for how the season would go. For Notre Dame it posed the first opportunity to display the toughness that had been honed in practices. The college football world's last images of the Irish were three straight defeats and manhandlings by Miami and Texas A&M.

Representatives from the Sugar, Orange, Cotton, Citrus, and Fiesta bowls watched the teams go through their pregame drills. Notre Dame warmed up in the north end zone, the one closest to the 134-foot-tall looming mural of a raised-arms Christ, dubbed Touchdown Jesus.* Both teams entered and exited the field at the

---

*The Word of Life is the formal name of the mural on the Hesburgh Library.

tunnel behind that end zone. Instead of Michigan players going around Notre Dame on their way to the locker room, a few players ran through the Fighting Irish drills.

Notre Dame sophomore cornerback Todd Lyght found himself running alongside Michigan's top receiver, John Kolesar. "What are you doing running through our drill?" Lyght asked, pushing the Wolverine.

The Irish took umbrage at the thoughtless intrusion. A dustup of forearms and shoves ensued.

Coaches broke it up, reported John Dockery, CBS's sideline man. "Talk about a ticking time bomb. That's what this is," he said.

Michigan forced Notre Dame to punt on the Irish's opening series. A speedy, swarming Notre Dame defense did the same to Michigan.

Sophomore Ricky Watters, who started the night at receiver, stood at the Notre Dame 30-yard line waiting to receive the punt from Michigan's Mike Gillette.

The year before, in the season opener at Michigan, Watters ranted and complained on the sideline in the fourth quarter, voicing discontent at his lack of playing time.

"He's yelling, going crazy. He's yelling at Coach Holtz!" Lyght told *Sports Illustrated*'s William Nack in a 1995 profile on Watters.

With Notre Dame in control and the outcome nearly decided, Holtz sent Watters into the game at running back. On his third carry, Watters ran 18 yards for a touchdown.

"Surrounded by teammates, within earshot of Holtz, he shouted over and over, 'I told you! I told you! Just give me the ball! I want to help this team win. All I want is the ball,'" Nack wrote.

That was Ricky Watters: an athlete supreme; a confident, cocky young adult hungry to win, willing to work for it; hard on himself and a bit selfish when it came to handling the ball.

"In all my times with Ricky Watters I only had two problems with him: one, he wasn't always on time; two, we only had one football and he wanted it. Now, that's an admirable quality and he deserved it, but so did Mark Green and Tony Rice, Rocket Ismail," Holtz said. "Sometimes you're wondering what they're doing off the field—I never worried about Ricky Watters and what he was doing."

Ricky came to his parents at a bus depot. He was the younger of two children adopted by Jim and Marie Watters. At a party in their Harrisburg neighborhood, Marie spoke to a woman whose daughter was pregnant and putting the child up for adoption. Marie contacted a lawyer to make the adoption legal, but the hospital did not want the exchange to take place on its property; hence the bus depot transfer.

According to Watters's self-published autobiography, at nine years old, an older kid confronted him on the YMCA basketball court, telling Watters his sister, Rhonda, wasn't really his sister. (In fact, the boy taunting Ricky was Rhonda's brother.) The older boy also told Ricky his mom wasn't his real mom. Ricky left the gym while the other kids laughed at him and yelled, "Go home and ask your mommy!"

"Everything that I had known up to that point in my life suddenly became a lie," Watters wrote.

At Bishop McDevitt High School, Watters became one of the most sought-after running backs in the Class of '87 (Another was Emmitt Smith, at Escandia High in Pensacola, Florida.) After Vinny Cerrato watched Watters's speed and explosiveness in a Thursday practice, he called Holtz.

"Coach, you've got to call this guy tonight. This is our back," he said.

With a promise of being an architect, playing running back, and wearing number 12, Watters, nudged by his mother, chose Notre Dame over Penn State.[*]

In practice at Notre Dame, Watters would run the length of the field to the end zone even though plays had been whistled dead. "I just want to get used to crossing that goal line, Coach," he said.

"He just wanted to play and have success. He was high-strung, too. He wanted to win. He could not deal with losing," said Tony Yelovich, the Irish assistant coach who helped recruit Watters.

Watters played backup running back as a freshman. As a sophomore, he moved to receiver, a change he felt broke the promise of playing running back.

On the night the Irish played Michigan, the position switch pegged Watters as the replacement for multithreat Heisman Trophy winner Tim Brown.

Gillette's 53-yard first-quarter punt sent Watters drifting backward. He caught the ball as he hopped back to the 19-yard line. Instantly, his legs churned. He took a few steps left and made a quick cut upfield before the hash mark, finding an open alley provided by blockers. With the ball in his left hand, he raised his right arm, waving a No. 1 finger starting at the Michigan 30-yard line. He looked back occasionally to make sure no tackler had a shot at catching him. Untouched, he sailed in for 6 points. He stopped at the back of the end zone, turned, and started to bow, but Raghib "Rocket" Ismail interrupted it by jumping on him in celebration. More teammates showed up, along with fans, and dog-piled on the star.[†] Notre Dame took the 7–0 lead.

---

[*] Tony Rice wanted to wear number 12, his high school number, but when he joined the team his sophomore year, the number had already been promised to Watters.

[†] Fans were able to join big-play celebrations because Notre Dame Stadium used to have wooden bleacher seating on the field behind the south end zone.

The Irish forced the Wolverines to punt after three plays. Notre Dame picked up a first down. Then Rice faked as if he were running the option, dropped back, and unloaded a 59-yard throw that slipped off Ismail's fingertips at the Michigan 14-yard line. With the closest Michigan defender lying on the ground 10 yards behind Rocket, a catch would have been another Irish touchdown. The play served its purpose anyway. Holtz had told Rocket he didn't care if he caught the ball. He wanted to showcase the blurring speed.

After the drive stalled, Notre Dame's punt team huddled. Pat Terrell and Todd Lyght were the gunners, the guys on the outside who sprint down the field as soon as the ball is snapped on a mission to tackle the returner.

"I'll see ya at the ball," they shouted at each other.

"It was fun. It was a race to get there. I was more worried about Todd getting there first than the defenders trying to block me," Terrell said.

Lyght knew Kolesar, the Wolverine from the pregame altercation, waited for this punt. He had an added message for Terrell.

"Listen, we're going to take this guy out."

Jim Sexton booted a 40-yard punt, and Terrell and Lyght took off like two hungry foxes seeking a chick that got away from its mama. The ball took one high bounce before Kolesar went to field it. Just as Kolesar caught the ball, Terrell and Lyght crashed into him, crunching his body to the ground. Kolesar wasn't heard from the rest of the game.

"That's the thing that separated that team," Lyght said. "We not only wanted to beat you, but we wanted to physically punish you, too."

Late in the first quarter, Notre Dame drove to the Michigan 16-yard line, but Messner, the All-American cover boy, blew up a play. Speeding by Andy Heck and fullback Braxston Banks, an untouched Messner tackled Mark Green for a 3-yard loss.

"He'll go under you. He'll go over you. He'll go inside, outside, whatever it takes. He's a little unorthodox, but he gets around the ball," said Pat Haden, who provided the color commentary for CBS broadcasts.

Messner could have easily been playing alongside Chris Zorich, Jeff Alm, and George Williams on the Notre Dame defensive line. The 6'3" 244-pound Hartland, Michigan, product took an official recruiting visit to Notre Dame. Messner, a Lutheran, attended Detroit Catholic Central High School, which, like many Catholic high schools, aspired to be a mini–Notre Dame. Messner had a great visit until he met coach Gerry Faust at a restaurant for dinner.

"Hey, Mark, great you're here. We're excited at Notre Dame," Faust said across the restaurant.

The big, loud greeting wasn't a fit for Messner, and it left him disinterested. "I was mortified and embarrassed," Messner said. "I just couldn't have worked for him. There was no way."

That eliminated Notre Dame. Indiana came off the list when head coach Sam Wyche took over the same role with the Cincinnati Bengals. Really, on the night Messner grappled with Andy Heck and Co., he should have been teammates with Troy Aikman as the No. 5 UCLA Bruins dusted off No. 2 Nebraska 41–28.

Messner took his recruiting visit to Michigan in December and then left the cold Midwest for sunny Southern California. UCLA coach Terry Donahue picked him up at the airport and took the kid from the all-boys high school directly to Venice Beach to see California girls dotting the bathing-suit, Rollerblading, boom-box scene. He saw koala bears and the UCLA Botanical Gardens. He was a Bruin. He told coach Terry Donahue he would be. He wore his new UCLA hat on his flight from Hollywood back to Detroit. He handed his mom and stepdad a UCLA car decal when he got off the plane.

"I'm a Bruin," he told them.

As the trio pulled up to their home, they noticed a big Oldsmobile

Delta 88 in the driveway. Messner and his parents parked along the sidewalk. The unexpected driveway visitors exited their car. Schembechler came out of the driver side. Defensive coordinator Gary Moeller stepped out of the passenger side. The larger-than-life head coach approached the home-state kid who was ready to leave for the West Coast. The meeting was brief, more monologue than dialogue.

"You're a Michigan man and you belong at Michigan," Schembechler said, gripping Messner's hand in a shake and handing him a VHS tape of Wolverine highlights.

That night, Messner watched the highlight video. He started thinking about his stepdad, who had been diagnosed with terminal cancer. Messner's parents had divorced when he was two years old.

His dad, Max, had played six seasons in the NFL for the Lions, Giants, and Steelers. His mom remarried Delbert Pretty, a silver-haired, slender accountant with an accountant's personality, not exactly the model to get along with a football-playing stepson.

"You would never know he and I had this wonderful, loving relationship," Messner said.

Del paid Mark's high school tuition. "When you know those are things he's doing and you're not a kid anymore, you know he loves you," Messner said. "It didn't matter if there was a biological connection there—a father is a father and he was that."

Del wanted Mark to experience the woods he loved. He took Mark hunting one morning in Alger, Michigan. Mark, with bow in hand, stood in a blind at daybreak. Still waking up, Del, who would hunt small game later, sat in a car 300 yards away. A deer walked out, and Mark quickly took aim and shot in the animal's direction. He had no idea if he hit the deer, but he started sprinting through the waist-high ferns to the car. Hearing the *thump, thump, thump* of Mark's steps, Del looked up. *Swoosh*, the football player disappeared into the ferns. He popped back up, not realizing a tree stump tripped him. Del's chipmunklike laugh greeted Mark when he reached the car. Mark hit the deer, but the unintended slapstick comedy overtook the hunting triumph.

Lying in his bed, Messner stayed awake thinking about Del and his college choice. With a limited number of games on TV, Mark knew if he went to UCLA, Del would hardly, if ever, see him play. If he played at Michigan, that would be different.

Messner called the UCLA football office in the middle of the night and left a message for Donahue. He thanked him for the opportunity and told him he would sign with Michigan.

The next morning, he walked into his parents' bedroom.

"I'm a Wolverine," he told them.

His mother sat up in bed. "I thought they were Bruins."

"Mother, I'm staying home. I'm going to the University of Michigan,"

She started crying. Del hugged him.

In his first collegiate game, Messner started against Notre Dame. He was so nervous he prayed Michigan would go on offense first. Those prayers went unanswered. He got down in his stance and looked up at quarterback Steve Beuerlein and running back Allen Pinkett behind him.

"I'm looking and listening to Beuerlein," Messner said. "The offensive lineman is locked and loaded, and I swear he's a bull who's going to come kill me."

Then everything slowed down in Messner's world. The nervousness reached a climax and Messner puked on the lineman's hand. The center snapped the ball. As the puked-on lineman blinked in reaction to the vomit, Messner shot through the gap and made a tackle for a 2-yard loss.

In the '88 game, Messner's tackle of Green forced the Irish into a third down and long, which they didn't convert. Notre Dame booted a 31-yard field goal.

Leroy Hoard fumbled the ensuing kickoff after D'Juan Francisco stood him up and backup quarterback Steve Belles popped the ball loose. Freshman Arnold Ale recovered the pigskin at the Michigan 22-yard line, and the sellout crowd of 59,075 spectators turned up their volume in approval. Michigan had not even made a first down on offense, and Notre Dame had the chance to go up three scores. The game had the makings of an Irish blowout, but the offense stalled, gaining no yards on five plays and settling for another field goal to take a 13–0 lead.

Michigan's Tony Boles took the following kickoff 59 yards. He would have scored, but Francisco shed a block and ran Boles down from behind at the Notre Dame 38-yard line. Notre Dame's momentum dissipated. The Wolverines converted two third downs and a fourth down on a twelve-play, 6-minute 18-second drive capped by a 1-yard touchdown leap from Hoard. For all the dominance Notre Dame had shown, the Irish led by just 6 points as the Michigan band played "Hail to the Victors."

The 13–7 score stood into the third quarter. The game had a proverbial old-school football feel with evenly matched combat between the offensive and defensive lines. The inexperienced Notre Dame offensive line held its own against Michigan, creating holes for Irish runners to gain 5.8 yards a clip in the first half. Notre Dame offensive line coaches Moore and Yelovich used quickness and technique to neutralize the Wolverine defensive front.

"That offensive line didn't muscle us to death. They just chipped us out of the way, and we were always arm tackling because we weren't in position to make plays," Messner said. "I felt as ineffective as I've ever felt in a game in that game."

On each play, the Michigan offensive line and the Notre Dame defensive line looked like two wrecking balls swinging into each other. Zorich mixed it up with Vitale, the All-American center. The Irish confused Michigan by using three inside linebackers to counteract the run-heavy Wolverine formations. In the first half, Michigan ran the ball 23 times and managed just 2.3 yards per carry.

"They couldn't move the ball on us," said Alvarez. "Bo was pretty predictable because he had better players most of the time."

Alvarez had a proclivity for studying opponents' tendencies. With Michigan he had years of knowledge with which to work. Alvarez and his defensive assistants had more than two decades of combined experience facing the Wolverines, and Notre Dame defensive backs coach Chuck Heater played running back for Schembechler at Michigan.

Alvarez installed a game plan knowing the opponent and knowing his defense needed a confidence boost after the close of last season.

"Coach, they're doing exactly what we practiced against," defensive end Frank Stams said during the game.

The small interaction proved critical. The players also needed to believe in the first-year coordinator, as well as themselves.

An attacking Notre Dame defense, which saw all eleven defenders pile up to stop a third down and 1, opened the second half. However, the Irish offense had to start at their own 8-yard line after Watters fumbled a punt into the end zone and returned it just a few yards.

Michigan got the ball back and did nothing. Gillette lined up for his sixth punt of the night. Watters waved his arms under the high hanging kick. He either called for the fair catch or for his teammates to back away from the ball—either way, he wasn't going to return it—but he slipped as he moved toward the dropping ball. It hit the ground and bounced into his legs, causing a fumble, which Michigan recovered at the Notre Dame 14-yard line. Earlier in the night, Watters had slipped on a pass pattern. The Tony Rice–thrown ball hit him on the numbers and ricocheted off his chest and into the hands of a Michigan defender for an interception. Before Watters even left the field after the muffed punt, tri-captain Mark Green stood in front of him, telling him to let it go. As the defense went to work, Watters stood on the sideline, his face pressed into the shoulder of Tony Brooks.

Pat Eilers, Watters's big brother on the team, Green, Ismail, and Brooks gathered next to him, offering words to make sure their teammate kept his focus on making the next play.

"He was so passionate. He wanted nothing but good things to happen all the time," Brooks said.

"Don't let it eat at you," Brooks told Watters. "Put it behind you. Put it out of your head."

In one of the more bizarre drives in college football, Michigan needed to move the ball 42 feet to take its first lead of the night. The Wolverines faced a third down and 7 and a roaring crowd. Michigan quarterback Michael Taylor claimed he couldn't call his signals because of the noise, and the referees awarded Michigan an official time-out. This failed to quell the student-section noise factory. On the field, the officials spoke to Notre Dame captain Ned Bolcar. Holtz turned to the crowd, waving his hands for them to calm down. It didn't make a difference.

Taylor broke the huddle and waved his arms for quiet. He waited 30 seconds at the line of scrimmage before calling for the snap. He threw a pass to the corner of the end zone. Greg McMurtry was the intended receiver, but the Notre Dame drum line had a better chance of catching it.

"It's field goal time," said Brent Musburger, the play-by-play man for CBS.

After the play ended, a referee threw his flag. The officials gathered for a discussion and called illegal use of the hands on Notre Dame. The penalty gave Michigan first down and goal. On second down, Taylor backed away from under center, again unable to call his signals because of the noise, and the officials flagged Notre

Dame. The referees met for another discussion. They withdrew the penalty and charged Notre Dame with a time-out. Through the break in the action, the Fighting Irish defense maintained its intensity. On third down, Bolcar shot through the line, leveling Tony Boles with the help of Todd Lyght and Andre Jones. The crowd amped up even more. Rather than kick a field goal, Schembechler went for the touchdown. On fourth and 1, Taylor faked a handoff and ran into the end zone untouched. Michigan took a 14–13 lead with the extra point.

It took the Wolverines eight plays to drive 14 yards for the score. It took 3 minutes 53 seconds off the clock, but after the official conferences and crowd-induced time-outs, it took 11 minutes 19 seconds in real time. Michigan's two touchdown drives totaled twenty plays and took more than ten minutes of game time, but the ball only moved a total of 52 yards.

Tony Rice had started with 8 consecutive incomplete passes when Notre Dame took over at their own 22-yard line. On first down, he completed his first pass for a loss of 1 yard. On second down, he dropped back and delivered a 23-yard strike to Steve Alaniz. Rice led the Irish on a twelve-play, 68-yard drive, chewing up five and a half minutes and sending the game into the fourth quarter. A 26-yard field goal and Notre Dame regained the lead, 16–14.

Michigan answered back, not with a quick strike but in the way both of these ball-control teams answered back. The Wolverines used nearly nine minutes to go 48 yards on sixteen plays. Mike Gillette kicked a 49-yard field goal and followed it with a celebratory double-gun finger point to the Notre Dame bench.

With 5:39 to play, the Notre Dame offense took the field at their 20-yard line. After a 15-yard pass interference call, Rice rolled left and kept the ball, bolting for 21 yards. Two plays later, standing in a collapsing pocket, he delivered an 18-yard pass to Tony Brooks.

With 1:18 left, the Irish made it to the Michigan 9-yard line and called on Reggie Ho, the 5'5" 135-pound kicker.

The walk-on from Kaneohe, Hawaii, with a very deliberate style had made all 3 of his previous attempts on the night.

Ho played soccer at St. Louis High School in Honolulu. The premed student with the 3.77 grade point average tried out for the Notre Dame football team because he didn't want to be a geek, something he defined to *Sports Illustrated* as "a nerd who studies too much."

He failed to make the squad in Holtz's first year, but he tried out again the following season and ended up kicking an extra point against Navy in '87. He kicked field goals in the winter snow and spent spring break kicking about six hours a day in the Loftus Center.

"The guy was driven to be a field-goal-kicking specialist," said George Stewart, who coached the special teams.

Sophomore Billy Hackett was expected to handle placekicking duties, but Ho's consistently accurate kicks in practice made him Notre Dame's kicker from 40 yards and closer.

"Watch his hands before he kicks it. He goes with this voodoo or this kung fu routine of his...He had to get his jersey, I think, in the bookstore. I don't know that the team had a jersey that fit him," Haden told the TV audience before his first kick of the night. "I love him."

"Voodoo, who-do? Three more for the Fighting Irish," said Musburger after the initial make.

The camera panned to the Leprechaun mascot doing push-ups while being held up by male cheerleaders.

"It's not true, Pat, that Reggie Ho was the Leprechaun a year ago."

"He's a lot bigger than Ho, isn't he," Haden said.

"He sure is."

When Ho took the field to attempt his fourth field goal,

Schembechler called time-out. The Michigan sideline razzed Ho during the break. Prior to this game, Ho's biggest field goal at Notre Dame came when he booted the game-winner for his Cavanaugh Hall dorm team in Notre Dame's full-contact interhall football league championship.

After the commercial break, Ho went through his process. He placed the tee on the grass, took two small steps and two big steps with his back to the line of scrimmage, then he took two side steps. He turned around, adjusted his feet, and took a shoulder-raising breath, nodding his head at holder Peter Graham. He twisted his body, his head focused on the tee, his arms raised to his chest, extending to the opposite end zone, his fingers waving, knees flexed to a bend. Tim Grunhard snapped the ball. With some torque, Ho stepped to the ball. He kicked it and followed through in a yogalike lunge with his head down, never watching the ball.

He made it. The band played the "Notre Dame Victory March." Ho tied a Notre Dame single-game field goal record and gave the Irish a 19–17 lead.

Tony Boles returned the following kickoff to the 37-yard line. With 1:06 to play, Michigan had two time-outs and needed to drive 30 yards to get in Gillette's range. A couple of long passes put the ball at the Notre Dame 32-yard line, where Michigan called time-out with 3 seconds left.

Gillette had the opportunity to point the finger guns at the Notre Dame sideline again. He had already made a field goal from a yard closer.

"He is one of the more confident kickers I have ever met. Most of them are kind of wimps and flakes. This guy is not," Haden said during Michigan's final drive.

The Kansas City Royals drafted Gillette to play catcher. Instead of playing pro baseball, he chose to suit up in football and baseball for the Wolverines.

He got a clean step and put his leg into the ball, driving it long enough and high enough toward the goal post. It floated wide right. Notre Dame students rushed the field, celebrating with players who raised their gold helmets toward the stands.

"There is no love affair like the student body at Notre Dame and its beloved football team," Musburger said.

The Irish escaped with a win. A folk hero emerged. The team's toughness had been on display for 3 hours and 1 minute. But Rice's stat line—3 of 12 for 40 yards and an interception—coupled with the offense's inability to score a touchdown didn't signal a championship run.

CHAPTER 9

Freaks

Inside linebacker Wes Pritchett made the call in the huddle. The first-team defense lined up against the scout squad. Clear skies topped the 75-degree scene on the Wednesday of Michigan State week.

The ball snapped; the play went off, and a scout team guard tried to put a cut block on Pritchett. The 6'4" 251-pound defender didn't take kindly to a lineman trying to take out his legs. Pritchett got into it with the guard, and the scout squadder didn't back down. They started fighting.

Senior Corny Southall, the starting free safety, came up to stop the fight and protect the offensive player. Michael Stonebreaker, Pritchett's inside linebacking mate, started in on Southall.

"We've got a free-for-all," Holtz said.

The defensive coaches broke it up, but Alvarez questioned his unit's bond. *Holy smoke! Do our guys like each other?* he thought to himself.

Pritchett probably gave the offensive lineman a kiss on the cheek after practice, but on the field it was football, and the fisticuffs were part of it.

"Football is not a nice-person sport...Football players are mean. It's not supposed to be pretty," Pritchett said. "It was the way we were."

Mistakes filled the rest of practice. Tony Rice continued to have trouble throwing the ball. Holtz sent him to play with the scout team. Four days before the Irish played the returning Rose Bowl champions, the starting quarterback called the signals for the practice squad.

Beyond the passing game, Holtz had worries about the offensive line. Even though the Irish ran for 226 yards against Michigan, Holtz wanted better play out of the guard position. Tim Ryan moved from backup center to starting guard, next to Andy Heck.

Ryan, a sophomore, came from Rockhurst High School, an all-boys Jesuit school in Kansas City, the heart of the Big Eight.* He visited Barry Switzer and the Oklahoma Sooners, but his mom told him he wasn't going there. Ryan's high school coach, Tony Severino, told him he would give his left arm to play for Holtz, which made the decision to play for the Irish even easier.

Nebraska still tried to de-recruit Ryan from Notre Dame. The Cornhusker coach recruiting Ryan said he would rather see him play at Oklahoma, an in-conference nemesis, than suit up for Notre Dame.

"It was the oddest thing I had ever heard," Ryan said.

It was a preemptive strike. The college football world knew Holtz kept adding to an arsenal of Notre Dame talent, and that would be tough to stop.

On Friday, the team ate lunch in the Monogram Room of the Joyce Center before boarding buses for the three-hour ride to East Lansing. In late November 1966, the No. 1–ranked Irish traveled by train to face No. 2 Michigan State in one of college football's games of the century. Without quarterback Terry Hanratty, who was

---

*The Big Eight grew to become the current Big 12. The eight schools were Oklahoma, Nebraska, Colorado, Iowa State, Kansas, Kansas State, Missouri, and Oklahoma State.

injured in the first quarter, and running back Nick Eddy, who didn't play because of injury, Notre Dame came from behind to tie the game at 10 in the fourth quarter. The Irish got the ball back at their 30-yard line, and instead of driving down the field, coach Ara Parseghian ran the ball and drained the clock, playing for the tie. Notre Dame came away with the national championship that year, even though Parseghian received criticism because he played for the tie.

National audiences watched that game on a tape delay. At the time, the NCAA limited the number of national TV appearances a school could have each season, so ABC broadcast the game live in local markets. Meanwhile, in other parts of the country, where viewers waited to watch the game, announcers warned people to turn away from their screens when the network posted live score updates. The '88 game did air live to a national audience, and it opened a doubleheader. The headline act came from the No. 1–ranked Miami Hurricanes' matchup with Michigan. The Irish and Spartans played in an ABC noontime tilt.

"We can't win unless we throw the football," Holtz said. "I know that, and you know that. The only problem is our players don't know that."

Six plays into the game, Tony Rice dropped back to throw his first pass. Michigan State's Kurt Larson intercepted it and returned it 7 yards to the Notre Dame 43-yard line. The Spartans used the turnover to take a 3–0 lead.

The white s logo adorned one side of Michigan State's green helmets, and the other side, which was normally blank, had number 79 stickers honoring their suspended teammate, Tony Mandarich.

Mandarich, the freakish specimen of an offensive tackle, watched the game from the stands in a Powerhouse weight-lifting T-shirt and a mesh-backed Michigan State hat with his mullet hanging out the back. He stood 6'6", weighed 315 pounds, and ran a fullbacklike

4.68 forty-yard dash. Media, coaches, and pro scouts drooled over him.

In the summer before his senior season, Mandarich wrote a letter putting himself in the NFL's supplemental draft. A month later, after having second thoughts about going pro, he wrote NFL Commissioner Pete Rozelle to rescind his entry. Even though he never signed with an agent or accepted any money, the NCAA ruled that Mandarich had lost his amateur status and suspended him for the first three games of the season.

The suspension didn't quell the media infatuation. *The New York Times* and the *Chicago Tribune* wrote pieces highlighting Mandarich's seven meals a day: three 3,000-calorie shakes, a three-pound chicken, or three three-ounce beef patties and two feedings of thin steaks.

Michigan State's head coach, George Perles, who was an assistant on all four 1970s Super Bowl–winning Pittsburgh Steeler teams, called Mandarich the "finest offensive lineman I've been around."

In the lead-up to the following year's NFL draft, *Sports Illustrated* put a shirtless, backward-hat-wearing Mandarich on the cover. The headline christened him "the Incredible Bulk" and declared him "the best offensive line prospect ever."

Of course people questioned if Mandarich used steroids. At the time, he denied ever using them. "They're drugs, just like cocaine, and they should be banned," he told *The New York Times*.

Without using their names, the *Sports Illustrated* article quoted a Big Ten assistant coach and a defensive player claiming Mandarich did use steroids. The feature then quickly pointed out Mandarich had passed three drug tests at that point.

Mandarich was a character in an era of marketed and mythologized sports rebels. The "Punky QB" Jim McMahon had led the Chicago Bears to the Super Bowl two years earlier. McMahon's college protégé, "the Boz," Brian Bosworth, wore mirrored sunglasses, a headband and dyed colorful streaks into the sides of his blond hair while playing for Oklahoma. Deion Sanders, the Florida State cornerback, created his "Prime Time" persona. Nike would soon be launching its "Bo Knows" ad campaign for Bo Jackson, who was initially viewed as defiant for playing baseball and football and not settling for one sport.

Writers ate up the Mandarich character, the obscenity-spewing, weight-lifting machine who worked out to the heavy metal sound of Guns N' Roses and emulated the style of Axl Rose, the band's front man. Mandarich said he wanted to be the first guy to play pro football and then become Mr. Universe, the ultimate bodybuilding champion.

"It was 100 percent marketing and calculated," Mandarich said.

Mandarich grew up in Oakville, Ontario, Canada. He embraced the gym-rat culture and found influences in the Arnold Schwarzenegger bodybuilding movie *Pumping Iron* and Sylvester Stallone's *Rocky*. He moved to Ohio to play high school football in the States and get a college scholarship. Nick Saban, then an assistant with the Spartans, recruited Mandarich out of Theodore Roosevelt High School in Kent. Even though he denied it back then, Mandarich started on the juice in the summer after his senior year of high school.

He cycled on and off steroids, taking low doses for twelve weeks and then staying off the drugs for twelve weeks, all the time working out like a fiend.

"Some people who are naive about steroids think that you can take them and just become strong. That's not the case. You still have to work out. Is it cheating? Absolutely, 100 percent it is. If the rules say you can't use steroids and you take them, you're cheating. Did I cheat? Absolutely. Did I know I was cheating? Absolutely. But did I know there was going to be consequences if I got caught? Yeah. Was it going to be long-term consequences with health? Probably," Mandarich said. "I thought of all of those things as time went on and my decision was still to do it."

After the suspension, when he returned to the Michigan State lineup the Spartans went 6-1-1. In a steroid-fueled rage, at the coin toss against Ohio State, Mandarich punched a Buckeye defensive lineman in the chest and told him, "You're going to die today."

While his team played Notre Dame, his biggest game action came in a sideline interview.

"Have you ever seen a more imposing offensive lineman than Mandarich?" asked ABC's play-by-play man Gary Bender after the interview.

"I never have," said former NFL and UCLA coach Dick Vermeil, who handled the color commentary.

With the game tied at 3 in the second quarter, Rocket Ismail sped through the Michigan State line and blocked a punt. He showed an uncanny burst of speed to get to the ball. He lined up in a three-point stance with his hand on the ground at the 20-yard line. In 2.1 seconds, the 5'10" freshman covered 10 yards. A blocker pushed his shoulder, but Rocket blew by him into the backfield and extended his body to the point where he nearly could have caught the ball off the punter's foot.

"Rocket Ismail may be the best player I've ever been around," Alvarez said.

The Notre Dame offense took over at the Spartan 7-yard line. In three plays the Irish gained 2 yards and settled for another Reggie Ho field goal.

After becoming the hero who beat Michigan the week before, the tiny man playing the big man's game went back to his dorm room and slept. Ho wanted to keep a low profile, but he had become a national story, a media fascination.

A blurb in the *Indianapolis News* wrote about Ho, surrounded by reporters in the locker room after the Michigan game, asking a student assistant in the sports information office if he had studied for their musculo-skeletal anatomy class.

"I don't want to let this get to my head, sir," Ho told the Gannett News Service. "I just want to be an ordinary, average person. I just want to be a doctor and help people."

A devout Catholic with siblings at Notre Dame, Ho never aspired to get an athletic scholarship. Even though he had another year of athletic eligibility, he knew he wanted to move on to medical school or maybe join the Peace Corps.

"I'm doing this purely for Notre Dame. They've done so much for me, no way would I ever take money from them," he told the press.

He called reporters "sir." He always credited his holder, Peter Graham, and Tim Grunhard, the long snapper. He tried to avoid attention by walking through campus with his head down, but he couldn't elude the spotlight.

College & Pro Football Weekly and eventually ESPN posted his course load. Besides the anatomy class, he took biochemistry, medical anthropology, computers, philosophy of science, and Western literature.

Cavanaugh Hall rector Fr. Matthew Miceli wrote a poem, "The Mighty Ho," and the student newspaper printed part of it.

Soon *Asian World* wrote about him, and *Sports Illustrated* devoted a three-page spread to the kicker.

Ho said he developed his kicking routine with his dad in high school. His "special voodoo" fingers, as he called them, relieved his stress.

In *Sports Illustrated*, William Nack described it poetically: "He swept his arms to his right, looking like a bullfighter holding an invisible cape, and began waving his fingers, strumming the air with them, as though he were playing castanets."

.   .   .

No. 8 Notre Dame went to the half up 6–3 against unranked Michigan State. The Irish had managed just 50 yards rushing. Notre Dame quarterbacks had completed as many passes to Michigan State as they had to their own team. Tony Rice and backup Kent Graham were 2 of 9 for 50 yards and 2 interceptions. Rice's 2 completions were near-lateral passes: a swing pass to Mark Green in the flat that went for 38 yards and a quick throw along the line of scrimmage to Ricky Watters, who ran with it for 12 yards.

Throwing only twice, the Irish pretty much shelved the passing game in the second half. Instead, Notre Dame asserted its dominance on the ground, rushing for 156 yards in the third quarter alone. Both fullbacks, Anthony Johnson and Braxston Banks, went down with injuries. With no preparation, tailback Tony Brooks moved into the position.

"I don't know of anybody mentally tougher than Tony Brooks," said guard Tim Ryan. "He got the ball and he ran. If he was banged up, you never knew. That guy was from a different planet."

Brooks actually had a stress fracture of the fifth metatarsal on his left foot, a break in the bone leading up to the pinky toe. He didn't have much support from the arch in his foot, and the constant running and cuts made by his 230-pound frame caused the break. Coaches expected him to miss the opener against Michigan, but he played, rushing for 48 yards on 7 carries and catching an 18-yard pass on the game-winning drive.

Even with the fracture, he wasn't going to sit out. The training staff put together an orthotic that reduced some of the pain, and Holtz tried to call running plays to Brooks's right to limit planting on the left foot.

Brooks relished the physical pounding of the game. He played running back like a linebacker. He ran into collisions. It started back in his hometown of Tulsa, Oklahoma, when Brooks first put on pads in third grade. His coaches cheered the contact, and Brooks enjoyed the bull-in-the-ring drill where one player chopped his feet in the middle, awaiting a charging hit from one of a group of players circling him.

In middle school he broke his ankle. The doctor put him in a cast that ended just below his knee. Tony kept playing tackle football in the neighborhood. Twice he broke the cast. Then his mother had the doctor cast his leg all the way up to his hip.

"His threshold for pain was ridiculous," said Reggie Brooks, his little brother and an eventual Heisman Trophy finalist at Notre Dame.

On Notre Dame's first offensive play of the second half, Brooks took a Tony Rice pitch to his right. He cut upfield, twisted out of tackles, leaped over his own downed player, and thundered up the sideline for 37 yards. Instead of going out of bounds, he finished the play by lowering his shoulder and running through a defensive back for the final 3 yards.

Five plays later, Rice kept the ball on the option and streaked 8 yards into the end zone. Ninety-one plays and 437 yards into the season, and a Notre Dame offensive player had crossed the goal line.

The Irish led 13–3. The offense continued to dominate on the ground, totaling 245 yards on the day with senior captain Mark Green picking up 125 yards on 21 carries. The next Irish drive stopped at the Michigan State 6-yard line, and a bad snap prevented a field goal attempt by Ho. Midway through the fourth quarter, Notre Dame went for it on fourth down at the Michigan State 14-yard line, and Rice coughed up a fumble on an option play.

The score may have indicated Michigan State had a chance to come back, but the Notre Dame defense never did. The Irish stifled the Spartans in the second half, limiting them to 118 yards on offense. Michigan State never advanced the ball past the Notre Dame 32-yard line, and the Spartans ran only five second-half plays in

Irish territory. Dropping back into pass coverage in the fourth quarter, Michael Stonebreaker put an exclamation point on the defensive play. He picked off a Bobby McAllister pass thrown into his gut and returned 39 yards for the touchdown. Barry Alvarez lifted Stonebreaker off his feet as the linebacker strolled to the sideline having given Notre Dame the 20–3 lead.

The week before, in his return after being academically ineligible for the '87 season, Stonebreaker posted 19 tackles against Michigan. He had already posted 10 tackles against Michigan State when he scored the touchdown, which came on his second interception of the day.

The Notre Dame fans in Spartan Stadium began singing, "Nah-nah-nah-nah, nah-nah-nah-nah, hey-hey-hey, good-bye." The announcers filled much of the remaining airtime by talking about the upcoming Miami-Michigan game.

"We find a way to win. It's not real pretty," Holtz said in the postgame interview.

After two games, the Irish had 2 wins, and the defense, special teams, and offense all had 1 touchdown each.

Notre Dame boarded buses in East Lansing, and sixty-five miles south the Miami Hurricanes took their thirty-three-game regular-season winning streak into Ann Arbor.

With 7:16 left in the game, Miami had the ball and trailed Michigan 30–14 before a crowd of 105,000 at the Big House.

Steve Walsh, the All-American quarterback, stepped into the 'Canes huddle.

"Don't worry about it. We've been here before. We can get this done," he said.

The previous season, Miami came from 16 points down to beat Florida State en route to winning the national championship.

He looked around the huddle again and noticed no one from the championship team was there.

"Just don't worry about it. I'll handle it," he said.

Without ever using a time-out, Walsh led Miami on a 17-point comeback. College football's bogeyman survived. Walsh threw for 335 yards and 3 touchdowns. He and Stonebreaker were named the college players of the week by *College & Pro Football Weekly*. The No. 1–ranked Hurricanes were less than a month away from bringing their winning streak to Notre Dame Stadium.

CHAPTER 10

Throwing Darts

Tony Rice stood calmly, eyed the target, set his arm back, and threw for the bull's-eye, literally.

Holtz suggested Rice throw darts in his dorm room because it requires the same release as throwing a football.

Even though Rice engineered more than 500 yards of offense in the first 2 wins, his passing numbers made him look like a one-dimensional quarterback. Rice started the season a dismal 5 of 21 for 90 yards and 2 interceptions. As the team prepared for Purdue, Notre Dame even began to practice the halfback option pass, letting running back Mark Green throw the ball.

The Fighting Irish could have a really good season with Rice solely as a running quarterback. They could run the ball with dominance. The defense would always keep them in games, but, for them to have a shot at greatness, at perfection, Rice needed to connect on his throws. He had to make opposing teams respect his arm or be embarrassed by it if they didn't.

"This is the year of the big-gun quarterback in college football," Ralph Wiley wrote in an early-October *Sports Illustrated* article. "You don't mean a thing if you ain't got that fling."

Rice could throw a deep ball. Fooling around after practice, Rice stepped back to the 20-yard line and launched the ball 80 yards, dropping it to an uncovered receiver crossing the goal line.

Up until this point in games, though, Rice lofted throws high in the air and sent them sailing over receivers' heads. While it looked unattractive on the field, Rice knew he could make accurate throws.

Back in Woodruff he and his older brother, Rodney, played with another set of brothers. The Rice boys split up in constant older-versus-younger tag teams. They wrassled each other. The older boys pretended they were the villainous "Minnesota Wrecking Crew," Ole and Arn Anderson. Tony and his partner were the good guys, Ricky Morton and Robert Gibson, the "Rock 'n' Roll Express."

One day, the pairs stood about 40 yards away from each other in a mud-ball fight. Rodney needed to sprint 15 feet for cover. He made his move, and Tony drilled him before Rodney found safe haven. Rodney dropped to the ground.

"From that distance, you wouldn't think it could get there that quick," Rodney said.

Turns out the mud ball had a chunk of red brick in it. Tony hit him in the head, splitting his skin open and sending him to the hospital for stitches.

Now, Tony needed that exactness on the football field, and he revived it with a game normally reserved for the corners of smoky bars. Every night in his room he threw a hundred darts, working on his motion, precision, and follow-through.

This wasn't the first time Rice had used his dorm room for supplemental football practice. He practiced pronouncing his play calls over and over again.

Gullah is its own language, a mixture of English and African languages once used by slaves. It is still spoken by the Gullah, or Geechee, people living on the islands off the Carolinas. Rice didn't speak Gullah, but it influenced his accent.

Quarterbacks have only seconds between snaps to spit out play names, identifying formations, motion and blocking assignments. Obviously, it is critical for everyone to understand the assignments.

During Rice's first Notre Dame season, running back Mark Green called some plays in the huddle because players couldn't understand the South Carolinian. Holtz simplified some play calls, reducing them to "Cowboy" and "RPG."

"After a while you learn to understand a guy's accent, but he was very tough to understand," said offensive tackle Andy Heck.

While the outside chatter on Rice questioned his ability to throw and left him with an indelible Prop 48 stamp, he just worked harder. His teammates watched their leader blossom. They never heard him speak of any difficulties. He never put forth an I'll-show-them attitude. He kept his desire to prove himself internal. His teammates saw a guy with a smile plastered across his face no matter the situation.

"No matter how hard a hit he took," Heck said, "he'd bounce up. He'd pick up the linemen. It's supposed to be the other way around."

Rice prided himself on getting up after plays. He knew it sent a message to his teammates, and he never gave a defense the satisfaction of thinking they had put a lick on him. "Hurry up and get up before you catch a cold," Rice said, describing his posttackle mindset. "I'll be right back at you."

When his offensive linemen missed a block, Rice smiled and patted them on the rear.

"I absolutely loved that guy and would've done anything for him," Heck said.

When the defense played, Rice stood close to the field to watch them. He cheered their big hits. Once a week, he would go to Macri's Deli and grab a sandwich with the linebackers. A quarterback needs talent to play the position, but to lead a team he needs the intangibles Rice displayed.

"Just from his attitude and the way he carried himself—I've never seen another quarterback quite like that," said center Mike Heldt.

Rice remained unruffled when Holtz put him through a meat grinder of scrutiny every day in practice.

"Lou got on any quarterback he ever coached every day in practice, unmercifully," Alvarez said. "He wanted game day to be easy for them. He wanted every day in practice to be hell for them. That was his philosophy."

"Hey, Ricky. Hey, Ricky," Holtz said, calling to Rice in practice.

"Yes, sir," Rice answered. Rice knew Holtz was referring to Rickey Foggie, an option quarterback out of South Carolina Rice played against in high school and Holtz started at Minnesota.

Man, this guy hates me, Rice thought.

Rice went to his position coach, Pete Cordelli.

"I don't think I can take him, man," Rice said.

"Always listen to the words that are coming out of his mouth, not the tone of his voice," Cordelli counseled him.

Rice constantly worked on fundamentals. To prevent a possible fumble during the quarterback-center exchange, he rotated down a line, taking snaps from every center on the roster. Rice ran down the field practicing the option, pitching with his left hand, then his right. He moved on to throwing on the run. He got back under center to polish the option attack. First, he took the snap and worked on handing off or faking to the fullback. The halfbacks joined, and they rehearsed the triple option. Then regular practice started.

On Thursdays, with no defense in their way, Rice had to lead the offense on a flawless 99-yard drive. Any imperfections reset the drill. An incompletion on third down sent the ball back to the 1-yard line. Missed assignments signaled a restart.

Players had to hustle. If they didn't, the team would hear from a coach. "He was lollygagging. Put it back. Start over again."

Back they ran, huddling in their own end zone to start the march again. Just as Rice drove the team within striking distance, a coach interrupted the rhythm.

"Holding on the offense."

Even though there was no one to hold, no one argued the call. They trotted backward and started the drive again.

In the midst of the action, Holtz quizzed Rice.

"What does your receiver do on this play?"

"What is your guard's assignment?"

"What's the tackle's technique?"

Holtz wanted Rice to think like the coach.

"If your quarterback is on the same page as you, you're going to be fine. The offensive line may not show up one week. The receivers might not. But your quarterback better show up each week and you better know what to expect. I want to know what to expect when we snap the ball. If I call this play and you're going to throw an interception one time and you're going to throw it into the stands the next time, a completion the next time, I can't live with that. If you're going to throw an interception, that's great. Throw it every time because I ain't going to call it then. But I have got to know what to expect, and the only way I know what to expect is to put pressure on you. I put on tremendous pressure," Holtz said. "Tony Rice, if I didn't get all over him, he wondered what was happening after a while."

One time in practice, Holtz told Rice to yell at his offensive linemen. This departed from Rice's leadership style. He was never the fiery quarterback who got in a player's face after a missed assignment. Still, he always listened to his coach and executed his directives.

"I was there, following orders. I'm yelling," Rice said.

A couple of plays later the offensive line responded. They let the defense through to crash the quarterback. "They knocked the hell out of me," Rice said. It is probably the only time Rice abandoned the coach's plan. He took a different tone in the next huddle.

"Hey, guys, I'm sorry. Coach Holtz told me to do it."

•   •   •

The starting quarterback at Notre Dame held status in the sports world, like the center fielder for the New York Yankees or a gold-medal sprinter. When a player crouched under center for the Irish, he entered a fraternity with an unparalleled lineage. Preseason Heisman Trophy candidate lists included a handful of All Americans and, almost by default, the Notre Dame quarterback.

Irish field generals had etched their names into the history of the game. The names Angelo Bertelli, Johnny Lujack, and Paul Hornung sounded like football. That trio, plus John Huarte, all won the Heisman Trophy. Two-time All American Terry Hanratty won a national championship, and so did All-American Tom Clements. After leaving Notre Dame, Daryle Lamonica became "the Mad Bomber" with the Oakland Raiders. He won 78 percent of his starts, played in Super Bowl II, and won one AFL Championship. Joe Theismann won an NFL MVP and a Super Bowl with the Washington Redskins. Joe Montana's spot on the Notre Dame depth chart fluctuated. Called off the bench in 1975, he led comebacks against North Carolina and Air Force. He won a national championship in 1977. The following year, hypothermia took him out of the Cotton Bowl. In the locker room, he received intravenous fluids and warmed himself up drinking soup made with chicken bouillon. He reentered the game and helped lead a 23-point fourth-quarter comeback for the 35–34 win against Houston. In the NFL, Montana became the best quarterback of his era. He had two of his three Super Bowl MVPs before Tony Rice stepped on campus.

In the Holtz system, Rice didn't have time to think about history. The coach's spotlight never shone on being the Notre Dame quarterback; it focused on doing your job.

"You'll either listen or sit on the bench," Rice said.

"Everything will fall in place if you do what I tell you to do," Holtz told him.

Rice wasn't the first black quarterback to start at Notre Dame.

That was Cliff Brown. After Theismann graduated in '71, for the
first time in years Notre Dame had no solid heir to the quarterback
throne. Brown, a sophomore playing his first varsity year, took hold
of the starting job after injuries sidelined two upperclassmen, Patrick Steenberge and Bill Etter.*

"For so long the black athlete was thought of as, 'Give him the
football and let him run—he can't think," Brown was quoted in a
1971 *New York Times* column. "My being first-string should convince
them that a black man can play at the helm anywhere if he's good
enough."

College recruiters constantly wanted black quarterbacks to
switch positions and play wide receiver, running back, or defensive
back. The general old-time bigoted arguments against black quarterbacks reasoned that they lacked the ability to understand playbook intricacies, they had trouble reading defenses, and white
teammates wouldn't take orders from a black leader. There were
concerns about alumni being less prone to support their alma maters
if a black player held the most important position on the football
team.

In 1988, the NFL had three black marquee quarterbacks. War-
ren Moon, who played in the Canadian Football League before getting an NFL contract, was a few years into a Hall of Fame career.
Doug Williams had just won the Super Bowl MVP with the Washington Redskins. At the end of the season, Randall Cunningham of
the Philadelphia Eagles would become the first black quarterback to
start a Pro Bowl. Yet even in the late '90s, NFL starters Charlie
Batch, Kordell Stewart, and Steve McNair would still be fielding
questions about being black quarterbacks.

---

*The 1971 Irish finished 8-2 and did not go to a bowl game. The following
season, without controversy, Tom Clements took over the quarterback
duties.

Seventeen years after *The New York Times* described Cliff Brown standing behind center with "the tufts of his modified Afro clinging to the rim of his football helmet," black quarterbacks had become regulars on the college level. In '88, 20 percent of Division I schools started a black quarterback. *The Sporting News College Football Yearbook* published a five-page article on black signal callers titled "Breaking the Color Barrier." The article focused on USC's Rodney Peete, the strong-armed Heisman candidate who also played third base on the Trojans' baseball team. It went into detail about Oklahoma's and Nebraska's option quarterbacks as well as Eric Jones of Vanderbilt, Terrence Jones of Tulane, and West Virginia's Major Harris. The only mention of Tony Rice came in a gray box listing the black starting quarterbacks.

Holtz received letters about it. Rice heard the talk. "They said Notre Dame couldn't win with a black quarterback," wrote Bill Bilinski, *South Bend Tribune* sports editor.

Rice avoided the subject of race himself, and it remains a topic he has little or nothing to say about. When it came up in interviews during his playing days, Rice changed the subject, telling reporters, "You kill them with your smile."

He did speak to his grandmother about it, and he took her advice.

"Turn the other cheek, and when your name is called upon to do something, you better do it with the best of your ability," she told him.

Holtz never touted offensive firepower as a key to victory. "If you play great defense, don't beat yourself on offense and have a good kicking game, you've got a chance against anybody in the world," he told the *Indianapolis Star* in the lead-up to the home game against Purdue.

Rice threw incomplete passes on his first 2 attempts. Then he completed his next 4 for 85 yards and 2 touchdowns. He played less than a half and racked up 67 yards rushing on 5 carries.

He opened the floodgates of scoring on an option play. Running to the left, the bowlegged quarterback cut up the field, slipping through an ankle tackle, then racing up the hash marks. He finished with his signature, and understated, end zone entrance, feet chopping to a stop and both hands raised, with one hand cupping the ball, forming a V with his torso. The 38-yard dash was the longest run of his career.

He connected with tight end Derek Brown for an 8-yard score, Brown's first career reception. Rice faked the option, dropped back, and threw a 54-yard touchdown pass to Rocket Ismail, which was Ismail's first career reception. After a Mark Green touchdown run the Irish led 28–0.

"Notre Dame is dominating this game. If that does not change, this stadium has been turned into a football classroom for the remainder of the game," said Jack Nolan, calling the game for a local South Bend broadcast.

Moments later Ricky Watters added a 66-yard punt return for a touchdown. Steve Belles, the third-string quarterback, entered the game in the second quarter. He floated a short pass to Tony Brooks, who had ducked through the line of scrimmage. No one came close to Brooks on the 34-yard score. The Irish led 42–0. On the ensuing kickoff, Belles made the tackle. It has to be one of the only times in modern football that the touchdown-throwing quarterback made the tackle on the following kickoff.

The Irish rushed for 236 yards in the first half and added 119 yards passing. Holtz, up 6 touchdowns, implemented a stone-faced media plan during the halftime TV interview.

He spoke about two penalties that hurt Notre Dame. "There

really isn't that much difference between the schools, I promise you," Holtz said to WGN, the network broadcasting the game throughout the country.

"This happens to be Notre Dame's day for a half. What we have got to remember is we have another half."

The Irish buttoned it up for the final two quarters. When Billy Hackett nailed a 44-yard field goal it gave Notre Dame 45 points, which is 1 more point than Purdue had baton twirlers at the game. In the fourth quarter, announcers had trouble identifying tacklers. The Irish played so many people that some wore duplicate numbers or numbers that weren't on any roster. Of Notre Dame's 7 touchdowns, 5 came on plays of 34 yards or longer. When Rodney Culver took an option pitch from Kent Graham and ran 36 yards for a touchdown, he became the third freshman to score a touchdown on the day. The Irish finished with a 52–7 win over the Boilermakers.

With losses by three teams ranked ahead of Notre Dame, the Irish climbed from No. 8 to No. 5 in the AP poll.

While the Fighting Irish headed into the Stanford game, a *Sports Illustrated* article touting USC's win against Oklahoma questioned how good Notre Dame would be if they had Rodney Peete.

As raindrops drizzled into Notre Dame Stadium, ESPN's broadcast opened with a similar refrain.

"There is a major question about the Irish ability to throw the football," said play-by-play man Mike Patrick.

"Tony Rice, the quarterback, has got to be able to throw, and the receivers have got to be able to catch the ball. That is a problem for Notre Dame. If they're going to challenge this year for the national title, and I believe that's what they want to do—every team does—then they're going to have to throw the ball, and Tony Rice is going to have to do it," added color commentator Kevin Kiley.

Rice believed in himself even if his stats said different. "These guys didn't think I could do it. Okay, that's fine and dandy," Rice said years later. "They can write about a lot of things that are not true. The only thing we were worried about was winning."

Against Stanford, the defense set the tone early. On the first play from scrimmage, Notre Dame's Chris Zorich stood up his blocker, tossed him aside, grabbed the Cardinal ball carrier, and pushed him backward as four other Irish players piled on. Zorich popped up from the pile, his shoulder and neck giving a twitch as he headed back into the defensive huddle. The nose tackle played at a simmer just below frenzy.

"You couldn't congratulate him because he didn't want you to touch him. He didn't want the opponent to touch him. He didn't want the referees or the coaches to touch him. I just remember Chris in the huddle saying, 'Don't touch me,'" said safety Pat Terrell.

When the Irish offense took over, Rice unveiled the best game of his Notre Dame career to date. He rushed for 107 yards and 2 touchdowns on 14 carries. He completed 11 of 14 pass attempts for 129 yards and a touchdown. For all the noise about his inefficacy throwing the ball, he tied a Notre Dame record by completing 10 consecutive passes.*

Rice's first score typified Notre Dame's unrelenting run blocking. Everyone hit somebody, and they didn't stop until the whistle blew. Sprung by blocks from pulling guard Tim Grunhard and fullback Anthony Johnson, Rice darted up an alley. He barely broke stride moving to the outside as a Cardinal tackler grabbed his arm and slid off him, spinning to the ground. One defender had a shot, but Ricky Watters laid a shoulder into him, and Rice headed to the corner of the goal line, finishing the 30-yard run.

---

*Rice completed his last four passes against Purdue and his first six against Stanford.

This was the first game between Notre Dame and Stanford since 1964. The most famous game in the rivalry played out in the Rose Bowl on January 1, 1925. Knute Rockne brought the Four Horsemen—Elmer Layden, Jim Crowley, Harry Stuhldreher, and Don Miller—to Pasadena, California, to square off against coach Glenn "Pop" Warner and All American Ernie Nevers. The Irish won 27–10 and claimed the school's first national championship after their first bowl appearance. For the next forty-five years Notre Dame, as a policy, stayed away from bowl games.*

The 1988 game got chippy. When Notre Dame went up 14–0 on a 2-point conversion by Rice, a Stanford player drew an un-sportsmanlike conduct flag for drilling the quarterback after the play ended. The Notre Dame defense responded. On the next Cardinal possession, George Streeter hit a Stanford running back out of bounds, though no official threw a penalty flag. Backup lineman Bob Dahl sacked Brian Johnson, whirling him to the ground.

Zorich went at it with the Stanford offensive line throughout the night. "They were talking some garbage," he told the *South Bend Tribune*, "but that just fires me up more."

With the Irish up 28–7, Anthony Johnson ran for 5 yards. Stanford cornerback Kevin Scott made the tackle and kept his arm on Johnson as both men tried to stand up. In a martial-arts-like move, Johnson swung his arm in a circular motion, knocking Scott's arm off his chest.

---

*"When we got to a certain point income became quite important, and football was very important here. We were in a building mode, and our budget was going up every year, and it was helpful to have a good team even though we didn't have a team for that purpose. But it turned out to be fortunate that the income that came in here went into academic advancement," Father Hesburgh said of the Irish's postseason return in the 1970 Cotton Bowl.

On the next play, Johnson ran up the middle for 3 yards. Cardinal linebacker Kevin Richardson hit him late. Richardson and Johnson jawed at each other while Notre Dame guard Tim Grunhard intervened, backing Johnson away.

"I'll tell ya, Anthony Johnson is tough," Kiley said on the broadcast.

Johnson had a quiet, laid-back personality. The second oldest of nine children from a deeply Christian family, he took an unexpected delight in the violence of football. He enjoyed "being physical and not having to hold back and be restrained from hitting somebody as hard as you could and to some degree—and this may sound kind of off—being hit."

Johnson entered Notre Dame's on-campus student boxing tournament, the Bengal Bouts, because "I'd never been hit in the face before and I wanted to see what it was like."

He went to John Adams High School in South Bend, where he lettered for four years in soccer, a springtime sport in Indiana at the time. The soccer footwork aided Johnson's balance when he ran the ball up the middle with his low-to-the-ground style.

"If you needed two yards, he'll get it," Rice said.

Growing up he worked as a messenger for the ushers at Notre Dame Stadium, though he remembers watching football more than delivering any messages.

During one of his high school football games he left the field for a few plays because of an injury. The pain didn't subside after the game like it normally did. His mother drove him to the emergency room, where Johnson had to provide a urine sample.

"I peed V8 juice, basically," Johnson said.

He had played the remainder of the game with a lacerated kidney.

During his first game at Notre Dame, a plane flew over the stadium dragging the sign SOUTH BEND LOVES ANTHONY JOHNSON. Friends, teachers, and students from Johnson's middle and high school alma maters paid for the aerial acknowledgment of their hometown hero.

In the Stanford game, Johnson rushed for 58 yards, had a juggling 9-yard catch, and irritated the Cardinal defense. "A couple of times they were a little upset because I was hitting so low and [they] let me know it. But they're in our house and we don't take that," Johnson said after the 42–14 victory.

After the game, Ricky Watters, who led the team in receptions, laughed at the *Sports Illustrated* notion of Peete playing quarterback for the Irish instead of Tony Rice.

"Peete doesn't even come close," Watters said in the *Chicago Tribune*. "Peete, Aikman, all of them. I'll take [Tony] over them."

In the postgame media session, Rice mentioned the darts to reporters. "This whole week Coach Holtz had been telling me to throw darts in my room, and that really seemed to help a lot," he said.

With that comment it became a national story.

The darts helped, but "people really blew it out of proportion: 'That's what really made him a passing quarterback,'" Rice said. "It was all up in here and that's what Coach Holtz was trying to show me. 'By throwing darts, I'm going to have you thinking the darts really helped you out, but no. You really did it yourself.'"

In its last two contests, Notre Dame had dusted off opponents 94–21. The offense found a rhythm, and the defense continued its stout play, having given up 41 total points in all four games. Naturally, Holtz turned his attention to the future when he took questions from the media after the game.

"We have never played well at Pitt, and that game scares me to death," he said in a quote that would prove to be more foreshadowing than media gamesmanship.

CHAPTER 11

The Triple Fumble

Pat Terrell stood in the South Dining Hall. Still unnerved over his most recent position change, he snatched a flyer for a summer study-abroad program in international marketing.

Terrell came to Notre Dame as an option quarterback in Holtz's first recruiting class. As a sophomore he started games at wide receiver, playing opposite Notre Dame's Heisman Trophy–winning flanker Tim Brown. Heading into that season's Cotton Bowl against Texas A&M, Terrell had caught 2 passes.

"It was an extremely embarrassing statistic," he said. "My main role was to run decoy routes. So I was a little frustrated."

The day before the Cotton Bowl, Notre Dame practiced at Southern Methodist University. Terrell's parents had driven from Lakewood, Florida, to see their son play. They sat in the stands with other families watching practice. The team looked lackadaisical.

The offense called a pass play. Terrell lined up on the outside. The ball snapped; he sprinted off the line of scrimmage toward the middle of the field. Tony Rice threw him a tight spiral, a perfect pass. The ball went through Terrell's hands, hit his chest, and dropped to the ground. Thud.

Holtz had been standing in the secondary watching the play unfold. Now he started running right at Terrell.

Aw, what's he going to do? Terrell thought.

Then Holtz ran by him, not even glancing at Terrell. He ran through the linebackers, through the defensive line, and past the offensive line until he stopped, nose to face mask with Rice.

Rice eyed the receiver. Terrell tried to have his look back at the quarterback say, "Sorry."

Holtz grabbed Rice's face mask and let it rip.

"That's your fault. I don't care how open Pat Terrell is—do not throw him the ball. Take the sack. I don't care if he is so open you could walk up and hand him the football. Take the sack."

"Not only was it embarrassing, he called practice immediately after that," Terrell said.

The team headed off the field to the locker room. Holtz jogged over to Terrell and put his arm around him. Terrell thought he was about to get consoled.

"Pat, let me tell you something. Son, you're the best receiver I've ever coached."

A smile started to spread across Terrell's face.

"The best receiver," Holtz continued, "until I throw you the damn football. I'm moving you to defensive back in the spring."

At age ten Terrell had been embarrassed when he froze at his piano recital, but this was his low point. Going into his junior season, Holtz moved Terrell to free safety, where Terrell sat behind a team leader and one of the most well-liked players. Senior Corny Southall had experience and a lock on the starting position. Terrell thought about transferring, but his dad didn't raise quitters, and he knew his father had no tolerance for Pat wanting to leave because he faced a little adversity. So he made a little pact with himself.

"I'm going to make my scholarship one of Notre Dame's most expensive scholarships they've ever had," Terrell said.

Academics sat atop the priority list on the Notre Dame campus, even for football players. Now, with no NFL future in sight, Terrell wanted to study abroad.

He walked into an assistant athletic director's office and requested to take the international business course. Because of the expense, it had to be cleared with the NCAA. Terrell asked if he could write the clearance letter. He expressed his gratitude for the opportunity his athletic scholarship provided, and he addressed it limiting him from doing something he always wanted to do—study overseas. The NCAA approved his request to take the course.

At first, Holtz expressed some apprehension about Terrell's idea, but he quickly supported it. It wouldn't interfere with any other summer course work or football, and the coach realized he and his staff could further bolster Notre Dame's academic credentials on the recruiting trail with evidence of players studying abroad.

"Who else is going?" Holtz asked.

Terrell offered up Anthony Johnson and Stan Smagala, even though his teammates had no idea about the program.

Johnson and Smagala did join Terrell. The trio, grouped with Ivy League students, traveled to London, Italy, France, and the Netherlands. They met with executives in the boardrooms of Gucci, Price Waterhouse, and Cadbury Schweppes. They discussed the challenges and different aspects of multinational marketing and marketing in the United States.

Terrell came back to South Bend and he hadn't left his irritated mentality overseas.

"I was mad at the world, but I knew I had a great opportunity. I knew I wanted to be on the field. I had a chip on my shoulder, and that helped me with my aggression," Terrell said.

For Terrell, football is a game of respect. He was either earning it or losing it. As a backup, shifted from position to position, he set out to gain respect by throwing his body at plays, disregarding his safety and being recognized as a hard-nosed hitter. "I wanted people to know number 15 is back there and he has a loose screw," he said.

Terrell had no idea Barry Alvarez had been in staff meetings battling to move him to the defensive side of the ball. "I had coached him as a sprinter on the punt team. He could run and he could really hit. He was a very physical player and a smart kid," Alvarez said.

Holtz was reluctant, but Alvarez kept saying, "I could use him at safety."

Terrell rotated into games playing in the secondary and on special teams during Notre Dame's 4 wins. Going into the Pittsburgh game, he had 9 tackles and 1 interception when he supplanted Southall as the starting free safety.

Now, when Terrell practiced with the first-string defense it was his job to call out the assignments in the secondary. The offense would come out of the huddle "and it looked like spaghetti. Guys were lining up all over the place and I have to make the call, and I missed it a couple times," he said.

George Streeter, the senior starter at strong safety, noticed the mistakes. The product of the Chicago public high school league had been through Faust's final year, playing on a team that crumbled, in part, because of poor practice habits. Now he was a senior on a 4–0 team ranked fifth in the nation, and he watched a younger player, who had taken his best friend's starting spot, act confused and misread the offense.

"Why are you even in here?" Streeter snapped at Terrell in the defensive huddle. "How long am I going to have to line up with you if you can't even make the calls?"

"We are not going to be the ones who will lose games for us. Your ass better step it up right now or I'm going to kick your ass," Streeter said.

Like any man in his testosterone-filled early twenties, Terrell had a multitude of options with which to respond.

A healthy tension existed between the young hotshots, whose moxie Terrell admired, and the veterans, particularly those from the Faust era. Younger players changed the music on the locker room stereo, trampling an unwritten etiquette, and this led to constant shouting matches.

"They were our brothers," said Frank Stams, one of three fifth-year seniors on the team. "We can get mad at them, but don't dare let anyone else get mad at them or pick on them. I'm not going to say it was all roses, but if we had some problems, we could get it settled as a team and it was done with."

On the practice field, if somebody missed a play, top-tier players—starters or not—got on each other. It wasn't chiding. It was the players' accountability code. They used different words, but it was no different than the intent behind the coaches' concentration on perfection.

When Streeter lit into Terrell, Terrell respected it.

"I'll never forget George Streeter going off on me in the huddle," Terrell said. "It made me understand the magnitude of how important it was for me to play well and get the defense lined up."

The live test for Terrell came at Pittsburgh. The Irish had not beaten the Panthers since 1982. Notre Dame lost to Pitt 10–9 in Holtz's first season. In the most recent meeting, Pitt jumped out to a 27–0 lead and held off the Irish for a 30–22 win. The Panthers had a 2–2 record, beating Northern Iowa and No. 18 Ohio State to open the season and then falling to No. 11 West Virginia and Boston College. They looked average, but they played far better against the Irish.

The Panthers came out throwing. Four straight pass plays and Pitt reached the Notre Dame 14-yard line. There the Panthers turned to the ground game. Quarterback Darnell Dickerson ran an option play and pitched to freshman running back "Swervin'" Curvin Richards. Sweeping around the left side, Richards headed for the goal line. In a textbook tackle, Notre Dame cornerback Todd Lyght wrapped up Richards and put his helmet on the ball, jarring it loose. Chris Zorich trailed the play, slid to the ground, and gobbled up the fumble at the 2-yard line.

Rice returned to the field where he had lined up under the guard the year before when he replaced an injured Terry Andrysiak. Rice moved the Irish out to the 21-yard line. On third down and 5, he rolled right and under threw Steve Alaniz. Pitt's Alonzo Hampton intercepted the pass, giving the Panthers possession at their own 46-yard line.

Four plays later, Dickerson dropped back 11 yards and unleashed a 53-yard bomb to the end zone. Reggie Williams beat the Notre Dame secondary down the middle of the field. He had two steps on Smagala when the ball dropped to him just beyond Terrell's outstretched arms.

Seventeen plays into the game and Pitt took a 7–0 lead. Each team had turned the ball over. Instead of Notre Dame setting the tempo, Pitt dictated it. The Irish defense put little pressure on Dickerson, who had so much time to move around it seemed like a street game of two-hand-touch. In its first two possessions Pitt averaged nearly 6 yards per play.

The Pitt defense forced another Notre Dame third down. Rice dropped back and handed the ball off to Tony Brooks on a draw play. The big halfback rumbled 52 yards to the Pitt 2. With the wishbone formation behind him, Rice dove into the end zone on a busted play.

Notre Dame asserted itself again on its next drive. The Irish went 86 yards on fourteen plays. With first and goal at the 2-yard line, Notre Dame dialed up the sexy monotony of smashmouth football. Fullback Anthony Johnson ran up the middle for a yard.

Second down: Johnson up the middle for no gain.

"I guarantee Lou Holtz will not call that play again," said Lee Corso, ESPN's color analyst for the game.

Third down: Johnson up the middle, no gain.

The Irish called time-out. They were going for the touchdown, not settling for a field goal. The offense huddled around Holtz on the sideline. Nothing creative came out of it.

The Pitt Stadium crowd stood and roared when play resumed. On fourth down, tackle Andy Heck pushed his defender 2 yards into the end zone. Johnson ran inside him for the score. The Irish took a 14–7 lead.

After the play, starting guard Tim Grunhard, the 6'3" 279-pound lineman, sat on the turf between two trainers. Holtz jogged out on the field and knelt in front of Grunhard to check on him. The lineman lunged over, grabbing his right ankle. He declined assistance, hopped up, and limped off the field.

With a little more than six minutes to play in the first half, Pitt lined up to convert fourth down and 4 at the Notre Dame 33-yard line. Dickerson dropped back to pass. He surveyed the field and moved to his left. Stams and Zorich closed in on him, but like a schoolyard QB, Dickerson launched a ball to the end zone, finding Henry Tuten behind Todd Lyght for the score. Pitt tied the game; Dickerson looked like an All American, and Notre Dame hadn't slowed him.

This was the first time all season that receivers got behind Notre Dame defensive backs, and it happened twice for touchdowns. The longest play the Irish had given up entering the Pitt game was a 37-yard pass to Andre Rison at Michigan State, a blip in a game the defense dominated. The highly ranked Michigan Wolverines never had a play from scrimmage for more than 20 yards.

No. 1–ranked Miami and its vaunted passing offense had the week off. The Hurricanes had to salivate at opportunities they saw in the Irish secondary. If Dickerson played a step ahead of the Irish defense, just imagine what Steve Walsh and the Miami speed would be able to do.

Notre Dame answered the touchdown pass with a Reggie Ho field goal. The Fighting Irish led 17–14, and rain began to fall toward the close of the first half. In Pitt's final drive of the second quarter, Dickerson led the Panthers to the Notre Dame 9-yard line with less than a minute to play. On first down, Dickerson ran the triple option.

He faked a handoff to the fullback. He ran left, saw an alley, and made a quick cut back to his right. He put on a stutter-step move. Linebacker Ned Bolcar slid to the artificial turf, trying to make the tackle. The crowd burst with noise anticipating the score. Dickerson had nothing but 9 feet between him, a touchdown, and a halftime lead for Pitt. The Panthers had not only shown they could play with the No. 5 team in the country, they had an edge on them.

Dickerson tried to bring the ball up from behind his right butt cheek up to the middle of his chest. Inexplicably, he fumbled. The ball spurted into the end zone. Dickerson trailed behind it, his eyes focused on the ball. He bent his knees, reaching down and locking both hands on the skipping ball. He slid to the ground and the ball squirted loose again. Dickerson popped up from his slide, his eyes fixed on the the ball, which rolled along the back of the end zone. He dove on it, hugging the ball to his shoulder, lying across the field. At the same moment, before he gained full possession, two Pitt team-mates and a Notre Dame defender pounced on Dickerson, popping the ball loose again. Instead of heading out of bounds, the ball rolled toward the field of play. Smagala swooped in, smothering it and making the recovery for Notre Dame.

"I've been coaching twenty-eight years and I've never seen a play like that, never," Corso said on the broadcast. "Let me tell you something, there is the Luck of the Irish."

"When I fell on it the first time I thought I had it," Dickerson said. "It was frustrating, because I can't figure out what happened," he said. "The rain had just started, but I can't really blame it on that. I guess I just didn't tuck it away. I couldn't believe it."

The game was tied at 17 with a little more than three minutes to play in the third quarter.

The Irish couldn't simply swat away this Pitt team. Nervousness seeped its way onto the Notre Dame sideline, but not with Tony Rice.

"Boy, it's a fun game, isn't it, Coach?" he said to Holtz.

"Hell, we're tied," Holtz said.

"Yes. We'll find out how good we are," Rice said before trotting on the field to lead the offense.

Rice led a touchdown-scoring drive that put the Irish up 23–17.

After starting slow in the passing game, Rice completed 5 of 7 second-half throws for 73 yards. All game he engineered an offense that answered every Pittsburgh score with a Notre Dame score.

Pitt pulled close again, adding a field goal to make it 23–20 with 11:19 to go.

The Panthers had one final chance to stop the Irish, but they extended the Notre Dame drive when they lined up with twelve men on the field on a punt play.

Notre Dame relied on its running game during its fourteen-play, 64-yard game-sealing drive. Mark Green capped the near-seven-minute campaign with an 8-yard touchdown run to put the Irish up 30–20.

Even though Pitt hung in the game, the Irish pounded the Panthers on the ground, rushing for 310 yards on 72 attempts. Seven Irish ball carriers had at least 2 rushes, and Notre Dame controlled the ball for 22½ minutes in the second half.

The defense settled down. After allowing 278 yards in the first two quarters. Notre Dame limited Pitt to 102 yards in the final two. Dickerson tallied 225 yards of offense before his fumble. After the flub, his play shrank to 70 total yards, including a 3-of-11 passing performance for 39 yards and an interception.

Freshman linebacker Arnold Ale intercepted Dickerson late in the fourth quarter and removed any thought of Pitt pulling out a victory.

With a little more than one minute on the game clock, the Notre Dame band began chanting, "We want Miami."

CHAPTER 12

Prelude to a Brawl

At dusk on a late-summer evening, the telephone rang in the office of the defending national champions.

"University of Miami Football, Jimmy Johnson speaking."

The caller was Doug Browne. He had just come back from an ice cream social during freshman orientation. He never thought the head football coach of the archenemy would be on the other end of the line.

"I'm beating the rush," Browne said. "I hate you now."

"What?"

"Yes. I'm a freshman caller from Notre Dame," he said from his Keenan Hall dorm room. "We're playing you in October, and I'm not waiting until then. I hate you now."

There was some very brief back-and-forth, and Johnson hung up the phone.

A classified ad in the school year's first edition of the student newspaper, *The Observer,* prompted Browne to call. "Beat the rush," it told readers before providing the telephone number and mailing address of the Hurricanes' football office.

This is what the rivalry had become.

There are other renowned college football rivalries—Auburn–Alabama; Ohio State–Michigan; Texas–Oklahoma—but those games mean less to fans outside those geographic regions. In the late 1980s,

Notre Dame–Miami was the equivalent of Lakers–Celtics. Everybody picked a side.

Notre Dame was the traditional college football power. Miami was the brash, unapologetic upstart that had rocketed to the top.

The Fighting Irish were steeped in history. Knute Rockne. "Win one for the Gipper." The Four Horsemen. The Hurricanes were steeped in "now," with alums Jim Kelly, Bernie Kosar, and Michael Irvin earning roles as NFL studs.

The Irish claimed an unmatched ten national championships. Miami had won two of the last five. With seven, Notre Dame had the most Heisman Trophy winners. In the previous two years, both schools were tied at one.

Notre Dame Stadium sat below the watchful eyes of Touchdown Jesus. The brick venue held 59,075 fans and the Irish mystique. "You could actually hear the echoes," said TV announcer Mike Patrick, who spent fifteen minutes soaking in the atmosphere a few days before he called the Stanford game for ESPN.

Miami played in the Orange Bowl, the same home field as the NFL's Miami Dolphins. Opponents watched the 'Canes enter the field through clouds of smoke while Luther Campbell, the leader of 2 Live Crew, a profanity-pushing rap group, patrolled the sideline as a team booster.

Notre Dame used to take trips to Miami for an easy win and a respite from the cold. From 1955 to 1980, Notre Dame was 13-1-1 against Miami, including an eleven-game win streak. As the 'Canes taunted and flaunted their way to national prominence, they started manhandling the Irish. Notre Dame's last win against Miami had come in 1982. Since then Miami had outscored the Irish 133–20 in the last four meetings. There was the 24–0 pounding in 1987 in Miami, where insults and objects were thrown at Notre Dame players and supporters, but it was the 58–7 pounding in 1985 that had Fighting Irish fans wanting revenge. The upcoming mid-October game, Miami's first trip to South Bend since 1984, was the best chance the Irish had to upend the Hurricanes and regain a spot on the top tier of college football.

Holtz watched Miami's ascent from college football doormat to elite program. When he wrote about recruiting the 1988 freshman class, the Hurricanes had become the measuring stick for all of college football. "There'll be people who can run," he wrote about the fresh crop of talent, but "we still don't match up with teams like Miami."

It had been eleven years since Notre Dame won the national title. Worse, the Irish had not even been in the national championship conversation. So for Notre Dame fans to "beat the rush" and hate Miami it was part adrenaline, part goofy college prank, and part coping mechanism—an attempt to maintain some level of superiority over this renegade outfit.

Freshman Doug Browne wasn't alone in heeding the call to vitriol. Soon after his phone call to Johnson, letters began arriving at the Miami Athletic Department. One was sent to "the Jimmy Johnson Fan Club" and postmarked September 12, two days after the Fighting Irish beat Michigan in the season opener. It came typed in three different styles of late-1980s word processor fonts:

"DEAR MR. JOHNSON,
   I AM BEATING THE RUSH!!!!!!!!!!!!!!
        I HATE YOU!!!!!
           I HATE YOU!!!!!!!!!!
             I HATE YOU!!!!!!!!!
          A **NOTRE DAME** STUDENT"

Another note altered Johnson's image into "pork-faced Satan," a moniker Irish fans created for him; the picture gave him horns coming out of his head, a black pointy goatee, a curling pointed tail, and a stick-figure body holding a pitchfork. A one-pager on lined notebook paper read, "Jim, EAT ME," and then used most of the page to write "N.D. #1" in bubble letters.

When Johnson got the call from Browne, the Hurricanes were getting ready to open the season against No. 1–ranked Florida State. At a pregame Miami boosters breakfast, Johnson told the crowd that in South Bend the Hurricanes were already the top priority. Johnson said he had received a call from a Notre Dame freshman who sounded "like a little girl."

Newspapers across the country picked up Johnson's breakfast anecdote. Shortly thereafter, Doug Browne returned to his dorm room to find news clippings taped to his door. His act of fandom had been verified.*

While Miami had the week off to rest before going to Notre Dame, the Irish headed into the showdown with a battered offensive line and bruised fullbacks.

"There was the general feel that Miami was going to win the game easily. Notre Dame had struggled a little bit against Pittsburgh," said Jeff Jeffers, the sports director for WNDU-TV, the South Bend NBC affiliate. "Notre Dame was a great team that year, but Miami was off the charts. I don't think too many people gave Notre Dame a chance."

Early in the week, Holtz wasn't giving the Irish a chance. "We're

---

*Though Browne had company hazing the 'Canes, new Notre Dame president Fr. Edward "Monk" Malloy called the freshman to his office to rebuke him for misrepresenting the university. Twenty-three years later, Malloy stayed overnight with Browne and his family while visiting a Notre Dame alumni club near Browne's home.

as banged up as I've ever seen a football team. Maybe we can get them to play eight-man football. Yeah, we'll play Arena Football," he said after the team's 30–20 win at Pitt.

Starting guards Tim Grunhard and Tim Ryan were both likely to be sidelined for the game; Grunhard had injured his ankle and Ryan his shoulder. Starting fullback Anthony Johnson was already beat up when he hurt his ankle. Braxston Banks, who shared time with Johnson, had a solid second half against the Panthers, running for a touchdown and catching 2 passes for 36 yards, but before the Pitt game Banks had been on crutches with a knee injury since he left the contest at Michigan State.

Outside of the injuries and the inevitable hype of the No. 1 team in the country playing at Notre Dame, Holtz did like one distraction his players had to focus on: midterm exams. "It will keep the players from thinking about the game too soon. I've never seen so many people on campus so excited about a football game, and that could have a negative effect. Hopefully, the exams will keep everything in perspective," he said.

While Holtz couldn't control the hype, he held command over practices. Holtz ratcheted up the already intense sessions. He admitted the practices were more physical than he would have liked that week, but with the injuries and subsequent personnel changes, he felt hitting was necessary for the offense to gain some continuity.

"He has always been a coach who put a lot of weight on attention to detail, but it was magnified that week," said Pat Terrell.

No one practiced under the microscope more than Tony Rice. The junior signal caller was the key to Notre Dame's run-heavy option offense. Holtz knew his team had to stop the Miami offense, but he also knew that in order to win, Notre Dame would have to score points against a Miami defense that hadn't given up a regular-season rushing touchdown in nearly a year.

The year before, when Notre Dame went to Miami, Holtz deviated from his typical offensive style. He tried to surprise the Hurricanes with a different game plan for Rice.

"I remember our preparation, 'We're going to make him a passer.' He wasn't a passer. He was a winner," Holtz said.

This year, the coach stuck to his system, but he added noise to practice. Loud music blared through speakers in anticipation of Saturday's raucous crowd. For the first time in his career, Rice wore a wristband with plays on it. In case it was too loud to hear the players who shuttled in the calls, Rice would have to use the wristband to set the offense.

"Tony, I want you to run the option and with your first step, stop and see where you're at," Holtz said at practice.

Rice crouched under center. He took the snap, pivoted, and planted his foot to start the play.

"Hold it." Holtz's voice cut through the music, halting the play.

Rice stood like a statue with his feet at what he thought was a 45-degree angle.

"No, you're not at a 45," Holtz told him.

"In my head, I'm thinking, *Yes I am. I know I am*," Rice said.

"Nope. You're not," Holtz said as if answering his quarterback's thinking.

"I don't want a 44.

"I don't want a 46.

"I want 45."

Rice got under center again, and the scene repeated itself... and repeated itself... and repeated itself.

"That's not what I want, son," Holtz said.

"I'm thinking, *He just wants to get up under my skin*," Rice said.

Rice never shot back at his coach. It wasn't his way to address the situation.

"If I was wrong, I was wrong. You go back at it again. But I never argued with him," Rice said. "It bothered you. But you listen to your elders. He brought me to Notre Dame and I was brought up by a lady from down South. You respect your elders."

Rice got under center again. The drill continued. Holtz barked about exactness. The quarterback thought about the guidance bestowed on him by his position coach, Pete Cordelli: "Listen to the words, not the way he's saying them." Rice smiled.

"Yes, sir.

"Yes, sir.

"Yes, sir.

"I'd be happy to."

As Miami week descended upon the Notre Dame campus, Holtz dialed Michigan's Bo Schembechler. The Wolverines had played both teams, losing both games by a total of 3 points.

"How good were they? What kind of chance do you think we have?" Holtz asked.

"We didn't get them playing their best," Schembechler said before talking about the wealth of talent on the Miami team. "But if you play very well, you can beat them," Schembechler concluded.

"I did that because that helped my confidence," Holtz said of the call.

Like the chop-busting conversations during two-a-day practices, Holtz shared this one with the team, too. "Hey, you know, they aren't from Mars. They aren't Supermen. They aren't from Krypton."

During his morning jogs around campus with defensive backs coach Chuck Heater, Barry Alvarez saw the bedsheets with anti-Hurricane messages hanging out dorm windows. "There was a buzz," he said. "An electricity in the air."

As he broke a sweat, the defensive coordinator pictured just what he wanted to welcome Miami. "A typical South Bend day. Gray. Cloudy. Misty. Get somebody from the sunshine of Miami and put them in that atmosphere," he told Heater.

Alvarez would have to slow the Miami offense, and he would need a better pass defense than the secondary had shown the week before. Pat Terrell knew this, too. The new starter watched extra game film throughout the week. He dissected the Pitt film, deconstructing the coverage breakdowns, and he watched as much of the Miami passing game as he could.

"I had a lot to prove there, not only in playing," Terrell said, "but in earning the confidence of my teammates."

The Hurricanes rode into South Bend on a thirty-six-game regular-season winning streak. They hadn't lost a regular-season game since the opener against Florida in 1985. Playing on the road, the Hurricanes had the same success, having ripped off twenty consecutive away-game wins.

Miami had gone from being the whipping boy to doling out whippings in only a few years. In the twelve seasons leading up to 1980, Miami had posted just two winning seasons, and those were both 6-5 campaigns. Overall, the team had amassed a 51-78 record from 1968 to 1979. The university considered dropping the program, but in 1979 Miami hired Howard Schnellenberger. The tweed-coat-wearing, pipe-smoking, mustachioed man brought NFL experience to a program that was using Burger King and the purchase of a Whopper to give away tickets to its season opener. Schnellenberger built the program by recruiting "the State of Miami," an imaginary roped-off area of South Florida that was mined for talent. He took his pipe and sports coat into inner-city Miami neighborhoods and found the talent to build a program in places national recruiters had overlooked.

In Schnellenberger's fifth year, Miami surprised the college football world by upsetting No. 1 Nebraska in the Orange Bowl to win the national championship. After that season, Schnellenberger left Miami to coach a USFL franchise that never played a game.

Enter Jimmy Johnson. He was an All–Southwestern Conference defensive lineman at Arkansas and a member of the school's 1964 national championship team. He went through the assistant coaching ranks at a high school and various colleges before landing the defensive coordinator job at his alma mater. Some assumed Johnson would become the Razorbacks head coach when Frank Broyles, the coach Johnson played for in college, stepped aside after the 1976 season. Instead, Broyles, who was also Arkansas's athletic director, hired Holtz.

A spurned Johnson became the defensive coordinator at Pittsburgh and the head coach at Oklahoma State before heading to Coral Gables, where he was greeted by some as a midwestern hayseed who didn't deserve the job.

Johnson didn't fit the standard football-coach image at the time. He wasn't Nebraska's Tom Osborne or Penn State's Joe Paterno. He let his players express themselves. He let their talk intimidate other teams, and he even did some trash talking himself. His eyes beamed with brightness and authority, and his lips curled into a slight but calculatedly noticeable shit-eating grin when he unloaded one of his arrogant comments.

He proudly, openly displayed a lack of reverence for the established college football hierarchy. About to play Penn State for the national championship in the 1987 Fiesta Bowl, Johnson sarcastically referred to Paterno, the *Sports Illustrated* Sportsman of the Year at the time, as "St. Joe." He responded to former Notre Dame coaching luminary Ara Parseghian's criticism of the 58–7 walloping with this: "Nobody cries louder and more pitifully than a bully who's just had the shit stomped out of him."

Johnson's football strategy was just as aggressive as his words. Rather than have defensive linemen who acted like lumbering oxen reading plays and then reacting, Johnson wanted speedsters attacking the play when the ball was snapped. "It's more than a technical strategy. It's a frame of mind that starts with the defensive line," Johnson said. "As soon as the ball moves, we are charging upfield."

Johnson had a psychology degree, and he used it to get more out of his team. While a 'Canes player might dance after getting a 4-yard first down, the players knew their job between the whistles was to fulfill Johnson's orders. If they didn't, they didn't get on the field. The falsehood about Miami during this era is that they were undisciplined. Evidence of that existed after the play or off the field. Were they dissidents? Definitely. Wouldn't a team that traveled to the 1987 national championship Fiesta Bowl in military fatigues be that? During games, however, they performed controlled demolitions of their opponents.

While the Miami defense had given up only 3 points in three of their four games, the offense excelled with a pro-style passing attack, something new to the college game. The 'Canes averaged 35 points per game going into Notre Dame, and this included games against No. 1 Florida State and at No. 15 Michigan. A cool-handed Heisman Trophy candidate, Steve Walsh hadn't been sacked in '88. The quarterback led an offense that averaged 451 yards per game. He came into the game with a national championship ring and had never lost a game as a college starter.

As Notre Dame's collision with the Hurricanes drew closer, whole oranges started disappearing en masse from the Notre Dame dining halls. Orange slices replaced that menu option because concerned school officials suspected students planned on throwing the fruit at players from the Citrus State.

This might seem ridiculous, but it was real. Officials from both schools monitored the situation and decided to beef up security for the game. There was an unhealthy hate flowing from fans, students, and subway alums alike.

"You would walk across the campus and looking at people you

got this sensation and you thought, *You guys think you're actually going to play in this game?* The students were talking more trash than some of us," Terrell said. "The student body wanted us to beat those guys as bad as we did."

If you were a Notre Dame fan during this period, the sight of the Hurricane logo led to an immediate and unexplainable surge of disdain.

"I personally hate Miami," John Smith was quoted in *The Observer* and *The Palm Beach Post.* "The players are a bunch of thugs."

"For me it's in good fun, but for some of the kids it's getting way out of hand," sophomore Lisa Mackett told the *Chicago Tribune.* "If I were a Miami person, I wouldn't feel comfortable being on campus."

All of this animosity flowed into a booming business—unlicensed student-made T-shirts.

There were simple designs like the one that read "Canes sUx" and used Miami's U logo as the *u.* Or the one that read "You can't spell scUM without UM." Another pronounced, "Even God hates Miami." Then there was this shirt: an interlocking ND logo on the front with the words above it "This is your brain"; on the back was the Miami logo and the phrase "This is your brain on drugs." Pop culture wedged its way into the pregame loathing. The "Hate Night at Notre Dame" T-shirt parodied *Late Night with David Letterman* on NBC. The back of the shirt offered the Top 10 Reasons to Hate Miami.

"It was like there were white hats and dark hats. Good guys and bad guys. We liked to think of ourselves as the good guys and Miami as the bad guys," recalled Fr. Tom Doyle, who was the student body president in '88.

By midweek, the fervor led a nun from Pennsylvania to call him and ask him to tone down the rhetoric because it didn't represent Catholicism.

"On one hand, the rhetoric was getting out of control and we sort of enjoyed it and it was laughable," Father Doyle said. "And all the while I think we were aware, too, that this was not the best expression of ourselves or the best manifestation of ourselves as a Catholic university."

The shirts poured salt onto Miami's public wounds. A string of incidents from 1986–87 had made the Hurricanes' outlaw label more reality than metaphor. The alleged crimes involved siphoning gas from a parked car, shoplifting sunglasses, choking a woman, and assaulting a girlfriend. The school investigated a group of players for leasing cars from a sports agent. Forty-seven players used a long-distance telephone code to make more than $8,000 in calls, which they paid back after getting caught. Nearly half the roster of players got into a shouting match with police at a campus party. Seven players lost some or all of their complimentary ticket privileges because of abuses. No one went to jail, and community service hours came down as the stiffest legal penalties, but the headlines cemented a guerrilla image for Hurricanes detractors.

Even though they were dropped after a month, separate charges of rape in a football dormitory peeled back a different layer of embarrassment for the University of Miami. School president Tad Foote wanted Miami to become an academic powerhouse, and the inquiry into the rape allegations revealed SAT scores for some Miami players. Selwyn Brown's verbal score was 270, the highest tally among a group that included wide receiver Michael Irvin, fullback Cleveland Gary, tight end Alfredo Roberts, and defensive backs Donald Ellis and Darrell Fullington. Ellis scored the minimum possible 200 on the verbal section. He and Gary were still on the Miami squad in '88. The others had gone on to the NFL.

"We had such a brash group of guys that weren't bashful about getting their names in the headlines for good things, and they understood that when you made mistakes off the field you were going to get your name in the headlines that way, too," said Rich Dalrymple, a Dallas Cowboys vice president, who was the Miami sports information director then.

With the 'Canes' position on the police blotter in mind, *the* T-shirt arrived. This one didn't use pop culture. Instead it created its own place in the sports lexicon. "Unfinished Business: Catholics vs. Convicts." The message was clear.

Dillon Hall, the same dorm where quarterback Tony Rice resided, served as the headquarters for the hottest shirt. The sellers couldn't make enough of them. Alumni clubs across the country ordered them. People wanted these shirts so badly that rather than paying the standard ten dollars apiece, they paid up to ten times that.

In making the shirts, the sellers deftly circumvented certain rules set forth in *du Lac*, Notre Dame's standards of student conduct; a copy is given to every student in booklet form upon arrival on campus. *Du Lac* sets out strict and clear Notre Dame rules, such as the university's ability to bring sanctions against students who engage in sexual union outside of marriage. The application is less strict now, but in the late 1980s, a student could easily be suspended for a semester or expelled for breaking parietals, which regulate dorm visitation from the opposite sex to between 9:00 A.M. and midnight Sunday through Thursday and 9:00 A.M. and 2:00 A.M. Friday and Saturday. Beyond upholding Catholic teaching on premarital sex, *du Lac* also set guidelines about merchandising: "The University of Notre Dame has entered into a licensing agreement for the marketing of 'Notre Dame' items. All items—hats, shirts, painter caps, glassware, etc.—which contain pictures or words 'Notre Dame,' 'ND,' the Leprechaun, the Golden Dome, 'Fighting Irish,' 'Irish,' must be ordered through the Bookstore." Notice, neither Catholics nor convicts made the list.

If Holtz wanted less hype and university officials wanted less hate, the shirts were no help. The media devoured the "Catholics vs.

Convicts" storyline. If a reporter wrote about this game, the T-shirts got mentioned.

"The pregame hype was loaded with all the stereotyping," said Sally Jenkins, who covered the game as the national college football reporter for *The Washington Post*. "Good and evil, which of course was utter nonsense...but the national press corps always finds it irresistible."

Holtz said it again.

"We're not a very good football team."

This was the fifth consecutive week Holtz, the coach of the No. 4 team in the country, had told the media his squad wasn't any good.

As for those shirts: "Our students have talked a lot about Miami and worn the T-shirts, but I think, honestly, they had better wear them now because they won't get to wear them after Miami plays us," Holtz said.

Classic Holtz. Build up the other team in the media; disparage your own. It was as if he had four parts of the game to master: offense, defense, special teams, and the media. Whereas some coaches survived press conferences and lived with the paranoid fear that they gave away too much information, Holtz talked and talked and talked. On the practice field Holtz brought a ferocious intensity, but in the press room the coach brought an aw-shucks tone that made for good quotes in the newspapers. Whether his words were true, false, or funny, it didn't matter. It worked for reporters because they had entertaining copy, and it worked for Holtz because he said all of it in an effort to win games.

"He did it for effect and he did it to give his team an emotional edge. He did it because he was a competitor," Jenkins said. "If he could get an emotional edge by painting his kids as the serious underdogs and Miami as the 'overdogs,' he was going to do it."

With the passion for the game rising, Holtz answered reporters' question about his pregame speech. No, he wouldn't be implementing a "Win one for the Gipper" or hollering. "All that says is, 'I'm really nervous,'" he said.

Would the Irish unveil green jerseys for a shot of luck?

No. "When I came here, Father Hesburgh informed me our colors are blue and gold and those are the colors we will wear," he told the sports scribes.

In an unusual use of media, Holtz penned a letter to the editor of *The Observer*. He called for good behavior, but at the same time gave readers every reason to know how big this game was. He asked students to respect Miami and reeled off superlatives about the Hurricanes' regular-season and road-game winning streaks. "That's an amazing record that few teams in college football history can match."

He wrote about how impressed he was by the Notre Dame student body's "competitiveness, its intelligence, its intense desire to succeed and its closeness and caring for other people," but he also noted the phone calls and letters that Johnson had been receiving. If Notre Dame students hadn't been excited and clued into the game, the letter from the head coach provided a clear picture of what was at stake.

Holtz engaged Johnson through the newspapers as well. Johnson had said Notre Dame players were faster than the ones at Miami.

"That encourages me, because I thought Jimmy Johnson is smarter than that. It shows there's some vulnerability in their evaluations," Holtz said, deflecting the compliment.

"They're a much better football team this year as opposed to a year ago," Johnson said.

"They just reload and go at it again, and everybody saw what they did to Florida State," Holtz responded, reminding everyone of how Miami thumped the preseason No. 1 team 31–0.

Then he put Johnson on the defensive, going after Miami's reputation for talking trash. "There were two games almost resulting in riots last year—the Miami–South Carolina game and the Miami–Oklahoma game.* That's the way some people play the game, but they aren't going to be able to play that way. There's a penalty for taunting, but it hasn't been enforced. It will be enforced this year," Holtz said.

This forced a response from Johnson. The Miami coach called Notre Dame a class operation. "They play the game the way it's supposed to be played, but we also feel we play the way it's supposed to be played. We play to win."

Holtz's chatter in the press finally tweaked Johnson. During one of the Miami coach's postpractice media sessions, Johnson spoke with some reporters while other nearby media members listened to a tape of a Holtz press conference. "What did he say?" Johnson asked about Holtz, interrupting his own Q&A session because he thought Holtz mentioned his name. "It's hard for me to concentrate with that guy talking."

Miami quarterback Steve Walsh made light of the crazed fanaticism, showing up at his Tuesday press conference in Notre Dame shorts. He got the shorts from one of his best friends from Cretin-Derham Hall High School in St. Paul, Minnesota, who played on the Fighting Irish hockey team.

While Walsh played things cool with the press, Miami defensive back Donald Ellis refused to view the Fighting Irish as a rival.

---

*Both the games Holtz referenced had stoppages in play because Miami and its opponents got into fights, though the Oklahoma game took place in 1986.

"People say Notre Dame and it's like that's supposed to mean something," he said. "I don't see Notre Dame as being greater than Toledo or Wisconsin or anybody else. I don't see them any different than Central Florida."*

Miami didn't have to be impressed with Notre Dame because the Irish hadn't given the 'Canes anything to be impressed with in recent years.

"We've been beating them every year, so they have a reason to be upset," Miami wide receiver Andre Brown told the *Chicago Tribune.* "I think we'll try to keep it that way."

When a Miami assistant coach spoke to players about not getting caught up in the hype of Notre Dame's tradition, guard Darren Handy had a question. "Who's Knute Rockne?"

Before the era of 24/7 sports news, Miami linebacker Bernard Clark remembered hearing a TV report about an 0–2 Notre Dame team being the best winless team in the country. He and his fellow 'Canes couldn't understand how they could have more wins than Notre Dame and get less attention.

"How in the hell can you call a team that hasn't won a game the best? That's what stuck out in our mind as Miami players. No matter what you do at Notre Dame you're still going to be a great player considering you're going to Notre Dame," Clark said.

Clark was the on-field Luther Campbell for Miami. He had a breakthrough performance when he replaced suspended linebacker George Mira Jr. in the national championship Orange Bowl win against Oklahoma the previous season. On the sideline and on the field he celebrated wins and big plays by moving and gyrating with the

---

*Wisconsin was a Big Ten football doormat, having gone to three bowls in twenty-five years. The program became a national power under the direction of Alvarez, who left Notre Dame to take the Badgers head coaching post in 1990.

running man or the cabbage patch dance. He was also good. In '88, he carried on the "U" swagger as it had been passed to him from Jerome Brown, Michael Irvin, Alonzo Highsmith, and Bennie Blades.

When it came to Notre Dame, the 'Canes wanted to prove they had earned a rightful place among the game's elite.

"Forget about their tradition. Forget about their history. That's not important to us. What's important to us is that we go out there and we win this football game. That's what bothered Notre Dame fans more than anything else. It wasn't that we were looking down on their tradition. It just didn't matter to us when we stepped on that football field. We respected it. We respected the Four Horsemen," Clark said. "But at the same time we're trying to beat your brains in. Those things don't matter. The Four Horsemen aren't on the field with you right now. That's a totally different era of football."

One thing that did matter was looking good while winning. When Miami players knew they were playing on national TV, they would talk at practice about what outrageous, rebellious dance they would bust out during the game.

"They thought their new way was the only way. They didn't like Notre Dame at all. They despised Notre Dame because of everything that Notre Dame stood for," said Jeff Jeffers, who covered the game for the local NBC affiliate.

Notre Dame players stayed away from inciting comments in the press. They talked about wanting to win and being prepared to play sound football on game day. If they strayed from those messages, they poked fun at the circus show.

"People talk about hating Miami," said linebacker and tri-captain Ned Bolcar. "I think that's mostly because of the press. There's no hatred between me and Miami.

"It's not Miami's fault they beat us 56–0 [actually 58–7] and 24–0 the last couple years. That's their job. If people are upset at Miami, fine, but maybe they should be upset at Notre Dame."

Because the phone book listed their numbers, Bolcar, Holtz, and other players kept receiving calls from alums and fans throughout the week. Alums called Holtz at home, talking to him about getting a good pass rush against Walsh. Somehow, Miami fans got the coach's private office number and began blitzing him. Bolcar regaled reporters with stories from his phone conversations. One friend back in New Jersey told the linebacker he hadn't slept all week. Then another guy started weeping when he talked to Bolcar about how important it was to beat Miami. "I thought, *Geez, I don't get excited until Friday night.* I told him, 'Don't worry. Stop crying.'"

The acrimony, the T-shirts, and the newspaper back-and-forth led Bolcar, tailback Mark Green, and offensive tackle Andy Heck to send a letter to the editor of *The Observer* a few days before the game. The tri-captains asked the student body to refrain from throwing oranges and to support the team "in a positive manner."

Then there was Frank Stams, the eccentric Irish linebacker whose candor masked a precocious media savvy. He once told an interviewer he pumped himself up before games by watching the Three Stooges. It wasn't true, but because he knew the reporter was a huge Stooges fan, Stams figured the opener would send the interview in a good direction.

Stams stayed away from all of the typical Miami talk—the hate, the cautions, even the seriousness of the game. Stams was the starting fullback for Notre Dame when Miami thrashed the Irish 58–7, but he didn't talk about the humiliation in '85. He went further back to the recruiting trip he took to visit the 'Canes.

"Personally, I like Miami. I took a visit down there, visited some of the players. I don't really remember many of the players, but I remember the Hurricane Honeys... Suzy, I'd like to say, 'Hi.' If anyone out there sees her..."

·   ·   ·

Olympic speed skater Dan Jansen was a highlight during Notre Dame Spirit Week. The Athletic Department planned a week of events to quell the animosity in the lead-up to the Miami game. The end of the week featured baseball games between the Irish and Miami, a perennial national power, as well as Jansen's visit.

Jansen wasn't an alum or even known as an ND fan, but he did represent something beyond sports, something Spirit Week planners thought would provide a different perspective than the "Catholic vs. Convicts" tone. Just like President Reagan's visit to campus, this was another time when Notre Dame's 1988 season crossed paths with something outside the football world.

Jansen was favored to win the Olympic gold medal in the 500 meters in Calgary earlier that year. On race day, instead of going through his typical routine, he was on the phone with his sister Jane. He did the talking. She couldn't. She lay in bed dying of leukemia. She died before Jansen, the youngest of nine children from a Catholic family in Wisconsin, lined up to skate. With a worldwide audience aware of his grief, Jansen lost, falling during the race. Jansen sitting on the side of the ice track, head in hands, legs extended, skates pointed toward the sky, is a lasting image of those Winter Games.

He had made public appearances before he arrived at Notre Dame, but something about this visit touched him. The twenty-three-year-old figured the applause he had received was from people feeling sorry for him, and he didn't want that. Seeing people his own age or younger rise to their feet to cheer him changed his perspective.

"They just really appreciate what I went through as a human being, not so much as an athlete. They could relate to that," Jansen said. "It wasn't so much out of sympathy as it was out of respect."

During Midnight Madness—the late-night practice to open the college basketball season—Jansen stood at midcourt at the Joyce Center, his hand raised, thanking the crowd for the encouragement.

He also heard the crowd erupt when the public address announcer informed those in attendance that Notre Dame beat the Hurricanes in baseball 11–2 and 8–7 in a come-from-behind win.*

More than twenty years later, Jansen's biggest memory of the visit is of Coach Holtz at the pep rally.

The coach had revved up his quips during the day at the regular Friday football luncheon, which had nearly two thousand attendees. The Miami football chaplain, a Catholic priest, gave the invocation. Before the visiting priest said the prayer he made it a point to tell the crowd he wanted Holtz to know God didn't care who won the game tomorrow.

When Holtz spoke, he concurred with the priest. "Father, I agree with you. God doesn't care who wins this game. But I promise you, his mother does." The crowd howled with laughter and clapping hands.

Initially Holtz wasn't going to attend the pep rally at the Stepan Center. Typically the event took place inside the building, but because of the large crowd they moved it outside, and people kept coming and coming. Crowd estimates counted more than 10,000 people in attendance.

Standing at the podium with a backdrop of cheerleaders, players, and coaches, and a sea of Irish faithful in front, Holtz kept his remarks brief. "I want you to conduct yourself in the Notre Dame fashion. Always exhibit class and character in everything we do. Number two, I want you to yell as loud as you can."

Then he shed the aw-schucks demeanor. "And number three, I want you to go tell Jimmy Johnson we're going to beat him like a yard dog."

.   .   .

---

*Harry Caray, the legendary Chicago Cubs broadcaster, threw out the first pitch at the baseball game.

When he reconvened with reporters after the game, Holtz told the media he stirred in his bed that night and woke before dawn at 4:45 A.M., about nine hours before kickoff.

"I was sort of like a guy who was drunk," he said. He looked to his wife. "I did *what* last night?"

The coach who would never even say his team could beat the Penn High School cheerleaders in a football game couldn't believe he said the Irish would beat Miami.

What he told the players after the pep rally was totally different. They met at the hotel off campus where the team stayed before home games.

"Now, why did I say that?" Holtz asked.

"Because you wanted to convince us?"

"No."

"That's what they wanted to hear."

"No, because I believe it. I believe it."

Holtz went over Notre Dame's plan. He asked the players a series of questions.

"Who's going to lose a fumble tomorrow?"

No one raised a hand.

"Who's going to get a fumble?"

Frank Stams gave a nod.

"Okay, Stams, how're you going to get it?"

"A sack."

"Who's going to have a foolish penalty?

"Who's going to have a missed assignment?"

On and on, Holtz kept bringing forward the plan to win.

"Let's follow the plan. If we follow the plan, it will work itself out."

When Jimmy Johnson checked into his hotel room, he found it covered with Notre Dame memorabilia. His message for the 'Canes was to embrace all the hate thrown their way.

"You are disliked so much simply for the reason that you have played good. If you hadn't been successful against Notre Dame in the past, then they really wouldn't care. They really wouldn't be excited about this game. But you should take pride in the success you had, and every time they boo you, you ought to be able to stick out your chest and hold your head up high, because you did good and you're going to do good in the future," he said on CBS in a pregame interview, summarizing what he told his team.

As daybreak lit the sky, defensive coordinator Barry Alvarez realized the typical South Bend weather he hoped would engulf Miami wasn't going to happen. The day was clear, 70 degrees with a slight breeze.

Stams left Elvis Presley a game ticket at will-call, or at least that's what he told reporters.

Tony Rice put on the Walkman and maintained his game-day program. "Don't change up the routine. I listened to the same song I had been listening to, imagining myself breaking out for the score," he said.

The student government began painting bodies in gold, blue, and green, and fans lit grills for tailgaters. With hopes of beating Miami, they spoke about tradition being on their side. The Irish had a penchant for stopping winning streaks. They ended Oklahoma's forty-seven-game winning streak in 1957, Georgia Tech's thirty-one-game unbeaten streak in '53, and Texas's 30-game run in '71. For all the glorious past, though, Notre Dame had not fared well against the No. 1 team in the country, amassing a 5-13-1 record.

Fans driving south from Chicago could listen to talk radio callers explain why Notre Dame could not beat the No. 1 team in the nation.

On ESPN's *College GameDay,* which was in its second year, Beano Cook picked the Irish to upset the Hurricanes.

Cook's cohost, Tim Brando, poked fun at Cook for being bad at picking games. "If I sit here and allow you to make this pick, then I look like a buffoon. There's just no way that Miami, with that attack, is going to lose to Notre Dame."

Cook shot back at Brando, "If Notre Dame wins, you go there and you sing the 'Victory March.'"

CBS had promoted the game for two weeks. It was the week's only matchup between top 10 teams and the first time since the 1968 Purdue game that Notre Dame Stadium was hosting a No. 1–ranked team.

Notre Dame fans, in their Miami-mocking T-shirts, gathered around the Hurricanes bus and smacked it with their hands when it pulled up to the stadium.

On the field, the teams went through their warm-ups. Holtz and Jimmy Johnson spoke briefly in the middle of the field and shook hands.

Notre Dame used the half of the field closest to the lone tunnel where teams entered and exited. Miami ran its pregame drills on the farther half.

"The reason we were so good on the road is we had the mentality that people were coming to watch us and we were going to put a show on for them. We didn't care about the home team," said Walsh, the Miami quarterback.

In the course of conducting their drills, Miami players ran onto the Notre Dame side of the field. In an attempt to stop that from happening again, defensive backs coach Chuck Heater yelled over to Dave Campo, his Miami counterpart, and Hurricane defensive coordinator Dave Wannstedt.

"The point was, I wasn't going to let our guys be intimidated. I wasn't going to be intimidated. That was their calling card in those days. That's who they were," Heater said.

When the yelling didn't work, Heater threw a ball into their vicinity.

This failed to deter the 'Canes. Not caring, they bumped into and disrupted a group of Fighting Irish defensive players near mid-field.

"We were not going to be pushed around. There was not going to be any showboating in Notre Dame Stadium," said strong safety George Streeter.

Michael Stonebreaker, a Notre Dame linebacker, charged after some Miami players.

"Michael took off," Streeter said. "I didn't need any prompting after that."

The groups exchanged blows and shoves. This turned out to be the undercard.

"They were there when Miami intimidated them and humiliated them," Alvarez said. "They were there when Miami ran it up and Jimmy Johnson rubbed their face in it. They remembered that."

Holtz set up his pregame warm-up in nearly the same fashion Woody Hayes did at Ohio State. Instead of finishing with field goal kicking, Holtz ended with the punt team and players lined the back of the end zone. When the Hurricanes finished their warm-ups, they had two options to get back to the tunnel—go around Notre Dame or go through them.

Clark, the Miami linebacker, spoke to fellow linebacker Maurice Crum.

"We were trying to figure out why Notre Dame isn't going to their locker room. Why are they stretching across the back of the end zone? We were trying to figure out why they're doing that," Clark said.

"Should we go around?"

"Screw that. We're going through them" was the answer, and everybody followed.

The 'Canes did their thing. They strolled up to the middle of the Irish line.

This Notre Dame squad was different than previous ones. The 1988 Irish weren't going to play patsy. Forget the letters to the editor and all the talk about proper decorum; the jawing commenced.

Bolcar got pushed in the back and had words with a freshman offensive lineman for the 'Canes. They went through some customary name calling. The lineman said something about Bolcar's mother, and then Bolcar unloaded a fist into his throat.

At the same time, Anthony Johnson, the laid-back fullback, had heard Streeter take enough trash talk. He was standing behind Streeter when he made his move. "I gave [the Miami player] a forearm shiver to the face mask to gently say, 'That's enough.' He didn't take it that way," Johnson said. "I had to defend what I thought was the honor of my boys and my school."

"The whole field started to erupt," Bolcar said. "I felt like a wave of humanity pick up my body and move it toward the tunnel."

CBS wasn't on the air yet, and the cameras only caught a few brief moments as the scene instantly escalated into a battle royal. From above it looked like two masses of bodies pressing into each other, but on the ground a bunch of separate donnybrooks unfolded.

"It was 'Katy bar the door,'" said Pritchett, the Irish linebacker who was standing next to Bolcar when the tussle exploded. "I was grabbing guys, hitting guys. I was trying to pull their helmets off. I mean, it was a fight."

Tony Rice threw a flurry of uppercuts. "I see my teammates fighting, I'm going to go to battle for my teammates," he said. "Here I am a quarterback and people might say, 'Stay out of it. You might hurt your hand.' I didn't care."

While the violence unfurled around him, Steve Walsh, Rice's counterpart, chuckled.

"I was surrounded by four freshmen on our squad, kicking and punching, and I didn't throw a punch and I didn't get hit. I was just sitting there watching because they weren't going to let me get hit," he said. "We were trying to stir things up and get ourselves even more ready to play and more hyped."

Coaches tried to break it up, but they couldn't.

"I remember a couple of coaches saying, 'We've just got to let them go. It'll break up,'" Alvarez said.

It didn't.

"I remember a couple helmets being thrown in the air. I remember looking up and the fans just going crazy," said Miami's Maurice Crum. "They were all leaning over into the tunnel and they were trying to get into the fight."

Finally, stadium security and police intervened, separating the two sides.

"It was like the first time you punch a bully in the face and he flinched. It was an affirming moment for our team," said Rocket Ismail.

Notre Dame retreated to its locker room. The savage postfight atmosphere settled momentarily. The players took a knee and braced for an upbraiding from Holtz for misrepresenting Our Mother's University. He was nowhere to be found. Then the whistle blew, calling the room to attention. Holtz walked in.

"Men, I have no doubt you'll do well today. You'll be fine. You'll be fine," he said, adding a few more words about the game.

"But I have one favor to ask of you," he said with his voice intensifying.

"Save Jimmy Johnson's ass for me."

CHAPTER 13

Catholics vs. Convicts

Anger and surprise filled the Miami locker room.

"We felt like they were trying to intimidate us and we were supposed to be the intimidators," said Maurice Crum. "It's really on now."

The sellout crowd at Notre Dame Stadium chanted a slow, rhythmic "We Are ... N-D ... We Are ... N-D," over and over and over. The 'Canes reentered the tunnel. Foghorns blew and the rain of boos came when the Miami captains ran out onto the field and the rest of the 'Canes gathered just outside the tunnel.

"You couldn't hear yourself think. It was absolutely crazy. They were all over us," Crum said.

Meanwhile, in the Notre Dame locker room the players rose to their feet, letting loose thunderous yells when they heard Holtz ask for a shot at the opposing coach.

"For him to say that, it brought goose bumps to my body," Tony Rice said. "Aw man, I believe in this guy. I always have. But when he said that, that just took me to a whole other level."

The Fighting Irish took off without any prompting. They didn't need to hear anything else from Holtz. They were ready. They left the locker room, smacked the PLAY LIKE A CHAMPION TODAY sign, and gathered in the tunnel, bubbling with anger, waiting to take the field for game time.

The "We Are…N-D" chant grew louder and louder. The crowd broke into applause when they saw the loyal sons of gold and blue huddle at the edge of the tunnel. The Leprechaun, waving an Irish flag, led the sprinting team onto the field, and a wave of crowd noise climbed to higher decibels.

The entire Miami team, hand in hand, walked out to the hash marks for the coin toss. Notre Dame reciprocated the team unity gesture, standing across their hash marks as the captains from each team met in the center of the field.

The Irish won the toss and deferred receiving the ball until the second half. Notre Dame kicker Billy Hackett placed the ball on the tee, stepped back, blessed himself with the sign of the cross, and kicked off a game that matched the hype it had received.

"From the pregame brawl until the last play of the game, the intensity never died down," said Pat Terrell.

Miami freshman Darryl Spencer caught Hackett's kick at the 3-yard line. He ran to his left and upfield before Notre Dame's sophomore linebacker Andre Jones wrapped him up and planted Spencer on the turf at the 16-yard line, eliciting a surge of greater loudness from the crowd.

On the 'Canes' third play from scrimmage, Walsh found a pocket in the Notre Dame zone defense and dropped a 20-yard pass to a diving Andre Brown for the first down.

Miami had a propensity for big plays. The team speed lent itself to tearing off long gains. The Hurricanes' 16 touchdowns had come at an average clip of 22.3 yards. They had 4 scores of more than 40 yards.

Notre Dame knew it couldn't afford to give up big plays. When the 'Canes got loose it not only meant yards but it inevitably included flashy, momentum-building celebrations. The Irish defense had worked all week in practice to keep the ball in front of them. Don't let a quick slant pattern over the middle end up with a Miami speedster streaking down the field with nothing but the end zone in front him. Don't let a short out pattern get turned up the sideline as a 'Cane left everyone behind to watch the back of his jersey. The Irish defense had to do something that hadn't been done in more than a season—fluster and disrupt a Miami offense that averaged 35 points per game.

In the production meeting with CBS before the game, Frank Stams talked about getting to Walsh. "My goal Saturday is really just to touch him, touch his jersey, see if he's real back there, see if you can tackle him and get pressure on him," he said. "Put him in a situation he's not comfortable with."

Two plays after Walsh's 20-yard pass to Brown, Stams shot off the ball on the left side. Offensive tackle Darrin Bruce tried to push him past Walsh. Bruce yanked Stams's jersey and draped his left arm across his chest, but Stams muscled through the lineman, freeing himself and pulling Walsh's throwing arm. All of a sudden, Walsh felt an unfamiliar feeling. The ball came loose and he crooked his neck, looking back at his arm as it moved forward, no longer in possession of the pigskin. Stams found out Walsh was real and fallible.

The ball shot forward on the ground. Nose tackle Chris Zorich covered it, giving Notre Dame the ball at the Miami 41-yard line. The Irish gained 1 yard before punting it back to Miami.

The Notre Dame defense continued to set a tone. While Walsh completed a 17-yard pass to Dale Dawkins, he had to throw it in the face of pressure from defensive lineman George "Boo" Williams. Miami tried to run the ball, but that wasn't happening. Four Notre Dame defenders greeted a 2-yard sweep from Leonard Conley. Michael Stonebreaker bolted into the backfield on a Cleveland Gary off-tackle run. Gary spun away, but six gold helmets instantly smothered him for a 2-yard loss.

The Fighting Irish attack mode was one part speed and the

other part attitude. Notre Dame wanted to permanently shed the perception that it was soft or overachieving on the football field. "I'm not an overachiever. I'm good," Terrell said. "That sounds arrogant, but football is a game of respect, and going into the '88 season we didn't feel like we were getting the respect we deserved, and that made us a . . . physical team."

The Irish defense mixed up their personnel. Freshman Arnold Ale made his first start at outside linebacker, leapfrogging fifth-year senior Darrell "Flash" Gordon and sophomore Andre Jones. Alvarez subbed multiple players in and out of the defensive line and secondary to go along with the usual middle linebacker rotation that included Wes Pritchett, Ned Bolcar, and Michael Stonebreaker filling two slots.

"The Miami team thought watching films of Notre Dame the last few weeks that they were vanilla on defense. They thought they could get a very good presnap read," said Pat Haden, the CBS color commentator.

The dull game film was part of the plan. Notre Dame coaches knew Miami would be watching. So early in the season the Irish played basic defenses, waiting to unveil a more complex scheme for this game.

"We were playing a lot of rush two and drop nine . . . We would rush three and drop eight so there was not enough room to throw. You could complete some passes, but you wanted to keep them in front of you," Alvarez said of the Miami game plan. "I kind of stole that from Penn State. When they beat them in the Fiesta Bowl they used the same thing."

The Irish were intent on rendering the Miami running game useless and forcing Walsh to continually adjust to different looks. On a second-and-10 play, Pritchett walked up to the defensive line. Walsh looked across the line of scrimmage at six linemen, but when the play started only three rushed him. Stams dropped into pass coverage, which led Walsh to loft an incomplete pass over his head in the flat. For good measure, cornerback Todd Lyght put a shoulder into Leonard Conley, the intended receiver. On the next play, Notre Dame showed a six-man rush again. This time the Irish dropped two players back, but in an unorthodox move Zorich, the nose tackle, backpedaled into pass coverage. Stams beat two blockers and got to Walsh again, causing the fumble no one talks about.

Stams hit Walsh's arm as the quarterback cocked it back to throw. The ball went backward, spinning like a helicopter propeller. The refs ruled it a pass—but it went backward. There is no such thing as a backward incomplete pass in football, but the officials ruled it that way. Had it been a fumble, Irish linebacker Andre Jones would have scooped it up at the Miami 26-yard line.

The Irish offense took the ball and faced an equally swarming Hurricane defense. "There wasn't a slow person or someone who didn't belong there," said Notre Dame center Mike Heldt.

The same went for the players on the Miami offense.

"They were solid," Stams said. "Some guys when you hit them, they're like rocks, and other guys when you hit them are like marshmallows. Well, those guys were tough, and when they hit you, you felt it."

More than an NFL team's worth of talent took the field in South Bend. In fact, sixty-three players from the teams' rosters went on to the NFL, thirty-four from Notre Dame and twenty-nine from Miami.

"You were playing a pro team. Those guys were the cream of the crop," said Notre Dame halfback Tony Brooks.

They hit like pros, too. As a freshman playing the year before at Miami, Brooks, the same guy who played on a broken foot, briefly left the game after getting blasted. "I got hit so hard I didn't wait for the coach to tell me to come out. I went to the sidelines. 'I need a medic,'" he said.

On the first play of the Irish drive, Brooks took a pitch, and the Miami defense, led by Russell Maryland, popped him for no gain. Notre Dame stuck to the run, marching 75 yards on twelve plays in six minutes to take a 7–0 lead. The Irish went to work behind an offensive line that included Mike Brennan and Joe Allen filling in at the guard spots for injured starters Tim Grunhard and Tim Ryan. Tony Rice accounted for more than half the yards and ran for the final 14. Rice gained 7 yards on a busted play where everyone went right and he ran left to the 7-yard line. On the next play, Rice faked a handoff to Banks up the middle and ran around the end, untouched, into the end zone. The crowd went ballistic.

Last year, the Irish had never crossed the Miami 26-yard line. This was the first meaningful touchdown Notre Dame had scored against Miami in years. It was the first regular-season rushing touchdown the 'Canes had given up in eleven months. It was the first lead Notre Dame had had on Miami since 1984.

John Dockery, the CBS sideline reporter, armed himself with a decibel meter to measure the crowd noise. "For much of this game it registered around 110," he said. "That means you're sitting in the fifth row at a rock concert or you're standing at O'Hare International Airport about 50 yards away from a 707 on takeoff. So this is really loud for the Hurricanes."

Five plays later, D'Juan Francisco intercepted a third-down pass from Walsh and returned it to the Miami 35-yard line. The undefeated, national-championship-winning Heisman candidate had completed 4 of 10 passes for 67 yards and turned the ball over twice.

Starting with the ball in Miami territory, in a rare occurrence, Rice fumbled the snap from center Mike Heldt, an eighteen-year-old sophomore. After the ball was initially mishandled, Heldt inadvertently kicked it, sending it rolling waywardly up the field. Miami's motormouthed junior middle linebacker, Bernard Clark, pounced on it.

Clark had been Heldt's teammate for the A. P. Leto High School Falcons in Tampa, Florida. Lining up across from the center, Clark spewed forth a perpetual stream of taunts at his former teammate.

"You just gave us the ball," Clark told him. "Mike, you've got to do better than that."

"Here I'm young, probably more nervous than anything else, and he's over there yelling my name," Heldt said. "That's the last thing I wanted to hear at that point in time."

Heldt was Florida talent that avoided the 'Canes. He took unofficial visits to the University of Florida and Florida State, but not Miami. "I was a different person than what they had playing there," he said.

The kid who completed the first and second grades in one school year went on recruiting visits to Duke and Georgia Tech and thought about going to Rice before he visited the Golden Dome.

"It was an aura they had," Heldt said of his weekend at Notre Dame. "They were going to win and they were going to do it the right way and it was going to be through hard work, and if you wanted to be a part of it you needed to come."

To this day, Clark still teases Heldt about kicking the ball. The Notre Dame center had to tolerate another distraction, too. He had hardly any feeling from his elbow down to his right hand, the one he used to snap the ball. It had been that way for a week since he took a hit in the Pittsburgh game. "I got hit upside the head. It was a classic stinger," he said.

In a drive bridging the first quarter into the second, the Hurricanes went 68 yards on eight plays in just under four minutes. Big plays—two 20-yard passes—keyed the march to the Notre Dame 8-yard line. On first and goal Walsh changed the play at the line of scrimmage and then called time-out.

"I was so in tune with that offense. I knew it so well, and Gary Stevens, our coordinator, and I had a great rapport. He had such trust in me, and anytime I wanted to change the play, he was never going to second-guess me," Walsh said. "They empowered the quarterbacks so much."

After the break, Walsh called an audible again. He took a short drop back and threw to Andre Brown on the wide side of the field. Streeter wrapped up Brown, but as the pair rolled to the ground, sliding out of bounds, Brown stretched the ball over the goal line and got the favorable touchdown call from the officials. The 'Canes tied the game at 7.

At some point in the first quarter, Notre Dame linebacker Wes Pritchett heard the bone snap in his right hand when he threw his body into a gang tackle. The Irish's defensive signal caller looked down. His hand had immediately started to swell. He'd broken the fourth metacarpal, the bone connecting the wrist to the ring finger. He never left the game. During a TV time-out he hustled to the sideline and spoke with Alvarez about the defense.

"Get over here," he yelled to the medical staff while keeping his eyes on Alvarez. "Tape my fingers together."

He kept his helmet on. He never looked down. Alvarez gave him the defensive call, and he ran back on the field.

Pritchett did not possess great speed, but he played with a fierceness that made up for it. He grew up wanting to emulate the vicious style of Dick Butkus and Jack Lambert. "I truly believed I was more intense and meaner than the next guy, and I willed myself to make a lot of plays," he said.

He doesn't remember many specifics from games because he worked himself up into a hypnotic state while playing them. The dark-complexioned linebacker of Welsh descent had thick eyebrows and bulging eyes that peered out atop his 6'4" frame. The warrior mentality came from his father, who was lying in a coma at home in Atlanta during the Miami game.

Ken Pritchett was born in the Great Depression. He remembered men in suits coming up to his family's back door asking for food. He boxed in the navy while serving the country during the Korean War. He was a high school star in East Point, Georgia, playing football and baseball and running track. He got injured playing running back at the University of Georgia. Partially paralyzed, he rehabbed with a chiropractor until he returned to 100 percent strength. He coached his two football-playing sons, and he provided for his family working as a stockbroker.*

"My father meant everything to me," Wes Pritchett said.

Ken Pritchett placed the Irish on a pedestal. He grew up listening to Notre Dame games on the radio. He took Wes to see a Vagas Ferguson–led Fighting Irish team play Georgia Tech.

When it came time to pick colleges, Georgia wanted Wes, a National Merit Scholar semifinalist, to make a commitment to the Bulldogs before he visited Notre Dame. Wes didn't, but he did call the Georgia recruiter, Bill Lewis, after he visited South Bend. Lewis told Pritchett he wasn't sure there would be a scholarship open for him, but he could walk on the team.

"Hang on a second, I think I made a mistake," Pritchett said before hanging up the phone and dialing up Notre Dame assistant George Kelly and committing to the Irish.

"Notre Dame stood for all the right things: Division I football at the highest level, great academics, integrity. It's a great school. Nobody loves Notre Dame more than me," Pritchett said.

Even so, he felt miserable throughout his freshman year. He called home. He wanted to transfer to Georgia and play ball and party with his friends from back home. Ken Pritchett had no tolerance for the bellyaching.

---

*Roland Pritchett, Wes's younger brother, played football at Boston College.

"Son, let me tell you something. You made a decision; quit feeling sorry for yourself and make it work," he told Wes.

"That was the greatest thing that was ever said to me," Wes said. "From that day forward I decided to quit whining, play hard, work out harder in the gym, practice harder on the field, and hit more people until they played me."

He solidified a starting role for himself going into the '87 season. During the summer before the '88 season, Wes was on the Notre Dame campus when he received word that his father had had a stroke and fallen into a coma, his survival aided by a feeding tube.

He didn't talk about it much. It didn't become a media storyline during the season. It received brief mentions in articles, but there were hardly any features about the *"heartbroken linebacker playing for his ailing dad."* This was private.

"I internalized all that pain and sorrow," Wes said. "I just internalized it into being the best I could be, being more focused, more intense on the field. I turned it, more than anything else, into rage on the field."

After getting the ball back with the score tied at 7, the Fighting Irish had third down and 12 yards to go at their 18-yard line. Rice took a deep drop back to the 6-yard line and unloaded a bomb down the middle of the field. After Russell Maryland decked him on the release, Rice watched the rest of the play from grass level.

"The ball hung in the air so long," Rice said.

The pass traveled 60 yards, landing beyond the mistimed arms of Miami safety Bubba McDowell and in the gut of Rocket Ismail. The freshman, making his first collegiate start, gained possession of the bobbling ball somewhere between his crotch and thigh. With everyone already dusted by his speed, it would have been an easy 6 points for the Irish had Ismail made a clean catch, but juggling the ball took him tumbling to the ground at the Miami 25-yard line.

Kneeling on the grass, Ismail leaned over, cupping his hands to his helmet, knowing it could have been a touchdown.

The Miami defense forced Notre Dame into a fourth down and 1. Holtz decided to go for the first down rather than try a 33-yard field goal. The Irish lined up in a wishbone formation with Tony Brooks and flanker Pat Eilers as the halfbacks and Braxston Banks at fullback. Rice handed the ball to Banks, and the left side of the Notre Dame offensive line moved Miami to the right, clearing the way for the first down run.

The Hurricane defense pushed the Irish into another third down. From the 9-yard line, Notre Dame needed 5 yards. Holtz sent Tony Brooks in with the play call. From the I-formation, Rice dropped back. Banks ran up to the offensive line pretending to block and then ran a delay route over the middle. Rice floated a touch pass to him. Tight end Derek Brown had run a drag route, drawing attention from both middle linebackers, so when Banks caught the ball at the 6-yard line no one came near him until he reached the end zone. The Irish regained the lead, 14–7.

"It was man coverage on the goal line," said Bernard Clark. "I took my eyes to the tight end and the back came on the crossing route and I gave up the touchdown. I went to the sideline and [defensive coordinator] coach [Dave] Wannstedt tore me a new one."

The Fighting Irish drove 80 yards on eleven plays and kept the Miami offense off the field for more than five minutes. Rice dispelled any notion that the Irish were outmatched at quarterback. He was responsible for both Notre Dame touchdowns. On the two scoring drives, he went 3 for 4 for 88 yards passing and accumulated 115 of the offense's 155 yards.

Miami came back picking up two big first downs, using just three plays to move the ball 38 yards to the Notre Dame 42-yard line. With the Hurricanes moving the ball with ease, Alvarez went away from the zone defense and called an all-out blitz for the Irish.

"Barry, you sure you want to do this? This is first down and 10. You sure you want this call?" Chuck Heater asked him through their headsets, seconds before the decision needed to be made.

"Yeah. What do you think?" Alvarez responded.

"Yeah, go with it. Go with it."

With so many players blitzing, the play call put more pressure on safety Pat Terrell and the secondary. Terrell was one of a few guys who did not get into a frenzy during or after the pregame fisticuffs. He wanted to stay calm. The aviation buff eased his nerves by thinking about World War II fighter pilots. "Those guys had a right to be scared. To go make a tackle, why fear that? That's nothing compared to what those guys went through."

Walsh crouched under center. The Notre Dame defense looked the same as it had all game, but instead of dropping multiple players back to defend against the pass, the Irish sent seven bodies hurling toward the 'Canes quarterback. Stams went untouched. Walsh tried to lob a pass over him to halfback Leonard Conley, but Stams leaped and got a piece of the ball. It went wobbling in the air.

"That was the money ball, right there," Terrell said.

Terrell had taken an angle on his old high school opponent, Conley, and darted in to make the interception. Everything in his world went silent.

Terrell raced 60 yards toward the end zone, and on the way a few thoughts popped into his mind. He had to score or he would be forever ridiculed in the defensive back meetings. All his boys at home in Florida were watching him, and he was playing against the same guys he competed against in high school—he could not let Walsh, a quarterback, tackle him. In the less than seven seconds it took him to return the ball, he turned his head four times to check Walsh's pursuit.

"And a third little thought was I always wanted to show Lou Holtz I could be a wide receiver."

Walsh dove at Terrell's legs at the 4-yard line, and the quarterback caught a cleat to the chin, busting open a gash that required bandaging.

Terrell never broke stride until he crossed the goal line, putting the Irish up 21–7.

In the first twenty minutes, Notre Dame had put 21 points on the scoreboard. Miami had allowed more than 20 points in an entire game only three times since the end of the 1985 season.

The Hurricanes didn't get rattled. In their minds, they had no reason to, and it wasn't just bluster. They had won so many games. In the past six years they beat the preseason No. 1 at some point during the year. They played big in big games, defeating the No. 1–ranked team six times in the '80s. Plus, they had confidence in their field general.

Walsh went to a Catholic high school in St. Paul, Minnesota. He would have liked to go to Notre Dame. "I would have been a good fit on paper," he said, but he actually was a better fit elsewhere.

No one really wanted Walsh, though, except for the Division III schools in Minnesota. One major problem was that the big in-state college football program had no interest in him. Ironically, that was the Minnesota Golden Gophers coached by Holtz. A thrower wouldn't fit Holtz's option offense. Because Minnesota had no interest, no other Big Ten schools thought Walsh was worth a scholarship. Walsh actually called them trying to get on the roster. They didn't budge.

"Oh, we've got enough guys" was Iowa's answer.

"There are guys who are redshirted. We're not interested," Wisconsin responded.

Iowa State, a Big Eight basement dweller, had some interest. Northwestern was curious, but Wildcats coach Dennis Green wanted Walsh to bring film of himself on a visit because he wasn't sure about offering Walsh a scholarship.

Late in the recruiting process, one of the assistant coaches for Walsh's high school team contacted Marc Trestman. The assistant coach had played ball with Trestman, who served as quarterbacks coach for Howard Schnellenberger at the University of Miami.

"You've got to come see this kid. He's not getting recruited," Walsh's assistant coach told Trestman.

The 'Canes sent a recruiter. Within a month, Walsh visited Miami, and the Florida school nabbed another member in its line of Catholic out-of-state passers. Jim Kelly came from Pittsburgh and ended up the fourteenth pick in the NFL Draft by the Buffalo Bills. Bernie Kosar suited up for the 'Canes and returned to Ohio to quarterback the Browns after being selected with basically the No. 1 overall pick.* Vinny Testaverde left Long Island, New York, won the Heisman Trophy at Miami, and became the No. 1 overall pick, taken by the Tampa Bay Buccaneers.

Though it looked like a long shot, Walsh landed where he wanted to go. He had a VHS tape of the classic 1984 Miami–Boston College game, the Kosar–Doug Flutie duel that ended in Flutie's iconic Hail Mary pass to Gerard Phelan.

"I remember taping the game and watching it after because I had a basketball game and just saying to myself, 'I want to go to a college like that' because Kosar and Flutie were just flinging it everywhere," Walsh said.

Walsh had already thrown for 154 yards when he and the Hurricanes offense took the field with 5:33 to play in the first half. Down 14 points, they drove to the Notre Dame 23-yard line and called time-out. Instead of kicking a field goal on fourth down and 4, Miami was going for the first down.

---

*The Browns took Kosar in the 1985 supplemental draft with a pick that equated to the following year's No. 1 overall pick.

Remembering a Notre Dame blitz he had seen on film, Walsh went to the sidelines with a play in mind.

"What about this?" he asked Stevens, the offensive coordinator. "If they come with this blitz, we're going to have a good chance at getting a back out of the backfield in a man-to-man situation and pretty good leverage on the corner."

"Great, let's go with it," Stevens said.

It unfolded exactly as Walsh predicted. He hit Leonard Conley in the right flat, and the running back raced into the end zone for the score.

With its lead cut to 21–14, Notre Dame tried to run down the clock, but the Miami defense held the Irish to three offensive plays. Notre Dame booted a 25-yard punt and gave the ball back to Miami at the Hurricane 46-yard line with 1:06 left in the half. The 'Canes tied the game, going 54 yards on seven plays in 48 seconds. Walsh ended the drive with his third touchdown pass of the afternoon, a 15-yarder to an uncovered Cleveland Gary.

On their final two drives of the half the 'Canes showed why they had been the dominant team of the era. Staring at a 2-touchdown deficit, they played with aplomb and tied the game at 21 with seconds to go before halftime.

At halftime, Holtz reiterated a message he had been sending the team since the previous season's Cotton Bowl loss.

"I always told the team that we didn't want to flinch. By flinching—don't show that things aren't going well in your life or in the game," he said.

The second half opened, and the teams exchanged turnovers. Rice, in a clear miscommunication with Ismail, lofted a pass where only Miami's Bubba McDowell could make a diving interception, charging in like a baseball outfielder snagging a pop-up. The Hurricanes gave it right back. Zorich shoved a blocker into Conley on a rush up the middle. As Conley spun away Zorich clawed at the ball, which ended up on Conley's back, where Jeff Alm finished stripping it. Stams dove in for the recovery.

The Irish immediately put themselves in field goal position with a 12-yard Rice run, but the drive stalled three plays later at the 27-yard line. Billy Hackett, the Irish's long-distance kicker, set up for a 43-yard field goal attempt. Bubba McDowell rushed in from the left end and blocked it, his ninth career blocked punt or kick.

The Irish defense stopped Miami in three plays. On 4th down and 3 the Hurricanes set up for a punt from their own 47-yard line. Steve Belles, the third-string quarterback, who played special teams for the Irish, picked up a tell in the Hurricanes alignment.

Notre Dame special teams coach George Stewart had showed his unit three years of Miami fakes during the week's film session. Even though the Hurricanes hadn't shown this formation in more than a year, because of the studying, Notre Dame knew that if two backs lined up closer than normal to the line of scrimmage and one stayed back, Miami was coming with a fake.

Belles had taken an odd path to ending up on the punt return team. He came in as a quarterback in Faust's last year. He roomed with Rice during road games and loved to watch ESPN's *SportsCenter* in the hotel rooms because cable TV didn't exist in Notre Dame dorm rooms. Belles knew that Rice and Kent Graham held the top spots on the depth chart and he wasn't going to rise above them. He asked for a meeting with Holtz.

"I don't care what I do, I just don't want to be a guy holding a clipboard. I just want to help the team," Belles said.

From his three-point stance, Belles and then other players started yelling out the team code word for the fake. Miami snapped the ball directly to Matt Britton, who typically played linebacker. Britton tried to run left. Belles grabbed him around the waist, and the fleet of Irish tacklers, including starting tailback Mark Green and linebacker Scott Kowalkowski, gang-tackled him for a 1-yard loss.

The crowd came back to life for the first time since Miami made its 2-touchdown run to end the first half.

"When they did that and didn't make it, we all said, 'They flinched. They don't believe they can beat us without trick plays. They don't think they're good enough to punt the ball and they've got to have trick plays,'" Holtz said. "That's why I never had a whole lot of trick plays. I never wanted to send the message that we're not good enough to win. But that was a big turning point in that game mentally."

The Irish seized momentum. Rice dropped back and aired out his best pass at Notre Dame. The high-arching, perfectly placed ball dropped over the shoulder of Ricky Watters. The flanker had started his route toward the middle of the field and then cut back to the corner, where Rice connected with him, giving him just enough space to tap both feet in bounds before going out at the 3-yard line.

The injured guards, Tim Grunhard and Tim Ryan, had entered the game.* Notre Dame lined up in the wishbone formation with flanker Pat Eilers in the backfield.

Eilers, the Ivy League transfer, took the pitch from Rice on a sweep to the left. He planted his feet to change direction, avoiding an ankle tackle and cutting back up a lane created by offensive tackle Dean Brown. Leaning over, reaching his hand to the ground to keep his balance, Eilers lunged into the end zone for his first touchdown.

The middle of five children, Eilers, like Miami's Steve Walsh, went to a Catholic high school in the St. Paul, Minnesota, area. He was the student council president and the captain of the football and baseball teams at St. Thomas Academy. He competed in downhill slalom at the Junior Olympics. His dad was a Class of '56 graduate of Notre Dame, and his sister was attending the school when Eilers was accepted out of high school. Instead he chose to go to Yale.

---

*Grunhard and Ryan ended up in the game for about ten plays each.

After his freshman year in New Haven, Connecticut, Eilers knew he wanted a different college experience. He wanted to compete for a national title in football without compromising academics. He set up a meeting with Coach Holtz that coincided with his visit to campus for his sister's graduation.

"If I transfer, would you afford me the opportunity to participate in the program?"

Holtz gave him an affirming nod.

"Is there an opportunity to earn a scholarship?"

"If you come in and you're competing for a starting job, I will give you a scholarship," Holtz said.

Eilers's coach at Yale didn't quite understand the switch.

"Pat, you're nuts. You'll never play. You'll go to Notre Dame and you can probably be on the scout squad. Why wouldn't you stay here and get a Yale degree and certainly be able to contribute significantly in the football program?"

"Coach, I don't want to ever look back and ask myself, what if I had transferred?"

Eilers spent his first season at Notre Dame as the scout team tailback. In the spring of '87, he competed for the starting position at strong safety.

During one practice, Andy Heck put a block on Eilers, sealing a long run for the offense. Holtz stopped the action and made a beeline to the walk-on.

"Eilers, I'm trying to find a place for you to play, son. Maybe you should've just stayed at Yale."

Not missing a beat, Eilers stood his ground. "Coach, I didn't transfer not to play."

Holtz paused, looked Eilers in the eye, and said, "Run it again."

Heck came out again, and Eilers blew up the play.

Head coach Lou Holtz leads the 1988 Fighting Irish onto the field for the No. 1 versus No. 2 clash with the Trojans of Southern California. *(Photo courtesy of Michael and Susan Bennett, Lighthouse Imaging)*

The quarterback-coach relationship is critical to the success of any team. Holtz scrutinized every quarterback he coached, and Tony Rice developed his own way to respond to Holtz's intense style. *(Photo courtesy of Michael and Susan Bennett, Lighthouse Imaging)*

Notre Dame President Fr. Theodore Hesburgh *(left)* credits Fr. Edmund "Ned" Joyce with overseeing the school's athletic programs during the duo's tenure leading the university. *(Photo courtesy of Michael and Susan Bennett, Lighthouse Imaging)*

Wes Pritchett and others raise their golden helmets to salute fans after a win on the road. *(Photo courtesy of Michael and Susan Bennett, Lighthouse Imaging)*

Pivotal move: In 1988, Barry Alvarez went from being the linebackers coach to the defensive coordinator for the Fighting Irish. He also revamped the entire defensive coaching staff. *(Photo courtesy of Michael and Susan Bennett, Lighthouse Imaging)*

The addition of Joe Moore to coach tackles and tight ends proved to be another key move in the coaching staff changes made for the '88 season. *(Photo courtesy of Michael and Susan Bennett, Lighthouse Imaging)*

Andy Heck as a college tight end prospect out of W. T. Woodson High School in Fairfax, Virginia. *(Photo courtesy of Tom Lemming)*

Heck (66) and Tim Ryan (52) pull to make a block at Pittsburgh. After playing tight end for three years at Notre Dame, Heck, a tri-captain, made the move to offensive tackle for his senior season. *(Photo courtesy of Michael and Susan Bennett, Lighthouse Imaging)*

Campus cult figure and starting nose tackle Chris Zorich sports the belly-showing half jersey, which he made a trend for those who idolized him. *(Photo courtesy of Michael and Susan Bennett, Lighthouse Imaging)*

While a few years away from dominating the college scene, freshman Raghib "Rocket" Ismail put his blazing speed on display during the 1988 campaign. *(Photo courtesy of Michael and Susan Bennett, Lighthouse Imaging)*

The legend of the diminutive pre-med major, walk-on kicker Reggie Ho, became a national story. Here he makes a field goal against Michigan. *(Photo courtesy of Michael and Susan Bennett, Lighthouse Imaging)*

Michael Stonebreaker sealed Notre Dame's 20–3 win at Michigan State with this interception return for a touchdown. *(Photo courtesy of Michael and Susan Bennett, Lighthouse Imaging)*

From Bishop McDevitt High School near Philadelphia, Ricky Watters was a highly touted running back coming out of high school. Nationally, he ranked second to Emmitt Smith, who went to Florida and went on to become the NFL's all-time leading rusher. *(Photo courtesy of Tom Lemming)*

While he played split end in '88, here Ricky Watters finds a gap running the ball between defenders. *(Photo courtesy of Michael and Susan Bennett, Lighthouse Imaging)*

Reggie Brooks breaks a run up the sideline against Michigan State as guard Tim Ryan trails the play. *(Photo courtesy of Michael and Susan Bennett, Lighthouse Imaging)*

Freshman tight end Derek Brown is about to snag a touchdown in the third quarter of a 42–14 win against Stanford. *(Photo courtesy of Michael and Susan Bennett, Lighthouse Imaging)*

Student government–sponsored body painting elevated the already intense stadium atmosphere for the game against No. 1 Miami. *(Photo courtesy of Michael and Susan Bennett, Lighthouse Imaging)*

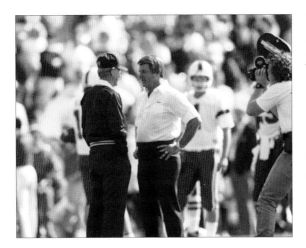

Notre Dame's Lou Holtz and Miami's Jimmy Johnson speak to each other on the field before things erupted between the two teams and before they coached their squads in an all-time classic. *(Photo courtesy of Michael and Susan Bennett, Lighthouse Imaging)*

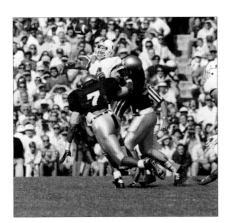

Frank Stams and Andre Jones (7) hammer down on Miami's Steve Walsh, dislodging the ball from the Hurricanes All-American quarterback. *(Photo courtesy of Michael and Susan Bennett, Lighthouse Imaging)*

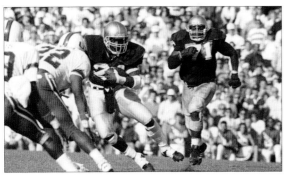

Tri-captain Mark Green makes a cut, attempting to avoid the tackle from Miami's Randy Shannon, while tackle Dean Brown trails the play. *(Photo courtesy of Michael and Susan Bennett, Lighthouse Imaging)*

Wes Pritchett played more than three quarters of the Miami game with a broken hand. Here a member of the medical staff tapes his gloved fingers together in an attempt to stabilize the situation. *(Photo courtesy of Michael and Susan Bennett, Lighthouse Imaging)*

While the deflected 2-point conversion attempt is what people remember most about Pat Terrell, he also had this interception return for a touchdown against Miami. *(Photo courtesy of Michael and Susan Bennett, Lighthouse Imaging)*

Pat Eilers, a transfer from Yale, who walked-on the Irish squad, and then earned a scholarship, scored this touchdown against Miami and cemented a Notre Dame moment for himself. *(Photo courtesy of Michael and Susan Bennett, Lighthouse Imaging)*

Pat Terrell batting down this pass from Miami's Steve Walsh stopped the Hurricanes 2-point conversion, secured the Irish win, and is widely viewed as the most crucial play in the championship run. *(Photo courtesy of Michael and Susan Bennett, Lighthouse Imaging)*

Not often seen in public settings, Holtz's pipe would come out at practice. *(Photo courtesy of Michael and Susan Bennett, Lighthouse Imaging)*

Holtz coaches Chris Zorich at the 1991 Orange Bowl. *(Photo courtesy of Michael and Susan Bennett, Lighthouse Imaging)*

Tony Rice breaks loose for a run against West Virginia. Rice was named the Fiesta Bowl Co-MVP. With 75 yards rushing and 213 yards passing on just 11 attempts, he accounted for more than fifty percent of the Irish offense. *(Photo courtesy of Michael and Susan Bennett, Lighthouse Imaging)*

Just like Holtz drew it up: With All-American safety Mark Carrier behind the play after overpursuing the option, Tony Rice had nothing but grass between him and the end zone on this 65-yard touchdown run at USC. *(Photo courtesy of Michael and Susan Bennett, Lighthouse Imaging)*

Wes Pritchett (34) and Frank Stams (30) chase USC quarterback Rodney Peete in the pivotal regular-season finale that pitted the No. 1 and No. 2 ranked schools against each other. *(Photo courtesy of Michael and Susan Bennett, Lighthouse Imaging)*

Unheralded as a recruit and viewed as possibly the lowliest member of what Holtz called his worst recruiting class, cornerback Stan Smagala quickly became a starter at Notre Dame. Here he celebrates his interception return for a touchdown against USC. *(Photo courtesy of Michael and Susan Bennett, Lighthouse Imaging)*

Frank Stams helped lead St. Vincent–St. Mary High School in Akron, Ohio, to back-to-back state championships before playing at Notre Dame. *(Photo courtesy of Tom Lemming)*

After the Irish defeated USC and sat one game away from winning a national championship, Frank Stams talked to ABC's Mike Adamle about the program's turnaround. *(Photo courtesy of Michael and Susan Bennett, Lighthouse Imaging)*

A combination of confidence in a Fiesta Bowl victory and the intention of having the players only think about winning led Holtz to have them practice carrying him off the field. *(Photo courtesy of Michael and Susan Bennett, Lighthouse Imaging)*

Known for goofy antics, the Notre Dame starting linebackers, Frank Stams (30), Michael Stonebreaker (42), and Wes Pritchett (34), flex for the camera. *(Photo courtesy of Michael and Susan Bennett, Lighthouse Imaging)*

From a game where the linebacker remembers "being completely possessed," Wes Pritchett drills West Virginia quarterback Major Harris during the Fiesta Bowl. *(Photo courtesy of Michael and Susan Bennett, Lighthouse Imaging)*

Even the Leprechaun gets into it as running back Mark Green (24) leaped, Andy Heck (66) signaled the touchdown, and Frank Jacobs (88) clapped for the score by Rodney Culver. *(Photo courtesy of Michael and Susan Bennett, Lighthouse Imaging)*

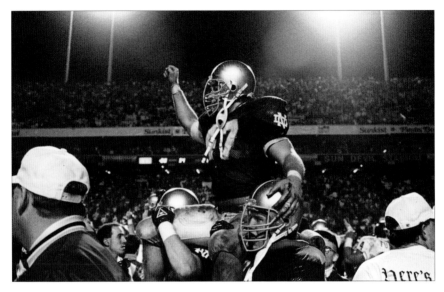

Notre Dame tri-captain Ned Bolcar is carried off the Fiesta Bowl field after the Fighting Irish clinch the national championship. *(Photo courtesy of Michael and Susan Bennett, Lighthouse Imaging)*

Holtz addresses the team in the locker room after the Fiesta Bowl win against West Virginia. *(Photo courtesy of Michael and Susan Bennett, Lighthouse Imaging)*

The players are aboard the plane and headed to Washington, D.C., to meet the president. *(Photo courtesy of the University of Notre Dame Sports Information Department)*

Holtz and his wife, Beth, ride the team bus on the national championship visit to the White House. *(Photo courtesy of the University of Notre Dame Sports Information Department)*

President Ronald Reagan wanted one of his last acts in office to be hosting the national championship Notre Dame team at the White House. Here The Gipper of American politics uncorks a pass during the ceremony. *(Photo courtesy of the University of Notre Dame Sports Information Department)*

Defending Champs: A bunch of smiling players pose for a personal photo after the spring football Blue-Gold game in 1989. *(Pictured, left to right: peeking back:* Ricky Watters; *standing:* Rod Smith, Jeff Alm, D'Juan Francisco, Stan Smagala, Todd Lyght, Pat Terrell, and Scott Kowalkowski; *kneeling:* Don Grimm, Ned Bolcar, Chris Zorich, Bob Dahl, and Bryan Flannery). *(Photo courtesy of Scott Kowalkowski's private collection)*

Holtz walked by Eilers, didn't look at him, but tapped him on the helmet. "Son, I think you're going to be just fine."

Later that spring, Eilers earned his scholarship. Unheralded players can usually break into the lineup by showing grit on special teams. Eilers did that. In the '87 season he made 224 special teams appearances, 64 more than anyone else on the team. With a love for blocking that fit well in Holtz's run-first offense, he made the switch to receiver for '88.

After his short run gave Notre Dame a 28–21 lead against Miami, he looked back at Touchdown Jesus and knew this was his Notre Dame moment.

"It wasn't often that we got the ball to me. Just given the other talent we had back there ... You don't get too many chances down by the goal line. But it's just a job to do," Eilers said.

Miami continued to show its resilience, driving deep into Notre Dame territory on its next possession.

"There's that man again," said CBS's Brent Musburger when Walsh connected with fullback Cleveland Gary for a 21-yard pass play, giving the Hurricanes the ball at the Irish 25-yard line. With the catch, Gary already had 8 receptions for 105 yards.

Walsh pitched the ball to sophomore running back Shannon Crowell on the next play. He gained 2 yards on the sweep before Terrell leveled him. Crowell let go of the ball and shriveled to the ground. The refs didn't call a fumble, but Terrell accomplished his goal.

"I just wanted to punish people," he said.

The Fighting Irish sent five pass rushers on the next play. Avoiding the sack, Walsh got rid of the ball quickly. Looking for Gary, he dumped the pass over the line of scrimmage, where Notre Dame's Jeff Alm had been crouched down, engaging a blocker and retreating back to pass coverage. The 6'7" 248-pound lineman jumped up and grabbed the pass with both hands. Notre Dame had the ball again.

"Of course, they brought in the bowling ball. Oh my goodness," Miami linebacker Maurice Crum said of Notre Dame's hard-running Tony Brooks.

Brooks brought the Irish offense to midfield on a 22-yard run in which he spun out of tackle behind the line of scrimmage, cut across the field, and hurdled a prostrate blocker before stumbling to the turf.

A play later, Rice dropped back, set his feet, and delivered a 26-yard strike up the middle of the field to freshman tight end Derek Brown. The Miami defense didn't expect the Irish to send a tight end streaking up the middle of the field.

"It was a new wrinkle, and we weren't prepared for it at the time," Crum said. "These guys really came out here to play."

The fact that Brown, who went to Merritt Island High School in Florida, chose Notre Dame over Miami shocked the 'Canes.

As one of the nation's most sought-after high school players, Brown found himself in a recruiting process that quickly became harried. To get away from the nonstop calls from coaches, he would go to the library after school and then sleep overnight at a friend's house.

For Notre Dame, this meant that recruiting coordinator Vinny Cerrato spent time talking to Brown's mother and twin sisters. Cerrato even befriended the local newspaper reporter who wrote about Brown's recruiting process.

Miami and Notre Dame had a showdown at one of Brown's basketball games. Jimmy Johnson attended the game with most of his staff. Cerrato cozied up next to Brown's mother and asked a friend to keep talking to the twins, blocking any possible communication from the Hurricane coaches.

Johnson and the Miami coaches went to Brown's house after the game. Brown's mother told Cerrato to stop by after the Miami entourage left, but the Hurricane crew stayed well past midnight.

"I got a call. It was two in the morning. It was from the lady writer, and she said they had just left and she said 'You're in good shape,'" Cerrato said.

Initially Brown saw himself as a Florida Gator, but then he took two unofficial trips to visit the Hurricanes. He liked Miami. Some of his friends played there, and some more of his high school teammates would be going there.

"He was talking like he was coming to Miami," said Bernard Clark, who spent time with Brown during the visits. "We continued to talk after the visit, 'Hey man, can't wait until you get here.'"

Brown remembers the moment he picked his school. He came home after school and no one was there. The phone wasn't ringing, and he popped a tape in the VCR. He watched "Wake Up the Echoes." More than a Notre Dame highlight reel, it was the Fighting Irish tradition captured on video and produced by NFL Films.

Goose bumps ran up and down Brown's arms. *You know what?* Brown thought. *Screw it. I'm going to go. I'm just going to go.*

"I totally went on my gut," he said. "There was just something about the place. Something intangible."

The decision jolted Clark and the Hurricanes. *You've got to be freaking kidding me. This bastard's going to Notre Dame*, Clark remembers thinking.

After the Brown reception, Notre Dame drove to the Miami 11-yard line before Reggie Ho came on the field to kick a 27-yard field goal. The Irish headed into the fourth quarter with a 31–21 lead.

The Notre Dame band played the "1812 Overture," and as per tradition the fans chanted "Lou," making *L*'s with their thumbs and index fingers, waving their arms from back to front.

At the same time, Miami displayed its own tradition. On the sideline, the players raised four fingers toward the sky, symbolizing the program's ownership of the fourth quarter.

"The worst thing about scoring a touchdown against Miami is you give the ball back to them," Musburger said during the broadcast in a line that has drawn historic ire from Irish fans.

It had some truth. The Hurricanes felt no need to panic. The last two double-digit deficits they faced came in road games against ranked teams and they came back to win both—Michigan earlier in the season and Florida State in '87.

Plus, great teams put mistakes—turnovers, blocked kicks, and failed trick plays—behind them. A common misconception about football games is that miscues somehow mar the contests. "The Greatest Game Ever Played," the 1958 NFL Championship between the New York Giants and Baltimore Colts, had 7 turnovers. If each team played flawlessly, the sport would be a demonstration, not a competition. Football is filled with constant action and reaction. Great teams force opponents to make mistakes. The games become classics when teams keep charging back after mishaps that would have broken the will of lesser squads. Notre Dame and Miami kept coming back at each other all day.

Walsh drove the Hurricanes to the Notre Dame 9-yard line. On first and goal, the quarterback threw to a leaping Andre Brown in the end zone. Brown had a run on a slant pattern and beat Notre Dame cornerback Todd Lyght by a step, but Lyght made up the ground and knocked the ball loose for an incompletion. The 'Canes came away with a field goal and trailed the Irish 31–24.

The ensuing kickoff went through Rocket Ismail's legs. He ran back and fell on the ball at the 12-yard line. With the lead and the ball deep in their own territory, Notre Dame's offense shed its running style. Rice faked the option, running into the line and then stepping back, launching a long ball to Ismail. Miami had two players on the speedster, and the ball fell incomplete. On second down, Rice rolled out and overthrew Steve Alaniz. Now, forced into a third down and long, Rice stayed in the pocket and delivered a 20-yard rope to Derek Brown on an out route. Rice and Ismail hooked up for 8 yards, moving the ball out to the Notre Dame 41-yard line. This was the farthest Notre Dame would go in the entire fourth quarter. On the next play, Ricky Watters mishandled a Rice option pitch, fumbling the ball for a 15-yard loss.

One play after forcing the Irish punt, the Hurricanes were back on the Notre Dame side of the field. On third down and 2, Walsh threaded a throw between two defenders, hitting Andre Brown on the sideline for 21 yards. On second down from the Irish 11-yard line, Walsh threw to Brown in the back left corner of the end zone, but again Todd Lyght made the play, diving back to knock the ball away. After another incomplete pass, Jimmy Johnson, down 7 with more than seven minutes to play, decided to go for it on fourth down.

Notre Dame rushed three players, dropping eight men back into pass coverage. The pocket opened up around Walsh. He threw to Gary at the 2-yard line, already past the first-down marker. Gary turned and dove toward the goal line, extending his arm into controversy and the end zone.

Safety George Streeter had lunged at Gary, getting an arm across his helmet, chest, and leg as the Hurricane reached for the touchdown.

The ball came loose. Gary tried to regain possession and pushed the ball out of the end zone to the 1-yard line, where Notre Dame's Michael Stonebreaker dove on it. After three seconds of discussion, an official waved his arm signaling Notre Dame ball.

"It would've been easy to stop a couple feet from where he was," Streeter said. "Everything was about feet and inches. We just didn't give up, and there was just some hope that we would make a play."

Johnson kept waving his arm forward, yelling, "First down," on the Miami sideline.

"It wasn't a fumble. The ball was in his hands when he went down. It had to be enough for the first down, but those things happen," Johnson said in his postgame media session.

Five years later, even after Johnson won a Super Bowl coaching the Dallas Cowboys, he addressed the play in his 1993 autobiography. "The ball hit the ground and the ground caused the ball to come loose, which of course meant no fumble."

Gary said after the game, "After I caught the ball I thought I broke the plane and scored a touchdown. The official said my knee hit the ground, and therefore I thought the play was dead. I don't understand why it was ruled a fumble."

Walsh went to the officials, screaming that Gary's knee had hit the ground. "One official turned to me and said, 'I know. We're just trying to determine whether it was a first down,'" Walsh said. "Another one got in there and said, 'No. Notre Dame ball.'"

Holtz did not believe Gary scored. "When you try to score and you put the ball out like that, you better make sure you have control of it," he said. "That's abnormal to see a ball out like that. You know, all this is judgment, and in a critical game like that, there are a lot of close calls."

A few days after the game *The Miami News* printed a story quoting an anonymous official who said, "There was no fumble. The ruling was the ball went over on downs. We were wrong in doing it, but the truth is we just had a very bad day."

Holtz responded in the media, saying he had talked to the head of the Collegiate Independent Football Officials Association, it was one of their crews that officiated the game, and confirmed that Gary fumbled and that no referee from the game had talked to the media.

Regardless of the argument, Notre Dame took over with the ball at its 1-yard line. The Irish used up a little more than three minutes and made it out to the 15-yard line before punting the ball back to Miami with 3:52 on the clock.

Starting at midfield, Walsh completed an 11-yard pass to his tight end Rob Chudzinski, who was hit out of bounds by Zorich, resulting in a 15-yard personal foul. Miami had a first down at the Irish 24-yard line.

Walsh took a 10-yard drop back. Notre Dame rushed three men, dropping Zorich back into pass coverage. Stam excelled at coming off a block and speeding to the ball. Chudzinski engaged him, and then Stams came looping around the left side. Walsh slid his feet up in the pocket and cocked his arm back, and Stams hacked the ball out of his hands. The ball bounced forward, and the torque on Stams's body sent him twirling forward, too. Zorich ran up to recover the fumble, giving the ball back to the offense at the 28-yard line. It was Miami's seventh turnover.

Up 31–24, Notre Dame ran the ball twice, draining the clock and forcing Miami to use a time-out. Holtz called a pass play on third down, but the Miami blitz got to Rice, sacking him and forcing the fumble. The 'Canes had the ball at the Notre Dame 14-yard line with 2:10 left.

Leonard Conley slipped through the line, running for 3 yards before Terrell tackled him. Walsh threw a quick-out to Gary, and Streeter instantly tackled him for no gain. On third down, Walsh threw behind Gary at the goal line, and Wes Pritchett broke up the pass. Just like the possession on the Gary fumble, Miami, down 7, had a fourth down and 7 from the 11-yard line.

"On those fourth-and-long situations I was taught, 'Hey, we've got these very athletic receivers. Just put the ball in a position for them to make a great catch,'" Walsh said.

He faced no pressure when the ball was snapped. He timed a pass across the field to the front right corner of the end zone, where Andre Brown ran under it to make the catch, rolling on the ground as he grabbed his second score on the day. Notre Dame 31, Miami 30.

Jimmy Johnson called time-out because the Hurricanes would go for the 2-point conversion. The 'Canes didn't play for ties. They played for wins.

Alavrez kept cool in his black-tinted sunglasses, gathering the Notre Dame defense on the sideline. The Irish knew Miami would run one of a few plays. There would be no surprise, just a test to see which team executed better.

Around the country, the Irish faithful said prayers in front of TV screens. Some of those in the stadium called on religion as well.

In the Miami huddle, Walsh called the same play the Hurricanes ran for a 2-point conversion during the comeback against Michigan. Two outside receivers would run up 4 yards and cut in while the running back came out of the backfield and ran a route to the corner of the end zone. Walsh could throw to one of the receivers when they broke inside or he could drop it to the corner.

Walsh dropped back and set to throw, but a bull rush from George "Boo" Williams forced Walsh to hold the ball and then throw it off his back foot to the corner.

Terrell had picked up Conley as the running back came out of the backfield. When the ball came toward the pair, Terrell leaped up and to the side, batting the ball down and securing the Irish lead.

The home crowd erupted. Rice ribbed Terrell when the defensive back made it to the sideline. "Pat, you could've intercepted the ball instead of knocking it down. You had to make it look dramatic."

Even when they didn't convert the 2-point attempt, Miami still believed they could win the game. They had a time-out left and 45 seconds left on the clock.

"I went over to the bench and sat down. I was starting to think about my next three plays to get in field goal position to win because I was convinced, well, we were going to get the onside kick. I mean, we just did it a few weeks earlier at Michigan. This is what we do," Walsh said.

Holtz sent Rice into the game on the hands team to recover the onside kick. Miami's Carlos Huerta dribbled the ball, and Anthony Johnson moved up and covered it. All Notre Dame had to do was hike the ball and let the clock run out.

The band played the "1812 Overture" again, and the stadium repeated a chorus of "Lou. Lou. Lou."

Two snaps later, the Fighting Irish had avenged the 58–7 debacle. They had unseated the team of the era, ending Miami's thirty-six-game regular-season winning streak and knocking the 'Canes out of the top spot in the polls.

"It seems like we had no way of losing that game even though it was close," said Rice, who recorded 2 touchdowns, 195 yards passing, 38 yards rushing, and 70 percent of Notre Dame's total offense.

"They say 'Catholics vs. Convicts.' God was on our side," he added with a quick laugh.

"We had no answer for Frank Stams," said Walsh, who finished the game with 424 yards in the air, 4 touchdown passes, and 5 turnovers. "We definitely underestimated Stams's ability because we couldn't block him. We were really struggling there... He alone was the difference in their defensive effort because he was constantly harassing me."

Holtz had an explanation. "This was won by the Notre Dame spirit," he said during the CBS postgame interview as the students and fans rushed the field. "Our players deserve a lot of credit, but hey, it's the spirit of Notre Dame."

Back in the press room, Holtz began to wipe away the unavoidable euphoria. "I don't believe we have the chance to win a national championship with six victories," he said.

Even though they had this historic win, Notre Dame did not control their own destiny, nor did they jump to No. 1 in the rankings. The Irish win put UCLA and Troy Aikman in the top spot in the polls and the national championship driver's seat. Notre Dame came away ranked No. 2. If the Bruins won out, there would be no denying them a share of the national title. Because of the Pac-10 conference tie-in to play the Big Ten winner in the Rose Bowl, there was no way Notre Dame could face them.

The Irish also had to finish the regular season at USC, which was undefeated and ranked third after the weekend. The Los Angeles Coliseum had become a place where great Notre Dame seasons went to die. On five occasions, unbeaten Fighting Irish teams traveled to Southern California only to return with a record blemished at the hands of the Trojans.

Ghosts of Notre Dame's past also included historic hangovers. The week after Knute Rockne used the "Win one for the Gipper" speech to inspire an underdog Irish team to beat Army in 1928, Notre Dame fell 27–7 at home to Carnegie Tech.* In 1969, *Sport* magazine listed the 1935 Notre Dame–Ohio State game as the best college football game in the first hundred years of the sport.† Down 13–0 in the fourth quarter, the Irish stormed back to beat the Buckeyes 18–13. They followed it up with a 14–7 home loss to Northwestern. Notre Dame stopped Oklahoma's forty-seven-game winning streak with a 7–0 win in Norman in 1957. The Irish flopped 21–13 when they returned home to face Iowa.

By Sunday morning after the win against Miami, Holtz had started rattling off stats about the next opponent, Air Force, and its prolific option quarterback, Dee Dowis.

"After the game you didn't feel like you've got it made now. I still looked at that schedule and we had Penn State and Southern Cal," Holtz said.

---

*The school expanded and is known today as Carnegie Mellon.
†The game was listed third overall. The 1958 NFL Championship came in first, and the Ice Bowl, the 1967 NFL Championship between the Dallas Cowboys and the Green Bay Packers, ranked second.

CHAPTER 14

Weekday Wars and Visualization

On Sunday morning after the Miami game, Holtz fixated on Air Force, Notre Dame's next opponent. His stress levels shot up when he eyeballed the Falcons' offensive production.

Around 10:00 A.M. in Connecticut, Tim Brando, the cohost of ESPN's *College GameDay,* awoke to a ringing telephone.

"Timmy, you may not like this call, but we booked a flight for you on Monday morning and you're going to South Bend," said the producer on the other end of the line.

Before ESPN's college football coverage spread across three networks and mobile apps with numerous highlight shows and a stable of hosts, Brando worked fourteen-hour Saturdays and forgot about his promise to sing if the Irish won.

In Coral Gables, Jimmy Johnson brought the Hurricanes together in a team meeting room. He turned on a projector and let the Cleveland Gary fumble run on the screen. The play ended, and he shut off the machine.

"The play's over. We lost. We're now going to evaluate every position on the team, and if we don't have the right guys playing, we're going to make a change," he said, putting everyone on notice.

Through the media, Johnson would politic for the top spot in the rankings, but the 'Canes knew other teams had to slip in order for Miami to get another shot at the title.

Steve Walsh sat with offensive coordinator Gary Stevens to watch the offense's performance. Stevens slowed down the film on the 2-point conversion attempt. The coach saw what Walsh saw in live action: Leonard Conley open for a fraction of a second coupled with a partially obstructed passing lane courtesy of Boo Williams.

"Steve, you realize if you had thrown this ball when you wanted to, there would have been a million Irishmen rolling over in their graves," the coach said.

On Monday in South Bend, Holtz halted practice with a whistle.

"I've got to stop the practice because I'm very concerned about our focus, and listen, we just have to tighten up. We've got to button it up. And by the way, gentlemen, on *College GameDay* last week Tim Brando made a complete fool of himself. He did not believe that we could beat Miami," Holtz said. "He made a bet with Beano Cook and now he's got to pay up."

Brando stepped in, raising a helmet and singing the fight song, nailing all the lyrics.

"Well, is that the way you guys do it?" Brando asked when he finished.

"Yeah, we usually do it with a bigger arm," Holtz said, referring to Brando's helmet holder.*

That would be the last of the light moments for the Irish that week. After the TV host left, Holtz warned his team about Air Force. The 5–2 Falcons averaged 46 points per game. The starting backfield had run for 31 touchdowns. Their rushing attack was the best in the country, averaging 432 yards a game.

If the players thought beating Miami, a team with enough players to field an NFL lineup, meant they would walk over an under-

---

*The following Saturday *College GameDay* aired a Keystone Kops–style segment, using sped-up film to show Brando leaving the ESPN studios, traveling to South Bend, and rushing up to practice to fulfill his bet.

sized service academy, Holtz disabused them of the idea, almost making it seem delusional.

Holtz raved to them about Dee Dowis, the 5'10" 160-pound Air Force quarterback who engineered the Falcons offense. He reminded them that last season Dowis had needed just 14 carries to pick up 132 yards. Holtz rattled off Dowis's season stats—7.9 yards per run and almost 100 rushing yards per game.

"I was scared to death. I was nervous and uptight," Holtz said.

Facing Air Force and then Navy meant that for the next two weeks the Irish prepped for option offenses. This made the defense leave its basic assignments and practice techniques and alignments it hadn't used before and wouldn't use again during its regular-season schedule.

On Tuesday, when he entered the coaching-staff meeting, Holtz had a plan only he knew. "Let me have it today," he told his assistants.

During the first fifteen minutes of practice he chewed out the entire team. He went on about Air Force and let loose a diatribe about how the Irish weren't working hard enough.

Twenty minutes into practice he threw them off the field. He didn't give them a specific reason, just told them to leave.

Between the preaching of impressive stats and calling off practice, Holtz had the team's attention. "We were worried. We were concerned," said strong safety George Streeter. "We were really on edge, the whole entire team...All of a sudden, [we're thinking] these guys can beat us."

"If we have a letdown, if we aren't ready...we don't deserve to wear the Notre Dame helmet," Holtz told reporters.

George Stewart, who coached the outside linebackers and special teams, knew this drill. He'd been through it in college when he played for Holtz at Arkansas.

The Razorbacks had just come off a big game, and they faced a lowly Rice team the following Saturday. Holtz wanted to jolt his squad and ensure focus. Early in the Razorbacks practice, after giving them a verbal pounding, he told the team to get off the field. Stewart left bewildered, not knowing what had happened. When it happened at Notre Dame, Stewart figured it all out.

"The purpose was to get them off the field and give them rest and get them sharp for Air Force," Stewart said. "They came back that Wednesday mentally sharp and physically ready to go to practice."

The Falcons hung in the game, taking an early 3–0 lead and finishing the first half within a touchdown of the Irish, 20–13. This did not sit well in the Irish locker room, where seniors began addressing the team during the break.

"I did some screaming," Wes Pritchett told reporters. "I told them we had come too far and worked too hard all winter, all summer, to let it slip away."

After giving up 168 yards and ten first downs in the first half, the Notre Dame defense shut down Air Force, limiting the Falcons to 48 yards, three first downs, and zero points in the second half.

Liz Holtz, the coach's daughter, devised the biggest highlight of the Irish's 41–13 win. After running the halfback option pass on her Notre Dame dormitory flag football team, she told her dad to install the play in his offensive repertoire. The Irish started practicing it the week before Michigan State. With Steve Belles, the backup quarterback, playing halfback, Holtz called it against Air Force.

Out of the I-formation at the 50-yard line, Rice pitched to Belles, who feigned a run right, stepped back, and threw a bomb to Ricky Watters, who carried an Air Force defender on his waist for the final 4 yards as he stretched into the end zone.

Tony Rice threw 2 touchdowns and ran for another. The quarterback had 123 yards passing and 36 yards rushing. One game past the season's midpoint and he had now surpassed Joe Theismann's eighteen-year-old record for single-season rushing yards by a Notre

Dame quarterback. "It is a nice honor for me to be up there with him," Rice said after the game.

On Monday after the Air Force game, fifth-year senior Irish linebacker Darrell "Flash" Gordon had to get something off his mind. How did he go from being the starter at outside linebacker to not playing a defensive down against Miami or Air Force?

"That experience is still raw today for me. It is one of the biggest games of all time...I watched the entire game from the sideline," Gordon said of his role in the win against Miami. "As a competitor you want to be able to contribute to such a thing."

Gordon didn't pout. He didn't go into a shell. He didn't get mad. He never whined to other players about it. He didn't want to be selfish. He knew his team had just posted huge wins, but back in his dorm room he kept thinking about his lack of playing time. He had practiced well. He couldn't figure out a reason why he ended up a spectator.

He went to Holtz's office, utilizing the coach's open door policy.

"I am excited about what transpired, but I didn't play...And if you can tell me today that all of a sudden...I am no longer good enough to even get on the field—to get on the field and play and compete—and help this team to win, I just want you to tell me that," he said to the coach.

Holtz called George Stewart, Gordon's position coach, into the office. The three discussed the situation. Gordon didn't head straight back to the starting lineup, but he garnered praise for how he addressed the situation.

"To still have the wherewithal to be a team leader said a lot about Darrell Gordon. He handled it as a man," Stewart said. "He didn't like it, but he accepted it."

Gordon figured a youth movement was afoot. Freshman Arnold Ale and sophomore Andre Jones started ahead of him in consecutive weeks. Of the top twenty-two players listed on the first- and second-string defense against Air Force, only five were seniors.

Seniority, on its own, held no clout. It didn't matter if players had been at Notre Dame for years or if they first stepped on campus in August, Holtz was going to field the best possible team. Missed practices reduced playing time. As a result, injured players came to practice on crutches, wearing their helmets and shoulder pads. They couldn't participate, but they did everything they could to maintain a starting spot or their game-day minutes.

The talent bottlenecked at certain positions, and this glared greatest at middle linebacker, where senior Ned Bolcar, a captain and second-team All American in '87, played behind junior Michael Stonebreaker, who had come back to the team after being academically ineligible the previous season.

Bolcar, the middle child from a Catholic family of five, signed with the Fighting Irish after a highly publicized recruiting process. He was the president of the National Honor Society and senior class vice president at Phillipsburg High School in Phillipsburg, New Jersey. *Parade* magazine named him the national high school player of the year. ESPN covered his Thanksgiving Day rivalry game with Easton Area High School. He detailed his recruitment in a diary published in *USA Today*.

Stanford enticed him with a Super Bowl party where he met Ted Kennedy and watched the game with John Elway. At Penn State, his mother shopped with Sue Paterno while Bolcar shared a meal with Joe.

The phone never seemed to stop ringing—recruiters, head coaches, and even pranksters pretending to be assistant coaches. Bolcar received more than five hundred calls during the process. In an age where high-profile athletes had a chance to be private, people knew Bolcar broke up with his girlfriend, flunked a history test, aced a calculus test, and got back together with Alice, the girlfriend.

The 6'1" 247-pound backer played with an aggressive, hit-everything style. He led the Irish team in tackles as a junior and received preseason All-American notice going into the '88 campaign. Yet he was still a backup. A backup who played major minutes—but a backup nonetheless.

"To have your role change to where you're splitting time with two other very good linebackers, it wasn't easy. It was absolutely difficult," Bolcar said. "I put the team first. I believed it was about Notre Dame. It wasn't about any individual players."

After the Michigan game, Bolcar spoke to the *Chicago Sun-Times* about his leadership role and his diminished playing time. With a bit of a dark laugh, Bolcar said the lack of snaps was meant to ensure his return for a fifth year.

After hearing about it, Holtz quickly summoned the captain and Alvarez to his office.

"Ned thinks he should be starting," Holtz told Alvarez.

Alvarez looked over the grades players received from practices and games. Wes Pritchett and Stonebreaker scored higher than Bolcar.

"You've got to go with who's playing best," Alvarez said. "It was clear Stony and Pritch were playing better, and that's nothing against Ned because Ned's a good player."

Bolcar disliked his new spot, but he knew that how he responded—positive or negative—would be noticed by coaches and fed off of by teammates.

"My role is to play my best when I'm on the field and be one of the leaders," he said.

Nowadays, for athletes, using visualization is as commonplace as stretching out and warming up before competition. Holtz had it as part of his holistic approach. He started using it with his team at Arkansas, and he brought it to Notre Dame.

On the night before every game he had the team lie down for group meditation, or "relaxation sessions," as it was listed on the itinerary. On the road the Irish gathered in a large hotel meeting room. At home they often met on the artificial turf at the Loftus Center.

"We were way ahead of our time. It's not something I thought about. 'Well, the country isn't doing it.' This is just something I believed and we did it," Holtz said.

Holtz had the team lie down and close their eyes. He dimmed the lights. The players had no clue what was about to happen.

What the hell's going on with this guy? Wes Pritchett thought during his first session.

"This is only going to take fifteen minutes, but it will be worth four hours of sleep. When you wake up you will be well rested," Holtz said, leading the group.

Typically there were a few snickers. Linebacker Andre Jones was known to whisper a few jokes or tickle the hand of an unsuspecting teammate.

"Your back sinks into the carpet. Your leg sinks into the carpet. Your arms sink into the carpet. Picture yourself in a calm setting. Picture Jesus at your hand," Holtz continued.

Then he talked them through the pregame locker room scene up until the end of the fourth quarter.

"Picture yourself in the stadium tomorrow. Picture yourself coming out of the tunnel."

He described each team's uniforms. He started talking about plays and game situations, watching the ball get snapped.

"Picture yourself on offense playing mistake-free. Picture yourself on defense doing all your assignments."

At the end, he had them picturing the postgame scene after a victory and then meeting up with their family, friends, and girl-friends after leaving the locker room.

"It's just about visualizing what's going to happen before it's going to happen," Holtz said. "It was more than just about football. It was about feeling good, counting their blessings for how lucky they were. Thinking about how fortunate they were to be at Notre Dame, to have the opportunity to be with these people, to have their families."

Pritchett and many others became believers. "I'm not trying to be hokey. He understood how to gain control of your mind," Pritchett said. "I truly believed everything he said."

Holtz wanted only good things floating in their heads. "I never wanted a negative thought in their mind in what we did or how we did it," he said.

A delayed flight caused the Fighting Irish to cancel their relaxation session the night before the Navy game. This was the first omen.

It shouldn't have mattered. No one expected this to be an actual game. The No. 2 Irish, a 34-point betting favorite, would roll over a 3-4 Navy squad. This was a game of blue chippers versus penny stocks. Notre Dame held a 51-9 lead in the series. The Irish had not lost to the Midshipmen since 1963, when Heisman Trophy winner Roger Staubach choreographed a 35–14 win. The Irish trounced Navy 56–13 the previous year in South Bend, gaining 630 yards and getting 4 touchdowns from Anthony Johnson and more than 100 yards from Mark Green.

In the locker room before the game, Holtz noticed Ricky Watters and some other players had written messages on the tape on their arms.

"I went berserk. 'That's not Notre Dame. You send the message the way you play—that's all,'" Holtz said. "I wasn't a happy camper."

The Irish defense took the field first. On the second play from scrimmage, Boo Williams got his paw on the Midshipmen fullback running a dive play. The ball popped up in the air, and Jeff Alm made the recovery. Six plays later Tony Rice connected with Derek Brown for a 10-yard touchdown pass. For the rest of the game, though, the Irish played flat. They gave up two fumbles and had seven penalties for 90 yards. The kicking game contributed a missed extra point and a 10-yard punt. At one point the Irish had to call a time-out because they lined up for a punt without the punter.

"We couldn't get anything going. It was like slow motion out there, and I'll take the blame," Rice said after the game. "I need to be a better leader, and get the team fired up."

Linebacker Michael Stonebreaker registered 18 tackles on the same field where his father suited up for the Baltimore Colts from 1964 to 1966.

"Our heads weren't into the game the way they should be. We came out relaxed and they came out and fought hard," he told reporters after the 22–7 victory.

Meanwhile, at the Rose Bowl in Pasadena, California, No. 1 UCLA had a 27–6 halftime lead at home against the 20-point-underdog Washington State Cougars. The Cougars, coached by Dennis Erickson and led by quarterback Timm Rosenbach, came back to tie the game at 27 in the third quarter. UCLA took the lead back with a fourth-quarter field goal. Washington State answered with a thirteen-play, 80-yard scoring drive to go up 34–30. All-American quarterback Troy Aikman drove UCLA to the Washington State 6-yard line with 35 seconds to play, but the Heisman-caliber passer threw four straight incompletions, and the Cougars preserved the upset. This propelled Notre Dame to the top spot in the rankings. The Irish now controlled their pathway to a national championship.

It was the first time since 1980 that the Irish held the No. 1 ranking this late in the season. In '80, a Dan Devine–coached team, like Holtz's '88 edition, became No. 1 in the first November poll. The 1980 squad relinquished the ranking after a 3–3 game at unranked Georgia Tech. Again, Holtz told the media the '88 team wasn't very good, but this time the 15-point win against what should have been an inferior Navy team strengthened his statement.

He also added that the lackluster play would be addressed. There would be no letdown the following week.

"Everybody sees the Saturdays, but there's a whole week of intense Lou Holtz. It's like boot camp. And everything has to be just so while you're running, and you're expected to be as aggressive as possible and you're expected to be perfect in your assignment," said halfback Tony Brooks.

Each day in the locker room players dressed, checked the practice schedule, and commiserated about the gauntlet headed their way.

"Practices were really, really tough. They were grueling, demanding far beyond what, in some ways, you'd experience during the game," said fullback Anthony Johnson.

That was the point.

"I always felt that if I made the practices really, really tough, the game would be easy," Holtz said. "You get out on the field: 'Thank God Coach isn't here. This is fun.'"

As players stretched, Holtz dropped in questions to make them think and to provide motivation. "Have you challenged yourself today? Are you doing the best you can be? Are you the person you want to be?"

He always spoke about the next, right thing to do. "First we'll be best, then we'll be first."

Once practice started, repetition dominated the sessions. "I don't remember practice. I remember drills," said free safety Pat Terrell.

Over and over again, defensive backs worked on keeping their outside arm and leg free from blockers, making sure they had leverage to turn plays back in toward the rest of the defense rather than let a ball carrier get to the sideline.

Line up. Do it. Line up. Do it again. Twenty straight minutes and practice *really* hadn't started yet.

The running backs had to have balance and run hard. To ensure this they ran through a funnel of buoys. If they kept their shoulder-pad level too high, coach Jim Strong knocked them to the ground in their first steps out of the funnel.

They had laughs, too. In a different drill, backs finished a run by popping a football dummy held by a student manager. Tony Brooks kept hitting the dummy too hard, knocking the student manager off his feet. Strong warned Brooks not to do it again, but the sophomore who loved lowering his shoulder into tacklers did it again.

"Okay, Bob, your turn," Strong said to the manager. "Brooksy, grab the bag,"

With a fleet of backs who would go on to play in the NFL watching, the manager gave his best effort, making the run and thrusting his body into the dummy. Brooks didn't budge. He chuckled.

"Come get your tickets to the County Fair. Everybody gets a ticket to the County Fair," Holtz would say at the start of some practices.

Immediately, the players rotated through four stations of non-stop, often full-contact, fundamentals. Offensive players banged against each other working on downfield blocking. Like snarling bulls waiting to see red, defensive players lowered into stances and charged into each other, battling for position in 1-on-1 drills. The entire defense lined up for a pursuit drill. They had to take the proper angle to chase down a runner on a sweep or a receiver cutting back across the field—all eleven defenders to the ball every time.

"It was all about fundamentals and toughness, and we started every practice that way," Holtz said.

Joe Moore, who coached the offensive line alongside Tony Yelovich, taught toughness and technique in an unorthodox but effective manner.

"The rules of the playbook, that's on you guys. You study those rules. I'm going to teach you how to get these guys," Moore told the unit. "You learn who to get, I'll teach you how to get them."

Moore likened blocking to boxing. He stressed keeping your eyes up, your hands inside, and your feet underneath your body, like a boxer. He built confidence in a unit that opened the season as an inexperienced question mark.

"He made us believe we had to fight for everything," said captain Andy Heck. "That we had to fight for respect."

Even though Notre Dame had a run-heavy offense, Moore practiced pass protection every day for no other reason than to get his players ready for the next level.

If a player failed in a 1-on-1 drill, Moore had him line up and do it over and over and over. The player had to succeed for the drill to end.

"He didn't give you room to think you couldn't do something," said tackle Dean Brown.

One time a player didn't fire low enough off the ball in a game. The following week, Moore had him firing into a fence post.

During one semester when guard Tim Ryan had bad grades, Moore took his car keys, VCR, and TV. The coach prohibited Ryan from leaving campus, and every morning at 7:00 A.M. Ryan had to crab—crawl with his knees off the ground—for 200 yards.

"Besides my dad, I don't know of anybody that is as instrumental in anything that happens as Joe Moore was," Ryan said. "He would put you through hell...It was some kind of bad joke. But looking back, it was the greatest thing ever."

Moore started practices with a ten-minute 1-on-1 blocking drill. He had his men go at each other for two minutes in what ended up looking almost like a fistfight. For the next eight minutes he let them get water and rest. It was their treat for going a million miles per hour.

"We're going to go as hard as we can possibly go, and then we're going to rest, because that's what football is. It's a four-second burst, then it's a rest," Heck said.

Holtz looked over and gave a shout. "Get to work, O-line."

"We're good over here," said Moore, cigarette in hand.

This built camaraderie among the linemen. They knew Moore had their backs, and, in a small way, they did their own thing.

The practice schedule called for twenty-four five-minute periods. Holtz never went more than twenty-four periods, but he did demand two good hours of practice, and sometimes it took three hours to get it. The field turned into football purgatory if Holtz saw careless mistakes, mediocrity, or players going through the motions.

A 21 lit up the play clock, showing the period and giving players some thoughts of showers and eating at the training table.

"Men, I ain't going to count a period if it isn't productive. Now, it's up to you how many periods there are," Holtz said.

He told the student managers to roll back the play clock to period 16.

"Okay, I don't think we got enough out of it. Let's try it one more time," Holtz said, followed by instructions to push the clock back to 16 again.

By the time he revisited the period a third time, it became clear he would do a fourth or fifth time if necessary.*

"It was perfection. There was one way to do it and that was his

_____

*This left an indelible mark that led to a team talent show skit featuring a *Twilight Zone* parody of an inescapable period 16.

way, and that's the right way, and that's how it was with everything we did that whole season," said cornerback D'Juan Francisco.

Holtz wanted game conditions for practice, which meant tackling every day. Linebackers tackled running backs. Defensive backs hit receivers. The quarterbacks never wore a red jersey, which would have signified they were off-limits.

"When you can play with one where they won't hit you in a game, then we'll use it in practice. But if they're going to hit you in the game, we're going to hit you in practice," Holtz said.

At a lot of programs, starters practiced against backups. Not at Notre Dame. The first-string offense lined up against the first-string defense.

Scott Kowalkowski remembered going up against fullback Anthony Johnson and his "razorlike" forearms in cut drills, where linebackers had to avoid blocks to the legs.

"He made me better, and that happened day after day after day in practice. Those practices, coupled with our nasty on-the-field attitude, made game day great," Kowalkowski said.

Fight Day was Wednesday. It was always a tough, physical practice with a lot of competition between the first stringers. Standing to the side, the coaches coached like it was a game, barking commands and encouragement.

"Those cats were tough, and they were trained that way," Alvarez said of the offense. "Our guys weren't backing off and they're not backing off."

The 1-on-1 matchups led to scraps. Players, mainly Chris Zorich, got thrown out of practice. The fights never traveled off the field. Later that evening, the combatants came back together at training table for steak night and plenty of fried shrimp.

Because the players practiced at a quick pace, Holtz reserved sprints for punishment. He never aimed for peak physical condition.

He sought game conditioning. "We aren't playing them in cross-country," he said. "We're playing them in who can play the best. So everything we did, 'Let's do it in how we can win and what do we have to do to execute.'"

He had little tolerance for players who didn't perform. For Holtz, lack of effort or consistent missteps failed the team and were an affront to teammates.

At one practice he called the left guard to the sideline and told the offense to huddle up without him.

Like a gap-toothed smile, the offense lined up for successive plays without the guard. The ball snapped, and Zorich charged unhindered to the ball carrier, whom he drove to the turf behind the line of scrimmage.

"I don't want a pretender, an imposter, an impersonator. His man made every play anyway. What's the difference? It's that simple," Holtz said.

If the offense didn't function as a whole, Holtz called fifteen scout squad players over to play defense. Holtz picked mostly freshmen hungering for stardom and looking to prove something after being relegated to practice-player roles.

The coach placed the ball on the ground and said it was third down and 2. He told the oversized defense exactly where the offense was going to run the ball. "You better keep us from getting it," Holtz said.

He stepped aside and watched the scout team stop the first-string offense for no gain.

"Run it," Holtz commanded.

The offense gained a yard but failed to get a first down.

"Run it."

The offense failed again and heard the same refrain.

"Run it."

The offense started to make gains, picking up 3, 4, and 5 yards.

"Now, think how good we'd be if they didn't know where we're going and they had only eleven. Now, that's the mentality we have to have on third and 2. I don't care if it's fifteen guys. I don't care if they know we're coming. We're going to run there and we're going to make it," Holtz said. "It's an attitude. It's a mentality."

During practices, Holtz mostly stayed with the offense. When he roamed, players knew to be on guard if they heard his golf cart or smelled the aroma from his pipe. The coach could certainly come across as harsh, but his rigorous and meticulous nature enveloped a teacher. Players weren't stranded with failing coachspeak advice: "You've got to catch that." Or "You need to make that tackle." If a receiver dropped a pass, Holtz spoke to him about where his hands were set as the ball approached. A missed tackle led to talks about taking the proper angle.

"Everybody is different. I tried never to criticize a performer, only the performance. I learned this from Woody Hayes," he said.

This coaching set the players up to succeed, and because of it his message reached the team. Even his talk about the spirit of Notre Dame, playing for the "Lady on the Dome," penetrated the group. Senior cornerback D'Juan Francisco moved to room 225 in Cavanaugh Hall to have a window view of the Golden Dome. Other players came up with the selfless rallying cry, "Give it up for the Dome."

Exhausting practice: "Give it up for the Dome."

Miserable weather: "Give it up for the Dome."

Grinding out the football schedule and classes: "Give it up for the Dome."

A week before election day, George H. W. Bush, the Republican presidential nominee and the nation's vice president, visited Notre Dame.

For more than forty years the university had invited presidential nominees to speak on campus. The last nominee to accept the invitation was Jimmy Carter in the fall of 1976. For Bush, this was his third visit to Notre Dame. He attended the Penn State game in Holtz's first season, and he participated in the closing ceremonies at the 1987 Special Olympics, which took place on campus.

Amid a series of scheduled events, Bush stopped by football practice and spoke briefly with the team. The straw poll among the players had Bush winning the election, but the Democratic nominee, Michael Dukakis, had a couple of supporters on the defensive side.

Zorich stopped the vice president before he left. The nose tackle joked with him about voting for Dukakis because Zorich's aunt by marriage, actress Olympia Dukakis, was the candidate's sister. The following day in practice, Frank Stams—a Greek—lobbied his undecided teammates to vote for the Greek Dukakis.

Bush was elected the forty-first president of the United States the following Tuesday. On the Saturday before that, Notre Dame played Rice in its first game as the No. 1 team in the country. The game against the Owls replaced one originally scheduled with Southern Methodist University. SMU had canceled its football season after receiving the NCAA death penalty for, among numerous violations, maintaining a payroll for its football players.

Instead of the Mustangs, the Irish played the team with the longest losing streak in Division I football. Rice had lost fourteen in a row, including seven straight to start the '88 season.

At 7:20 A.M. on game day, an usher found a pipe bomb lying on the ground a couple of feet away from a wall of Notre Dame Stadium. An unlit fuse snaked out of the nail-studded 4½" plastic pipe. Security scoured the stadium, and no other suspicious objects turned up. The South Bend police bomb disposal unit took the device to a rural area and tried unsuccessfully to detonate it. The incident had no impact on the game.

Notre Dame trounced Rice 54–11 on a wet, gray South Bend

day with temperatures in the mid-40s. The Irish defense held the Owls without a touchdown—3 field goals plus a blocked extra point attempt returned for 2 points. Raghib "Rocket" Ismail provided the big plays, returning 2 kickoffs for touchdowns. The Owls scored on the game's opening drive and then kicked to Ismail at the Notre Dame 13-yard line. He strode by a couple of would-be tacklers, shimmying his shoulders, before blazing up the sideline for a score. Less than a minute into the fourth quarter, Rice kicked a low dribbler down the middle of the field. The ball scooted back to Ismail. He ran back through the middle, breaking to the left and speeding his way to an 83-yard touchdown.*

"That's what they call him the Rocket for," Ricky Watters told the *Chicago Tribune*. "At least three guys had the angle on him. He just took all the angles away."

Ismail's speed was something the college game had seldom, if ever, seen. Watters was right. Defenders had great pursuit angles on Rocket, and then he simply sped away. In the next couple of years, Rocket would become the most feared offensive threat in college football. After returning 2 kickoffs for touchdowns at Michigan in an early season 1-versus-2 matchup, Ismail—a sophomore—graced the cover of *Sports Illustrated*. Michigan coach Bo Schembechler called him "faster than the speed of sound."

"He's not a track guy playing football," Notre Dame assistant coach Pete Cordelli told the *Chicago Sun-Times*. "He's a football guy that has track speed."

Until age thirteen, Raghib grew up in Newark, New Jersey, the

---

*In an era predating fear of terrorism targeting stadiums, a sportswriter could pen tongue-in-cheek words like these from the *Chicago Tribune*'s Andrew Bagnato: "Authorities safely removed the incendiary device, but they allowed another one to walk on the field, with devastating results. Raghib 'Rocket' Ismail exploded."

oldest of three children born to Ibrahim and Fatma Ismail. His father died from kidney failure in 1980. Soon after that his mother could no longer afford tuition at the Sister Clara Muhammad School. The crime and drugs in the Newark public schools led Fatma to send Raghib and his younger brothers, Qadry and Sulaiman, to live with their father's mother in Wilkes-Barre, Pennsylvania. There— blowing out of sprinter's blocks—Raghib became Rocket, a nickname given to him by his eighth-grade track coach.

In high school, Rocket converted from Muslim to Christianity. Even though he wasn't Catholic, he performed baritone vocal solos at at least three consecutive Christmas Midnight Masses in Wilkes-Barre.

In the tunnel before his first game as a Notre Dame freshman, he filled with nervousness until Holtz came up to him and told the rookie he believed in him. By the middle of his junior year the naturally quiet and modest Ismail was trying to avoid the constant attention that came with being a Notre Dame legend. In order to elude postpractice interviews or autograph seekers, Rocket folded his 5'10" 175-pound body into a covered laundry cart. Student managers wheeled him out undetected by the crowd waiting for him.

After his junior season, Rocket would leave school and turn pro. A February 1991 *Sports Illustrated* cover showed Rocket giving a thumbs-up above a gold Notre Dame helmet adorned with a large green dollar sign. He had assembled Team Rocket and was about to become the next sports-marketing myth. The second paragraph of Austin Murphy's piece conveyed both the opportunities and expectations.

> Ismail's marketeers can see a day when America's young will be able to pull on Rocket hightops—careful not to snag the laces on the tiny metallic afterburners—and pop into convenience stores to pick up milk chocolate Rocket

Bars. The candy could be right next to the microwaveable Rocket burritos, and only one aisle over from a soda cooler filled with Rocket Fuel, the sports drink in the bottle with the aerodynamic fins. Back home again, the kids could flick on the tube and watch Rocket the cartoon hero go head-to-head with Rocket J. Squirrel for the four- to 24-year-old viewing audience.

Ismail caused some NFL Draft Day hijinx when he decided to sign an $18.2 million contract with the Toronto Argonauts instead of playing in the NFL, where he would have been the No. 1 overall pick of Jimmy Johnson and the Dallas Cowboys. He played two years in Canada before having a nine-year NFL career.*

Against Rice in his freshman year, he thanked his blockers for clearing the way on his returns. "I have to give credit where credit is due, and none of it goes to me. The whole key to the returns was getting through the first line of blocking, and nobody got a clean shot at me," he said after the game.

The Irish had a week off. Then they hosted Penn State and played at USC. They were two games away from an undefeated regular season.

"We turned up the intensity in practice. We concentrated very hard on having a good week, and I believed that caused today's results," Andy Heck said. "We are in charge of our own destiny, and that's the place we want to be."

---

*Ironically, Ismail caught his first professional pass from Rickey Foggie, the quarterback Holtz started at Minnesota and whom he referred to Tony Rice during Rice's first year playing football at Notre Dame.

CHAPTER 15

Backers and Zorro

With his shorts dropped to his ankles, middle linebacker Wes Pritchett stood in front of a weight room mirror doing curls and reciting Shakespeare.

"In military rules, humors of blood,/ He was the mark and glass, copy and book,/ That fashion'd others. And, O wondrous him!/ O miracle of men! Him did you leave,/ Second to none, unseconded by you," Pritchett said, lifting 75-pound dumbbells to his shoulders, tearing through lines from the grieving Lady Percy in *Henry IV, Part 2*.

This was his Sunday morning routine. Why not just lift weights and listen to music like everybody else? "'Cause I'm nuts," Pritchett said.

Pritchett, the defense's vocal leader, represented one-third of what Barry Alvarez called the "Three Amigos."* The other two-thirds came in the form of inside linebacker Michael Stonebreaker and Frank Stams, who played a hybrid role of outside linebacker and rush end.

---

*The nickname originated from the 1986 *¡Three Amigos!* movie starring Steve Martin, Chevy Chase, and Martin Short. In '87, the Denver Broncos receiving corps of Mark Jackson, Vance Johnson, and Ricky Nattiel started using the nickname.

"The biggest improvement in the Notre Dame program is defense. This defense plays as well as any Notre Dame defense I remember," Air Force head coach Fisher DeBerry said after his high-scoring Falcons scored just 13 points against the Irish. "The defense is the unsung hero of this Notre Dame team."

Going into the ninth game of the season against Penn State, the defense had forced 27 turnovers. In the second half of games, the Irish defense allowed a stingy 6 points on average.

"When there's eleven hungry guys chomping at the meat, it wears teams down," said Pat Terrell.

The linebackers led this armada. Pritchett and Stonebreaker tied for the team lead with 95 tackles each. Stams had become a disruptive force. He had decent statistics—3.5 sacks, 3 forced fumbles, and 40 tackles—but the numbers alone couldn't chronicle his impact on the game. His speed rush from the outside had harassed opposing quarterbacks. His brightest game thus far had come against Miami. All day, he zoomed into the backfield, knocking around the previously untouchable Steve Walsh. He forced 2 fumbles and batted a pass into the air that resulted in Terrell's interception return for a touchdown.

Like Pritchett, Stonebreaker and Stams had close relationships with their fathers. At age thirteen, when Stonebreaker's parents divorced, he moved in with his dad, Steve Stonebreaker, who played seven NFL seasons. Stams, who kept his watch on Ohio time to remind him of his family, attributed his wit, and therefore his media relations acumen, to his dad.*

The Notre Dame linebackers, fortified even further with Bolcar, were being called the best corps in the country, but few

*South Bend is now on East Coast time, but back then that area of northern Indiana never changed clocks, so for part of the year Ohio was an hour ahead.

prognosticators had the starting trio on the radar in the preseason. Pritchett was the only returning starter. The last time Stams had started a game, he was playing on the offensive side of the ball. Though he met NCAA standards, Stonebreaker's grade point average fell below Notre Dame's requirements, and he had been academically ineligible for the previous season.

"They had been jackoffs throughout their career, and all of a sudden they became serious about football," Alvarez said. "They had their fun, too. Everybody knew they were going to be the ones pulling the pranks. They were the ones that were the clowns, but everybody knew they could depend on those cats to put their necks on the line. Those cats were going to play their fannies off."

Alvarez empowered the trio. He would have them in his office early each week before practice to go over the defensive game plan.

"Look, listen, I need you to get these guys up today. It's going to be a hell of a game," Alvarez would tell them. "You guys are going to need to pick it up."

Alvarez knew the confidence the Amigos exuded rubbed off on the rest of the team. He relied on that. Nevertheless, when he became the defensive coordinator, he set a clear tone in his first meeting with the trio.

"Guys, I know you like to have fun. We'll have fun. Winning is fun," Alvarez said.

Stonebreaker was the quiet one, the handsome little brother in the threesome. The 6'1" 228-pound junior from River Ridge, Louisiana, had a surname that screamed linebacker, and his thick brown hair crept out from under the back of his helmet. Sportswriters unleashed breathy prose to describe him. "He's got a drop-dead beautiful girlfriend and the kind of looks that make the women at a local TV station faint when he walks in," Andrew Bagnato wrote in the *Chicago Tribune*.

Stonebreaker fell out of a car at two years old, breaking his eardrum and fracturing his skull. The eardrum injury caused hearing loss. Pritchett hosted him on his recruiting trip to Notre Dame, and the upperclassman thought Stonebreaker ignored him.

"I'm thinking, *Who is this kid?*" Pritchett said. "And then I found out he had a bum ear."

Stonebreaker had surgery on his ear the same summer he failed a statistics class that made him academically ineligible.

When he returned to the team for the '88 season, Stonebreaker played eagle linebacker. He lined up with a defensive lineman in front of him, shielding him from an offensive blocker. This left him free to beeline it to the ball carrier, combining his speed and instincts to find the football. At one point during the Michigan game, Notre Dame lined up in the wrong defense and Stonebreaker still made the play. He possessed talent that couldn't be taught, Alvarez said.

Pritchett and Stams were the comedians.

They beat on Reggie Ho's shoulder pads before practice, telling the diminutive kicker he better make his field goals or they would date his sister, a student trainer on the team.

"I don't think Ho wants either of us for a brother-in-law," Pritchett told reporters.

If out-of-town reporters didn't recognize them, Pritchett and Stams used an arsenal of pranks. They would tell the media members they modeled in their spare time—and the journalists bought it. They would pretend to be each other in interviews. "I'm having a good year, but that Pritchett is having a great year. He's an All American," Pritchett said, masquerading as Stams.

CNN interviewed Holtz with the special teams running drills in the background. It looked like practice. So Stams and Pritchett stood within earshot of the camera, shouting as if they were assistant coaches.

"Great job, Frank Stams! What a player!"

"Way to go, Pritchett! I don't know another linebacker in the country who could have made that play."

During a two-a-day practice, Pritchett and Stams, one by one, told different freshmen Holtz wanted to see them immediately.

"You want to see me, Coach?" the unknowing first-year guy asked Holtz.

"Who told you that?"

"Pritchett and Stams said you wanted to see me."

After a while, Holtz caught on. "Yes, son, I just wanted to tell you what a great job you're doing."

Pritchett and Stams were known to rub Bengay or hot sauce in teammates' helmets. They got into snot fights, blowing streams of boogers on each other in between plays at practice. Sometimes Pritchett held straight-faced conversations as he walked the locker room in only his jock, the straps stretched up over his shoulders.

Asked if Elvis Presley picked up the tickets Stams left for him at the Miami game, the player responded, "Sure did. Sat in Section 30 . . . I got a nice note from him after the game. He said, 'Thanks a lot and I'll see you at USC.'"

One day in practice Alvarez hawkeyed the second team defense while the starters went to the sideline. The coach heard an unusual amount of chatter behind him. He turned around and saw plumes of smoke rising out of Pritchett's helmet. The linebacker had taken the cigar of beat writer Tim Prister and puffed on it from behind his face mask.

The week before the Stanford game, Stams picked up the phone in the sports information office. The caller asked what time the game started. In a drop-dead serious tone, Stams told the caller the two schools had agreed to cancel the game. He kept the gag going for a little bit and then confessed. The caller finally asked who was on the other end. "Michael Stonebreaker," Stams said.

Defensive line coach John Palermo had a friend bring him a bag of Philadelphia hoagies during home game weekends. After practice, Pritchett and Stams led a few underclassmen in devouring the East Coast delicacy. Stams left a signed napkin: "Thanks for the sandwiches. Michael Stonebreaker."

"Those guys were out there with their enthusiasm, with their personalities, with their energy, and that's huge for a team," said captain Andy Heck. "You can't just have a bunch of guys who quietly lead by example."

Pritchett and Stams met in their first few days at Notre Dame. Both were walking across campus, with their dads at their sides. Pritchett figured the 6'3" 230-pounder he spotted must be a football player, so he stopped and introduced himself to Stams.

"What position do you play?" Pritchett asked after exchanging salutations.

"Fullback."

"Fullback?" Pritchett said to his dad after they walked away. "He's huge."

Stams left St. Vincent–St. Mary High School in Akron, Ohio, and chose to go to Notre Dame after a pivotal meeting with a priest during his recruiting visit. The priest asked him what school he would want to attend if he ruined his knee on the first day of practice and never played football again.

"We all went to Notre Dame because we wanted to go to Notre Dame. Gerry wasn't having a great year when we were being recruited," Stams said. "I went because of the institution."

Stams started in the backfield as a sophomore. A couple of injuries—a broken leg, followed by a torn quadriceps—kept him out of action the following year, Holtz's first year. His 5.0 forty-yard dash became a 5.5 after the injury. He was no longer fullback material for a Notre Dame system that now ran the veer option offense. He could try to be a tight end or move over to defense. He chose defense, but he played sparingly.

"It finally got to a point at Notre Dame where I was pressing way too much. Everything was too serious. I lost an attitude I had in high school, and football became too much work and not enough fun and play," Stams said.

During a game in '87, he had watched Tim Brown come to the sideline and say, "Hey, Coach, you've got to get me the ball. I own this guy." Stams remembered the interaction as the player and coach discussed a play as if they were drawing it up in the dirt during a pickup game.

"They were laughing, having a good time. He couldn't wait to get back on the field," Stams said. "That had been gone for me. I used to have that, and somewhere along the line I lost that."

He came back for a fifth year determined to rejuvenate his game. He wanted to play football and not worry about making mistakes.

"He was a washed-up fullback. But [on defense] he'd come off that edge, man. You could wire Frank up. You could really get him cranked up to play. Especially once he understood that position and could turn it loose," Alvarez said.

Stams and the other Amigos had a great rapport with Alvarez, who brought a low-key style that got through to them.

"He didn't come off as some hard-ass coach. It wasn't about Barry," Stams said. "He made you feel that you were special. You had value. You had worth. You were a part of what we were trying to accomplish."

Alvarez knew he had unanointed leaders in his fold and could run his defense through them. "Those guys really had a lot to do with the success of that team," he said.

Just nine starts into his college career, Chris Zorich had already become a cult figure. High school football players started wearing belly-showing half jerseys to look like Zorro, the beast who played nose tackle for the Fighting Irish. Before the Miami game, a group of Notre Dame students pulled names out of a hat to determine which one would win the privilege of painting his body with Zorich's number 50.

"I had no idea. I was out there trying to have fun—and really, survive," he said.

Zorich is a sports rarity. In the lionization of athletes, his story is more truth than fable. He went to the same high school as Chicago Bears Hall of Fame linebacker Dick Butkus. He grew up with his mother, Zora, in a one-bedroom apartment in a two-story brownstone on the corner of Eighty-first and Burnham on Chicago's South Side. Rent was $140 a month. Zora, a diabetic on welfare disability, received $200 a month. She slept on the couch, and Chris slept in the bedroom.

When the money ran out each month, Zora put young Chris on her bike and she pedaled to the local supermarket shortly after closing. There she parked next to the Dumpster and lifted Chris over her shoulders into the trash. He picked through what the grocer had thrown out, handing his mother partly rotten meat and produce. Zora would cut away the spoiled parts, and they had their food until the next check came or until they needed to return to the Dumpster.

"She did the best she could, but there were times things were tight," Zorich said.

Dope fiends, drug dealers, gangs, and prostitutes colored the neighborhood scene. No one went to college. If someone graduated high school, it was a major accomplishment. Zorich never knew his father, but that was never an issue. Most kids in the area didn't know their dad. There were only about a half-dozen dads in the neighborhood of about sixty families.

It was more of a big deal that Chris was part white and part black, the ridiculed child of a Slavic mother and the African American father who left before he was born. Chubby, half-white Chris got beat up because he looked different. His near-debilitating stutter didn't help matters. When he rode bikes with his black friends, people shouted "cracker," "white boy," and "oreo" at Zorich. He took different routes to and from school to avoid beatdowns. One time when he was seven he didn't escape a sixteen-year-old girl. She left him bloodied. Later she was found dead in her early twenties. This was life in the neighborhood. This was the seminal environment for the man *Sports Illustrated* eventually called "the toughest, most vicious player in college football."

He wanted to play football when he entered Chicago Vocational High School as a freshman, but Zora refused to sign the paperwork allowing her boy to participate in the violent sport. In his sophomore year, Chris begged and pleaded with Zora to sign the permission slip. She refused. On the way to school the next day, Chris forged her name.

He lied to his mother, telling her he was getting home late because he was in the school play and participating in other school activities. The ruse fell apart when Zora found his football gear in the apartment.

"You've been lying to me, haven't you?" she asked, confronting Chris. She sat him down on the couch and told him she was doing her best to raise him on her own.

They talked for several hours. Chris told her football taught him discipline and he was around people who set goals. She allowed it, but she didn't see him play until the last game of his senior year. She was too worried he would get hurt. Chris had the assistant principal and some friends bring her to the game and sit with her in case she got upset witnessing her son on the gridiron.

"Oh my God. You're good," she told Chris after the game.

Illinois, Michigan, Miami, and Notre Dame showed interest in Zorich, but coaches were prohibited from visiting the apartment. Both he and his mom feared potential embarrassment—a coach sitting in their home spotting a roach crawling out from behind a picture on the wall or a mouse scurrying across the floor.

Zorich didn't understand how playing college football worked. He couldn't believe someone would actually pay for his education.

"I thought I was working a scam," he said.

He scored in the 700s on his SATs and had to rework his senior class schedule once going to college became a reality. He dropped the auto mechanic courses and added extra math classes, eliminating his lunch period in order to qualify with the NCAA.

At Notre Dame, Zorich found a utopia. There were tree-encircled lakes, with ducks and squirrels to hand-feed. The dining hall had all-you-can-eat food. Some students complained about it. Not Zorich. He didn't even share his. People left bicycles unlocked overnight in front of dorms. "And they were still there in the morning," Zorich said. "Are you kidding me?"

His freshman year, he did not play a down. On the night before home games, he slept in his dorm room while other classmates, ones who had a chance to see action, stayed with the team.

He moved from middle linebacker to nose tackle in his first year. Playing on the scout team during a practice leading up to the Michigan State game, he caused havoc for the first-team offense when he put a hand on the ground on the defensive line. After practice, Holtz announced to the team that they had found the next nose tackle.

Classes proved difficult. He stayed up late into the night studying and still ended up on academic probation during his first semester. Zora had gotten mugged back home. Chris wanted to return to the South Side and forget college. He packed his stuff and called her.

"I'm going to come home and be with you."

"You know, I'm not going to be here forever," Zora told him. "You have a chance to be the first person in our family to graduate from college, but more importantly there is nothing for you to come back to."

She was right. What was back home? Poverty. Food stamps. Crime.

Zorich had a realization.

"Here, I had an out."

His weight room sessions were performances. He curled as much as the punter bench-pressed, and he bench-pressed 500 pounds.

While Zorich grunted and maxed out on the bench, Ricky Watters leaned over in his face and mocked his stutter. The next thing everyone saw was Zorich chasing Watters around the weight room until the flanker escaped. Zorich wouldn't forget. Later, at training table, he might sneak behind an unsuspecting Watters, who had sat down to eat, and clamp a headlock on his tormentor.

Part of Zorich knew it was in jest, but he only knew one way to react. "Where I'm from, when you talk shit, you've got to back it up, and that meant fighting," Zorich said.

On road trips he always attended the private Mass in the hotel. Zorich always sat in the back, not wanting to be noticed. One time Holtz called on him to do one of the readings.

Are you freaking kidding me? Oh my God, Zorich thought.

He stood up, walked to the front of the room, and stuttered his way through the Bible passage.

After Mass, Holtz approached him and told him to come to his office on Monday.

Holtz had done some research by the time Zorich arrived for the meeting. The head coach, who had dealt with his own lisp, found a speech therapist at St. Mary's College, the women's school across the street from Notre Dame. For a couple of years, Zorich worked with the therapist, and the stutter became manageable.

On the field, his rage came unhinged. In games, he mocked opponents, laughing at them. "What do you got, chicken legs for arms?" he cackled at opposing linemen after he glanced at his own sleeveless arms and then stared at them.

A couple of years later, a *Sports Illustrated* profile wrote about Zorich's dream of sacking the quarterback and watching his head roll down the field. It mentioned the plaque John Potocki, his high school coach, gave Zorich with the saying about fearing no evil in the valley of the shadow of death because he was the meanest son of a bitch in the valley. Potocki mentioned that Zorich had some hate within him. Zora loathed the comment about the loving son she reared with poetry and short stories, but Zorich understood what the coach meant.

"I have all this aggression inside of me," Zorich said, "and the only way I can release any of this stuff is on the football field."

Coaches routinely kicked him out of practice for playing dirty or starting fights. He played with a fury to prove himself every day.

"It wasn't, 'Hey, I'm going to the pros.' It was, 'Hey, I need to keep my spot,'" he said.

"You could actually get a good block on Zorich, but if you didn't maintain it, he still would be able to make you look stupid," said starting offensive tackle Dean Brown.

Because they lined up across from each other, Zorich consistently had run-ins with center Mike Heldt.

"I don't remember too many days that would go by without us fighting on the field," Heldt said.

Zorich would dole out a cheap shot if the first-team offense scored and started taunting the defense. With his reputation for ferocious play, Heldt would occasionally set Zorich off with a sneaky cheap shot of his own. Then he'd watch Zorich get scolded while nothing happened to him.

Through their bond in the trenches, Heldt understood Zorich beyond the colorful ways he intimidated opponents and the clichéd praise he received for his football warrior status. "The game was his life," Heldt said.

CHAPTER 16

TV Revolution and the Renegade Bowl

When Notre Dame and Penn State met, it looked like throwback football. The helmets had no decals. The jerseys had no names. The cleats were black. Only yard lines and white, slanting primitive end zone chalkings decorated the grass field. Even the weather cooperated, with gray skies, intermittent rain, and temperatures in the low 40s.

The season's race to the national championship had been playing itself out like a tournament. Top teams squared off and eliminated each other from contention. Of the top 10 teams in the Associated Press poll on the day Notre Dame met Penn State, four were unbeaten, and the six others had just one loss—four lost to other top 10 teams, and the other two fell to opponents ranked in the top 20.

No. 1 Notre Dame, second-ranked USC, fourth-ranked West Virginia, and tenth-ranked Arkansas had won all of their games. No. 3 Miami had lost to Notre Dame, but the Hurricanes accounted for the lone loss for No. 5 Florida State. No. 6 UCLA had lost to No. 19 Washington State, but the Bruins were the only ones to defeat No. 7 Nebraska. No. 8 Auburn had fallen to No. 11 Louisiana State, and the No. 9 Oklahoma Sooners received a 23–7 beating from USC.

The 1988 season was the 120th for college football. Since its birth, the sport had evolved. From its round ball and rugbylike style to leather helmets, face masks, the forward pass, and the wishbone, football constantly updated itself. The most significant transformation for the college game in the mid-to-late 1980s had little to do with play on the field. The '88 season continued a TV revolution. A Supreme Court decision and a surprise national championship bowl game forever changed the game.

The Notre Dame–Penn State matchup was a noon showdown in a CBS doubleheader. The Big Eight rivalry game between Oklahoma and Nebraska followed.

It was the third time this season CBS used its airwaves to broadcast Notre Dame or Penn State. It was the Nittany Lions' fifth time on national TV and the sixth for the Irish.

Before the Supreme Court changed the system, no team was allowed to play more than two games on national TV, no matter the school's ranking or following. The NCAA held a vise grip on college football broadcast rights. The organization restricted schools' TV opportunities because it believed if more football appeared on the tube, fewer people would attend games, and that would mean less revenue from ticket sales.

Up until the late 1970s, all of the NCAA member institutions—even the ones without football programs—voted on measures affecting major college football. The big gridiron schools recoiled at the notion that they should share revenue with the entire NCAA membership.

"So, for example, Notre Dame's vote would be canceled by Wabash," said Chuck Neinas, the Big Eight commissioner during this period.

Unable to overcome the voting bloc of smaller institutions or have the NCAA effectively restructure its legislative process, a group of schools with major programs formed the College Football Association (CFA).

Notre Dame's executive vice president, Fr. Edmund Joyce, was instrumental in forming the CFA, which originally started as a lobbying group. When the CFA first formed in 1977, it accomplished restructuring the NCAA into Divisions I, II, and III, but the TV issue worsened.

The Fighting Irish had a history of using football broadcast rights to establish Notre Dame football as a national brand and elicit a following throughout the country. It started with radio broadcast rights during the Rockne era and continued with nationally syndicated next-day game replays.*

The NCAA's approach to TV rights started with fearmongering and ended with bullying. The University of Pennsylvania had broadcasted its home games from 1940 to 1950. In 1950, the NCAA formed a three-person Television Committee. At the convention the following year, the committee presented a study stating TV had an "adverse effect on college football attendance and unless brought under some control threaten[ed] to seriously harm the nation's overall" system. The committee made a proposal calling for only one game a week to be telecast in each area and a blackout on three of ten Saturdays during the season. This proposal also included the measure limiting teams to two national TV appearances per year.

The University of Pennsylvania challenged the proposal. The school planned to move ahead and broadcast its home games. In response, the NCAA threatened to declare Penn "a member in bad standing." The four schools scheduled to play in Philadelphia backed out. Penn changed its mind and went along with the NCAA TV plan.

That system lasted until 1977, when the NCAA signed a multiyear deal with ABC. This new deal gave the network more games to

---

*While the NCAA controlled live broadcasts, Notre Dame could set up the replays outside the governing body's purview.

broadcast, but the NCAA stuck to its 1951 appearance limitations. More televised games just meant viewers saw more teams instead of seeing the nation's best teams more often. The CFA, which represented a little more than sixty schools, made its move to break away from the NCAA constrictions.

"We all learned from [NFL Commissioner] Pete Rozelle: if you use television right, it's one of your great marketing tools. The popularity of the game has certainly benefited from the fact that people can watch it on television," said Neinas, who served as executive director of the CFA from 1980 to 1997.

The CFA inked a contract with NBC. It included $180 million over four years and twelve prime-time games per season.

"This was going to be great," Neinas said.

The NCAA responded with force, insisting that if the CFA fulfilled its NBC contract all the schools involved would be ineligible for postseason play in every sport. The CFA retreated from the deal, but the Universities of Georgia and Oklahoma went to court representing the CFA's desire to control broadcast rights.

The NCAA contended that, as an obligation of membership, schools must relinquish their football broadcast rights.

In court, the CFA schools used an example of a 1981 game between two schools ranked in the top 5, Oklahoma–USC, which aired on more than two hundred ABC affiliates. Those two big schools shared equal money with Appalachian State and the Citadel, whose games aired in a few local markets.

In June 1984, the Supreme Court ruled in favor of the schools in the case of *NCAA* v. *Board of Regents of the University of Oklahoma*. With just a few weeks before the start of the season, the CFA scrambled to put together a TV package.

"We were at the mercy of the networks," Neinas said. "They got it for a paltry sum."

The power shift occurred in 1986 when the CFA signed a deal with CBS and ESPN to air games on network and cable TV.

At the same time, Notre Dame, along with eight independent schools in the East, created a deal for secondary rights with Jefferson Pilot Communications.* If CBS and ESPN passed on a Notre Dame game, Jefferson could broadcast the game on independent stations throughout the country.

In the same season the CFA struck its new deal, the Fiesta Bowl hosted an unofficial national championship game between Penn State and Miami.†

The Fiesta Bowl had been a second-tier bowl, the punky little brother to the major bowls—the Orange, Sugar, Cotton, and Rose. Those were the elite bowls. They predated World War II, and the oldest one, the Rose Bowl, started in 1902. Having started in 1971, the Fiesta Bowl was literally a teenager.

The major bowls had automatic tie-ins to certain conference champions. The Big Eight winner went to the Orange. The Southeastern Conference champion played in the Sugar Bowl. The Southwestern Conference champ had a spot in the Cotton, and the winners of the Big Ten and Pac-10 met in the Rose Bowl. With the exception of the Rose Bowl, this system ensured the champions of these different conferences never faced each other in bowl games. All the games took place on New Year's Day, and fans glued themselves to the TV because any number of scenarios could see a team jump from No. 5 to No. 1 the way Notre Dame did in 1977. Rarely did fans get to see No. 1 versus No. 2 in a bowl game. Before the 1987 Fiesta Bowl, the two top-ranked teams in the country had met in a bowl game on only six occasions.

---

*The eight schools were Army, Boston College, Navy, Pitt, Rutgers, Syracuse, Temple, and West Virginia.

†The NCAA holds a championship in every sport except football.

The bowl in Arizona was about to interrupt the shotgun approach to crowning a champion. The outsider wanted in on the major-bowl party, and it had an aggressive and innovative style to disrupt the traditional order.

"They were resting on their laurels. They hadn't done anything. Example: the Rose Bowl, they were more interested in the parade than the game," said Don Meyers, founding member of the Fiesta Bowl and its second president. "They were a bunch of old guys who ran that bowl. They're the nicest guys in the world, but they didn't really do anything to enhance the bowl."

Technically, there was a date in November when bowl invitations could be offered, but bowl representatives constantly courted key school administrators, and handshake deals cemented postseason appearances prior to any official date.

With the Rose Bowl tied to the Big Ten and Pac-10 winners, the Fiesta Bowl positioned itself as the only warm-weather western bowl for the rest of the country. The reps sold schools on enticements that had nothing to do with football: trips to the Grand Canyon, rounds of golf, and spa visits for the wives in the travel party.

Meyers kept the Fiesta Bowl in the college football consciousness year-round, hosting up to sixty events tied to the game but spread throughout the calendar. During the first week in May, Meyers and Co. hosted the Fiesta Frolic. They put the coaches, athletic directors, and conference commissioners up in the Biltmore Hotel and plied them with golf, sightseeing, and even fishing expeditions, if that was their thing. The Frolic became an informal meeting ground for schools to schedule regular-season games with each other while administrators met over coffee or a beer.

The renegade bowl began to land marquee matchups from the conference castoff pile. In 1982, No. 7 Penn State defeated No. 8 Southern California and Heisman Trophy winner Marcus Allen. At the end of the '85 season, No. 5 Michigan beat No. 7 Nebraska, and the Wolverines finished the season ranked second. The major bowls had to take notice.

"They were really unhappy with us. They didn't want any more bowls, first of all, and secondly they didn't want any bowls that could compete with them," Meyers said.

The Fiesta Bowl became the first game to have a sponsor with naming rights when it generated a deal with Sunkist, the citrus growers association in Southern California and Arizona.

With Penn State and Miami—two of the NCAA's twenty-four nonconference independent schools—heading toward undefeated seasons, Meyers seized the opportunity. Joe Paterno and No. 2 Penn State were in, but No. 1 Miami didn't necessarily have to leave the state of Florida. The Hurricanes could have just as easily played in the Citrus Bowl, which vigorously pursued the home-state school. Meyers appealed to Jimmy Johnson's ego with the 1-versus-2 matchup. The Fiesta Bowl's head man spoke to Johnson's wife and the wife of Miami Athletic Director Sam Jankovich about a deal he worked out for all the coaches and administrators' wives to spend the day at Elizabeth Arden's Maine Chance, a spa normally reserved for the spouses of presidents and CEOs. Then Meyers offered each team a $2.4 million payout. He worked with NBC to move the game away from New Year's Day. Forget muddling with those contests of pride; this was the only game that mattered, and it had its own night on Friday, January 2.

The game had a good-versus-evil feel—Penn State with its drab, but winning, tradition coupled with Coach Paterno, the *Sports Illustrated* Man of the Year, against the brazen Hurricanes who stepped off the plane in Arizona in military fatigues. The Nittany Lions upset the 'Canes 14–10, intercepting Heisman Trophy winner Vinny Testaverde five times, but the TV audience had the biggest impact. Nearly 22 million homes tuned in to the game for a 25.1

rating. Networks and advertisers saw an enormous captive audience. The gold mine in college football had been discovered.

In South Bend, two years removed from a national championship, Penn State needed a win against Notre Dame to avoid its first losing season in fifty years. That didn't happen. The Fighting Irish gained 502 yards and limited the Nittany Lions to 179 in the 21–3 Notre Dame victory.

In his final home game, halfback Mark Green rushed for 64 yards, including a 22-yard touchdown run. Tony Rice tallied 275 yards of offense and 2 touchdowns, highlighted by a 67-yard third-quarter scoring pass to Rocket Ismail.

For the second year in a row the Irish went undefeated at home, building a twelve-game win streak at Notre Dame Stadium. After the game, Penn State coach Joe Paterno downplayed any Irish mystique.

"I'll be honest, I just don't see it," Paterno said. "Notre Dame has good players and a good team, but I didn't see any ghosts making any tackles today."

The Fiesta Bowl had been eyeing Notre Dame since the beginning of the season. During the week before the Penn State game, Notre Dame officials said the Irish would accept a bowl bid to play in Tempe, Arizona, if the Fiesta extended it.

In the locker room, after the game, Fiesta Bowl officials made the formal invitation to Athletic Director Dick Rosenthal, Executive Vice President Fr. William Beauchamp, Holtz, and the team. Notre Dame would play undefeated West Virginia. At the time, bowl games had no desire for a Notre Dame–Miami rematch even though the Hurricanes were ranked ahead of the Mountaineers in the polls.

The Irish had one more obstacle to overcome to ensure two

undefeated teams met in the Fiesta Bowl. Notre Dame had to travel to Los Angeles to play its longtime intersectional rival USC. Historically, the late-November games against the men of Troy had been national championship spoilers for the Irish.

When both teams met a week later, the 10-0 and No. 2–ranked Trojans had just as much at stake. The winner had the straight track to the national title.

CHAPTER 17

Suspensions and Hollywood Underdogs

Every Notre Dame player got a needle on the Monday before the USC game. As the team doctor inoculated them for measles, the nearby picture of Trojans quarterback Rodney Peete reminded them why they needed to receive the shot.

Medical staff injected the vaccine into every person in the Fighting Irish travel party—coaches, Athletic Department administrators, cheerleaders, priests, and the Leprechaun.

Health officials in California had recorded thirty measles cases on the USC campus, none more high profile than Peete, the All-American Heisman Trophy finalist.

Peete held sixteen USC records and ranked sixth in the NCAA in passing efficiency. Before donning a USC uniform he spent three years excelling at Sahuaro High School in Tucson, Arizona. With his dad working as an assistant coach for the Kansas City Chiefs, the Peetes moved to Kansas for Rodney's senior year, where he attended Shawnee Mission South High School in Overland Park. Multiple colleges wanted Rodney to play wide receiver or defensive back in college. He quickly removed those schools from his list of potential landing spots and arrived at USC as a quarterback.

At Southern California, Peete played baseball, football, and the role of charismatic joker. He'd call the sports information office impersonating a Los Angeles police officer and tell the staffer on the phone the cops had just picked up Rodney Peete.

In the summer before Peete's senior year, USC and UCLA worked collaboratively to push him and Bruins quarterback Troy Aikman for the Heisman campaign. Rather than the East or the Midwest taking the spotlight, college football pundits had to look to Hollywood.

"A lot of attention was focused on the city of L.A.," said Tim Tessalone, the longtime Trojans sports information director.

By the middle of September, both schools planted themselves in the top 5. After Notre Dame beat Miami, UCLA claimed the top spot until its loss to Washington State. On their way to a 9-0 start and the No. 2 ranking, the Trojans peeled off wins against No. 3 Oklahoma, No. 16 Washington, and No. 18 Oregon. Their regular-season schedule culminated against their two biggest rivals: a cross-town game with a Rose Bowl berth on the line against the No. 6 Bruins and a home game against No. 1 Notre Dame.

During the week of the UCLA game, Peete fell ill with the measles. He had to be hospitalized. Attempting to avoid publicity, he checked into a hospital away from the USC campus, but a local sportscaster happened to be visiting the same facility. With Peete's location disclosed, USC officials moved him again because so many people began dialing the telephone in his hospital room, Tessalone told the *Los Angeles Times*.

Uncharacteristically, USC closed its workouts to the media that week. Peete remained hospitalized until Friday, when he went through about an hour of very light work at practice. The next day, playing before a crowd of more than 100,000 people at the Rose Bowl in Pasadena, Peete led the Trojans to a 31–22 victory.

Aikman completed a school record 32 passes on 48 attempts for 317 yards and 2 touchdowns. The quarterback, who wisely transferred away from Barry Switzer's Oklahoma wishbone offense, was already being tagged as the No. 1 overall pick in the following spring's NFL Draft. But USC won the Pac-10 Conference and Peete walked out the winner. He accounted for 2 touchdowns, 1 throwing and 1 rushing, and he completed 16 of 28 attempts for 189 yards through the air. *Sports Illustrated* put him on the cover with the headline GUNNING FOR NO. 1.

With Peete behind center, the men of Troy fielded a nearly unstoppable team. They outscored opponents by a three-touchdown average, and they kept the ball an average of ten minutes more per game than the other team. The defense, which had seventy years of future NFL experience on its depth chart, smothered opponents' running game, holding teams to a nation's-best 68.1 yards rushing per game. The last five teams to face USC gained a total of 163 yards on the ground.

"Southern Cal combines running and throwing so well, and it starts with Peete, who is the best quarterback in the country," Holtz said. "They have averaged 35 points a game, and that's unheard of if you look at their schedule. They stopped the Oklahoma wishbone, and nobody runs the wishbone better than Oklahoma—nobody."

In only two seasons, USC head coach Larry Smith revived the program. The Trojans' fourteen consecutive regular-season wins was the longest streak in the country.* In '88, USC had reached ten victories in a season for the first time since 1979.

Dipping back into the final three Gerry Faust years, the Irish had beaten Southern California five times in a row. Outside of the come-from-behind 1-point victory in Holtz's first year, the Irish defeated USC by an average of more than 19 points per game during this stretch.

Except when travel was restricted during World War II, the

---

*The Trojans' last regular-season loss had come at Notre Dame in a 26–15 defeat the previous season.

schools played each other every year since 1926. The two top-notch programs had combined for nineteen national championships and eleven Heisman Trophy winners.

Notre Dame traveled to L.A. for a 13–12 win in the inaugural contest. The following year an estimated crowd of 120,000 spectators attended the game at Soldier Field in Chicago. In 1931, the first season after Rockne's death, USC rallied from a 14-point deficit at Notre Dame to beat the Irish 16–14. When the Trojans reached Los Angeles by train, a parade route lined with 300,000 fans greeted them, according to the *Los Angeles Times*.

"It is the greatest intersectional rivalry in the country. There's none that even comes close to it," Tessalone said. "People tend to mark moments in their life with where they were during [these games]."

In 1972, USC's Anthony Davis crushed Notre Dame with 6 touchdowns in a 45–23 win. He added 4 more scores in 1974, a game in which the Irish led 24–0 just before halftime and lost 55–24. Sandwiched between the Davis highlight reels, Notre Dame ended a twenty-three-game Trojans unbeaten streak with a 23–14 victory in South Bend in 1973.

In 1977, Irish coach Dan Devine busted out the green jerseys, and Notre Dame thumped Southern California 49–19 during a national championship season. The following year, Joe Montana rallied the Domers from 18 points down in the fourth quarter to take a 25–24 lead, but USC prevailed 27–25, kicking a field goal with 2 seconds left.

Before the 1988 contest, the highest-ranked matchup in the series came in 1947, when No. 1 Notre Dame beat No. 3 USC 38–7.

The Irish ended USC's attempts at unbeaten campaigns in 1969, 1952, and 1927. Notre Dame held a 32-23-4 advantage in the series. When playing at home, the Trojans had a knack for wrecking Notre Dame seasons.

"I grew to call the Los Angeles Coliseum the Wailing Wall of Notre Dame football," said Lou Somogyi, who has chronicled the Fighting Irish for decades.

In 1938, USC posted a 13–0 shutout against No. 1–ranked 9–0 Notre Dame. Looking for two consecutive perfect seasons under Frank Leahy, in 1948, the Fighting Irish had to come back to settle for a 14–14 tie in Los Angeles. In Ara Parseghian's first season, he took an undefeated top-ranked team to the Coliseum and lost 20–17 after leading 17–0 at the half. In 1970, an unbeaten Irish club, led by 526 passing yards from Joe Theismann, lost 38–28 to a 5-4-1 USC team. In his final year, Devine had the 9-0-1 Irish ranked No. 2 when they headed to California. The national championship hopes ended with a 20–3 loss.

When Holtz first asked his team what made the rivalry so special, the answers showed an insufficient knowledge of the names, games, and traditions. Holtz went back and studied the series. When the calendar turned to Southern California week, Holtz started each practice with a fifteen-minute lecture on the history and importance of Notre Dame–USC. He also added warnings against being distracted by the beautiful Trojan cheerleaders on game day. Toward the end of the week, Holtz gave the team a handwritten quiz.

"They knew everything they needed to know, if they listened," he said.

One of the questions: From either school, name four great coaches who coached in this game.

One sheet came back with "John McKay, Knute Rockne, Frank Leahy and I can't think of a fourth."

"I coached in it. You could've at least put me," Holtz said with a laugh.

The game had special importance to Holtz because Wade Watts would be in attendance. Watts was the high school coach who suggested to Holtz and his parents that young Lou become a coach.

During Holtz's first year at Notre Dame, Watts's wife called and told him her husband was in poor health and it would mean a great deal if Holtz reached out to him. Holtz invited Watts, who now lived in California, to the USC game.

"The next year, he is still living. I had him attend it at Notre Dame. He attended every one for eleven years," Holtz said.*

With a tough road game on the docket, Holtz called the most successful road coach in the game—Jimmy Johnson. At the height of the Notre Dame–Miami rivalry and with the 'Canes still having an outside shot at the national championship, Holtz wanted to know how Johnson's teams played so well away from home.

"I had a lot of respect for him as a coach and as a person even though we always seem to be on opposite sides," Holtz said.

Johnson told Holtz he had his teams treat road games like a business trip. They weren't leaving town to have fun or experience the social scene in the away city. They were there to play and, more important, win a football game.

One of Johnson's support staff asked the coach why he took the call.

"It doesn't matter," Johnson said.

While Johnson gave Holtz a coach's courtesy, some of the other 'Canes couldn't bring themselves to be as kind when asked who would win the showdown between No. 1 and No. 2.

"USC will win. They have much more talent than Notre Dame," Maurice Crum said in the *Chicago Tribune*.

A few other players, including receiver Andre Brown and linebacker Bernard Clark, echoed Crum's opinion. Of the small group asked to make predictions, guard Mike Sullivan, an Irishman from Chicago, was the only Miami player to offer a compliment for Notre Dame. He called the Gold and Blue a "legitimate team."

---

*Watts died two months after Holtz left Notre Dame.

Rodney Peete remained silent. Laryngitis, a measles side effect, had taken his voice. At his weekly meeting with reporters, Peete sucked on a lollipop, rested his vocal cords, and wrote his responses on a pad. Tessalone read the answers, such as "cherry," the lollipop flavor; "very difficult and frustrating" about not being able to speak; and "I will play."

In practice that week, redshirt freshman quarterback Todd Marinovich called the cadence from behind the backfield while Peete ran the offense. If Peete's voice remained mute, coach Larry Smith planned to have the tailbacks shout the signals during the game while Peete lined up under center.

Since the Associated Press established a poll in 1936, this Notre Dame–USC tangle would be the twenty-fourth time the top two teams met and the sixteenth time they played each other in the regular season.

"This is why you come to Notre Dame," halfback Mark Green told the press. "You came here for games like this. We all dream of playing great teams in national-championship-type games, and now here we are."

Green, a captain, playing in his final regular-season game, returned home to the L.A. area as the ninth-leading rusher in the Notre Dame record book.

Even though they took Holtz's quiz, many of the Notre Dame players had watched the games against Southern California, and the annual battles played a role in their choosing to play for the Irish.

Notre Dame captain and starting offensive tackle Andy Heck loved that the big-time programs squared off against each year and he abhorred the Trojans.

"I was definitely confident we would out-physical any team from the West Coast. There was great confidence that we could and should beat this team," Heck said. "I had a great distaste for any team from the West Coast... As a young person, I thought of them as soft at heart, surfer boys, pretty boys, Hollywood. I despised everything about them that I could. I hated Southern Cal."

The oddsmakers installed Notre Dame as a slight underdog. The spread had more to do with home field advantage than one team's supremacy over the other.

The talking heads of the day started to tout USC as the winner. The Trojans did just have a quarterback come out of the hospital and beat the sixth-ranked team on the road. They defeated Stanford by 4 and Washington by 1, but the other eight wins were by an average margin of victory of nearly 26 points. At least one Notre Dame player publicly bristled when asked if his team had a chance to win against the Trojans.

"You've got to be kidding me. I guess we'll find out Saturday," Chris Zorich told the *Chicago Sun-Times*.

Thanksgiving morning, the Notre Dame team practiced, hit the showers, dressed, and met for an early dinner before they boarded a chartered Northwest Airlines flight to Los Angeles.

"Please be on time, because I want to say a prayer and we have a lot to be thankful for," Holtz told the squad about the meal when practice ended.

All but two of the players showed up on time. Sophomores Ricky Watters and Tony Brooks walked in about forty-five minutes late.

"Tony Brooks was a great person by himself. Ricky Watters was a great person by himself. But you put those two together—it was a bad combination," Holtz said years later with a laugh. "They would encourage one another and challenge one another."

They missed the prayer. Holtz wanted to eat with his family, but instead a livid coach met with Watters and Brooks, who had no real excuse for running late.

This wasn't the first time Holtz spoke to the talented duo about promptness.

"I told them how important it was and how little respect they showed for their teammates by coming late and they should not even go [to USC]. I should not even take them," Holtz said.

He knew what happened when you suspended prominent players. He did it at Arkansas before the 1978 Orange Bowl. Now Notre Dame's leading rusher and leading receiver sat in front of him. In forty-eight hours they would play on national TV against the No. 2 team in the country in what amounted to an elimination game for the national championship. Holtz did not want the distraction that suspensions would bring. He didn't want a national story. However, he made Watters and Brooks a promise.

"If you're late one more time—your fault, my fault, bus driver's fault, heart attack—you aren't playing."

In California the team stayed at the Newport Beach Marriott. They practiced Friday morning. Holtz attended the "The Game Is On" luncheon, a traditional get-together for supporters of both schools held the afternoon before the game. The players had time to themselves. They could swim. Sleep. Watch TV in their hotel room. Go to the mall. They had to be back for a team meal.

Watters and Brooks, along with freshmen Derek Brown and Rod Smith, borrowed a car and went to the mall. When they exited the mall they couldn't find the vehicle. The mall had parking lots and stores on both sides of a street, and a pedestrian overpass connected the facility. The foursome couldn't recall where they parked when they looked out at the sea of vehicles.

Notre Dame Athletic Director Dick Rosenthal received a call letting him know the situation with the players. He told Holtz. When the foursome made it back to the hotel forty-five minutes late they found themselves closed out of the team meal.

Holtz met with the coaches. He had decided Watters and Brooks would not play.

"It's the right thing. You're going to be on time—you do it. You give your word on something; you honor it. That's part of being Notre Dame. That's part of being a man. We don't need to write a big contract. We need to shake hands, look one another in the eye. That's the way we operate, and it's all about *being it* at Notre Dame," Holtz said.

He met privately with the seniors and a small group of junior team leaders. Holtz wanted to gauge their opinion.

"If their decision is the same as mine, let's move on. If it was different, then they've got to convince me or I've got to convince them," Holtz said.

The leaders agreed. Nobody was bigger than the team.

"We didn't care how good you were. They were good, but it wasn't about one player," said senior cornerback D'Juan Francisco.

Holtz had the leaders vote on whether or not to send them back home to Notre Dame.

"Keep in mind we need to win this game to play for a national championship," Holtz said before the vote.

The players voted to send them home.

After the meeting between Holtz and the team leaders, the entire squad met to discuss the resolution on the Watters and Brooks situation.

Outside the meeting, assistant coach Joe Moore pulled Frank Stams aside. The coach fired Stams up, talking to him about what it meant to be on a team and how that had to be treated with honor.

"We all abide by the rules. They were stated early on. So there is no confusion on what we're supposed to do, and what we're not supposed to do, and if there's a violation of the rule, no matter who it is, nobody is bigger than the team. A rule is a rule. If you don't follow them, there are consequences," said Mark Green, a captain and the starting running back.

Andre Jones, a sophomore linebacker who had started some games, spoke up in favor of letting Watters and Brooks play.

It could have split the room and created cliques in favor of what Jones said and others in favor of discipline for the pair. It didn't.

"It's another moment where you can see the type of players and the character we had," said Derek Brown. "The fact that he can get up and say that, it meant two things: one, it wasn't the swagger of us-versus-them, old school/new school; it was we're all in this thing together and even though I'm a young guy you'll respect me by, at least, letting me voice my opinion, whether you like it or not."

The players in the room knew it took guts to speak up. They respected that.

It didn't change anything.

Stams stood up and addressed everybody. "I don't give a shit who's out there, or if I have to play offense. It doesn't matter. We're going to kick some ass tomorrow."

"And everybody just went nuts. That was it," Green said.

Later that night, Holtz spotted D'Juan Francisco grabbing a snack before going to sleep. They spoke about Francisco coming back for a fifth year. At the end of the conversation, Holtz asked Francisco if he did the right thing by sending Watters and Brooks home.

"Coach, you didn't make that decision. We did. We'll be all right."

"All right, DJ, I look forward to you coming back next year," Holtz said.

"I wanted to make sure that was the attitude they had," Holtz said years later of the interaction with Francisco.

At 5:00 A.M. Rosenthal barely tapped Holtz's hotel door and the coach opened it. There was no retreat from the consequences.

"Glad to see you," Holtz said. "I prayed on this all night. I've got to send them home."

An athletic department staff member drove Watters and Brooks to the airport.

"I didn't see it coming. I know Rick didn't see it coming," said Tony Brooks. "That was our wake-up call."

They watched the game in O'Hare International Airport when they arrived in Chicago. They sat in a restaurant, missed their connecting flight, and saw their headshots on the TV screen as the announcer spoke about their suspension.

"We both had ego issues," Brooks said of himself and Watters. "It was always something that we were being talked to about. We weren't the angels on the team, that's for sure."

"We screwed up and he stuck to his guns," Brooks said. "It was the biggest game of the year."

The press release issued by Notre Dame said Watters and Brooks had been sent home for "repeated irresponsible tardiness."

On the ride to the Coliseum, Holtz kept his thoughts on what Notre Dame had to do to win. When he arrived at the stadium he felt the buzz about the suspensions. He knew it would be compared to what happened at Arkansas, and it was so different from what happened then. He knew it would be a national story. How could it not be? The leading ground gainer and leading receiver on the No. 1 team in the country—suspended for being late.

"These were good young men," Holtz said. "Everything led up to it, and it started over Thanksgiving dinner, where I was so irate that I should've done it then. But no. One more time. Never in your wildest dreams do you think it's going to happen again, and it happened twenty-four hours later. After you warn them. It's like 'I don't care about the team—you need me.' . . . It seems so trivial unless you were there Thursday at Thanksgiving dinner and heard the conversation."

As the 93,829 spectators waited for kickoff, Anthony Davis, the USC hero, waved to the crowd from a Mercedes convertible being driven around the running track at the Coliseum. The game had been sold out for a month. It was the first time in forty years that a Notre Dame–USC game filled the venue. It was the first time both teams came into the game unbeaten and untied. The *Orange County Register* reported that tickets, which normally sold for $22, had a $1,000 value on the scalpers market.

ABC carried the game, with Keith Jackson and Bob Griese handling the announcing. Notre Dame's radio voices, Tony Roberts and Tom Pagna, would be heard on 212 stations across the country.

" 'All week long we've been hearing about how the Irish are going to be our biggest challenge,' " ABC sideline reporter Mike Adamle said, relaying pregame words USC senior fullback Leroy Holt told his team in the locker room. " 'That's wrong. We're going to be a challenge for them. This is all-out war. I don't want you guys playing four quarters. I want you guys playing five quarters.' "

The Trojans ran onto the field as their famed marching band played "Fight On" and the home-team fans waved pom-poms of the official school colors—USC Cardinal and USC Gold.

The USC band played "Tribute to Troy," the incessant refrain heard throughout Trojan football games, and Notre Dame walked out from the Coliseum tunnel, some players with their hands raised signaling No. 1 with their fingers.

USC received the opening kickoff and started at its 26-yard line. Peete and the Trojans moved the ball to the 45-yard line. On a second-down play, Michael Stonebreaker reached Peete and wrapped his arms around him, but the 6'2" 195-pound passer let the linebacker slide down his legs as he completed a 2-yard pass. On the next play, Notre Dame lined up with nine men at the line of scrimmage. This alignment served as a harbinger of things to come. The play's result did not. With the Irish sending almost every defender, Holt, the fullback, charged up the middle for 13 yards.

On first down from the Notre Dame 40, the Irish sent six rushers after Peete. The quarterback unloaded a pass. The crowd

roared as the ball traveled toward open All-American wide receiver Erik Affholter, but Peete underthrew the corner route, and
cornerback Todd Lyght made up the lost ground, batting the ball
to the turf.

The Trojans reached the Notre Dame 33-yard line as the artificial sound of a male cheerleader using a portable speaker system led
USC fans in cheers.

"One-two-three!" he'd count in the metallic tone.

"Let's go, Rodney," he and the crowd responded.

The Irish defense forced a punt. The Trojans pinned Notre Dame
just outside its 1-yard line when Mark Carrier caught the high-
hanging kick.

All week, Holtz had told the team he wanted the first offensive
play to be a big pass. They practiced a play-action fake. Rice would
pretend to hand it to Green out of the I-formation. He'd step back
and hurl a bomb up the sideline to a speeding Rocket Ismail. Holtz
wanted the fake so precise that Rice actually gave the ball to Green
sometimes during practice and carried out the rest of the play with
an imaginary pigskin in his hand.

"If the quarterback gets sacked, I'll take responsibility for it. If
the running back gets tackled behind the line of scrimmage, you're
responsible for it," Holtz told the offensive unit at practice.

"In other words, I wanted them to give that run just a tremendous look, and we worked on faking it and walking back, hiding the
ball," he said.

The fake needed to draw the attention of Carrier, USC's All-
American free safety. If Carrier moved up to play the run, Rocket
would easily get behind the defense.

In all this planning, Holtz never thought he'd start out backed
up against his own end zone. He balked at calling the play.

"What play do you think we should run?" he asked Rice.

"Hey, they would never expect me to throw the ball."

The quarterback convinced the coach. Rice called the play, broke the huddle, and lined up with his feet in his own end zone.

"Hands it off," Jackson told the TV audience. "No he doesn't. He stepped on the back of the end zone, but they didn't see it."*

Rice faked to Green and gingerly dropped back 9 yards deep in the end zone. Trojans cornerback Ernest Spears, the one supposed to be covering Rocket, bought the fake and peered into the pileup of USC defenders and Green.

Rice tapped the ball once with his left hand and hurled the pass 53 yards in the air to a waiting Rocket. Ismail, who had his man beat by 6 yards, lost his balance making the catch. Spears closed the gap, pushing Rocket out of bounds after a 55-yard gain.

"You've got to give credit to the magic of Lou Holtz," Griese said. "He just suspended two of his best players. He's on his own 1-yard line. He's traveling two thousand miles away from home and he calls the biggest play of the ball game so far to get them out of the hole."

"That's my play call," Rice said watching the highlight more than two decades later.

The Irish drive stalled three plays later, but the long pass accomplished its purpose.

"It sent a message," Holtz said.

The teams exchanged punts, and Notre Dame took possession of the ball at its 28-yard line. Two dive plays from Anthony Johnson covered 7 yards. The Irish faced third down and 3 yards to go.

"Then we ran a special play we had put in," Holtz said.

---

*Rice didn't come close to stepping out of the back of the end zone. He stepped beyond the paint of the Trojans logo. Jackson corrected himself twice during subsequent plays, but when Rice and Holtz talk about the play today they are quick to correct the error made by the well known college football announcer.

Holtz respected the USC defense and its linebackers so much, he created a play to false-key them.

Rice started with a reverse pivot to the right. He quickly spun around and ran a trap option to the left. The pivot created the briefest moment of hesitation from the linebackers, and it allowed pulling guard Tim Grunhard and fullback Anthony Johnson to seal blocks on players coming across the field attempting to catch Rice.

By the time Rice got outside, Carrier had come up to the line of scrimmage from the secondary, but Carrier focused on Mark Green, the option if Rice wanted to pitch the ball. Rice saw this and made a swift cut back inside. Rice was only 2 yards off the line of scrimmage, and no one was left in his way.

"I know if I saw green, I'm not going to let anyone catch me," Rice said.

He took the ball 65 yards to the end zone, the longest run of his career. Notre Dame took the lead 7–0.

On USC's second offensive play after the touchdown, Peete completed a swing pass to Aaron Emanuel. The Trojans tailback escaped Jeff Alm, who had already rushed into the USC backfield. Emanuel held the ball away from his body and lost control of it trying to avoid the oncoming tackle from George "Boo" Williams.

Frank Stams had rushed from the opposite side of the field. He fell to the ground after leaping over an attempted block from Leroy Holt. As Stams rose up, USC's right tackle Darrell Marshall hardly got in his way. Stams kept moving, running through Marshall's nonchalance toward the ball Emanuel fumbled. Stams dove on it, making the recovery at the 20-yard line.

Sitting on the bench after the play, Stams looked up and turned to the TV camera after someone called his name. He waved a No. 1 finger and offered a "Yeah baby!"

On the field, the Irish ran the ball five straight times until Mark Green scored from 2 yards out, leaping over a pile of would-be tacklers. The Irish led 14–0. In less than one quarter, Notre Dame had gained 83 rushing yards, 15 more than USC averaged giving up per game.

The Irish defensive game plan had a schoolyard look: kill the quarterback. On the second play of the second quarter, Notre Dame blitzed eight players. A backpedaling Peete threw across his body before getting knocked to the ground. George Streeter, one of the three Irish players in pass coverage, cut off Peete's pass, making the interception. Notre Dame fumbled it back to the Trojans, and the Fighting Irish kept coming after the USC quarterback.

USC had first down and 10 at the Notre Dame 35-yard line, and for three straight plays the Irish harassed and battered Peete. Sophomore linebacker Andre Jones knocked him to the ground on an incomplete pass. Boo Williams batted a pass into the air and, showing an equal-opportunity approach to hitting, cornerback Stan Smagala popped Affholter, momentarily sending the Trojans receiver out of the game. On third down, five Notre Dame rushers chased a scrambling Peete 22 yards behind the line of scrimmage before the quarterback threw an incomplete pass and hit the ground compliments of Jones and Wes Pritchett.

"We were sending those cats and I tell you, we wore Rodney Peete out," said defensive coordinator Barry Alvarez.

Midway through the second quarter, USC finally threatened to score. On first down from the Notre Dame 19-yard line, Peete handed off to sophomore tailback Ricky Ervins, who fumbled. Ervins started to chop his feet into a cutback at the line of scrimmage; Notre Dame defensive lineman Jeff Alm reached out his paw and knocked the ball loose as he was being blocked out of the way. Boo Williams made the recovery.

The USC defense stymied the Irish on three plays. When the Trojans took possession of the ball, they drove 66 yards on eleven plays and scored a touchdown on a 1-yard pitch to senior tailback

Scott Lockwood. With 2:24 to play in the half, Southern California had made it a 14–7 game.

The Trojans shut down the Irish offense again, forcing Notre Dame to punt with less than a minute to play in the second quarter. The Irish booted the ball 21 yards. USC had two time-outs and the ball at the Notre Dame 49-yard line.

Peete lined up in the shotgun. Notre Dame, unfazed by the possibility of giving up a big play, blitzed seven men. Peete had good protection. He threw to a receiver running an out to his left at the 36-yard line. Irish cornerback Stan Smagala intercepted the pass and sprinted 64 yards untouched up the sideline to the end zone for the touchdown.

Smagala was the guy Holtz thought couldn't play at Notre Dame. He came as the lowliest member of what Holtz called his "worst recruiting class." Hard to imagine, but Smagala's college career looked even worse after his first practice.

Coaches put players through a conditioning test. They had to run around the football field, and Smagala had an asthma attack. He left the field on a stretcher. Holtz shook his head as he watched the player get carted off.

"I'm sure he was just imagining, *God, this is a waste of scholarship*," Smagala said.

His teammates busted his chops because the asthma put a great reduction on practice time for the sub-six-foot cornerback with the thick Chicago accent.

"But I was able to play in the games and do it halfway decent," he said.

"Stan played four years here with a chip on his shoulder," said Pat Terrell. "He loved his school, loved his teammates, but he always wanted to prove he's one of the best guys and fastest guys on the team."

On the touchdown against USC, Smagala eyed USC receiver John Jackson. "As soon as I saw his hips drop, I just shot to that angle," Smagala said.

Smagala went to the spot where Jackson was headed. Jackson slipped to the ground, "which I didn't realize, I just ran," Smagala said. "The ball came to me and I caught it and I ran to the end zone."

After Smagala's teammates congratulated him in the end zone, the next image on the TV screen was of Peete, slumped to one side on the ground being tended to by medical personnel.

Stams had rushed in from Peete's right side. The USC linemen did a good job protecting the quarterback by pushing Stams upfield, behind Peete. After the interception, Peete started to take strides toward the action, his eyes looking at his mistake.

"I'm so far behind him upfield that I'm in a perfect position to just peel back on him and I've got a kill shot," Stams said.

Being a former fullback, Stams knew exactly how to position himself to throw a devastating block: stay high and get in front of him.

If a snarling bull charged a defenseless Bambi, it would look like Stams's block on Peete. He leveled the unsuspecting quarterback. Peete's head jostled back and forth before his body flopped to the turf. Stams finished the play by covering Peete on the ground.

"I'm just glad he got up," Stams said.

USC had only 14 turnovers in its first ten games. The Irish had forced 4 in the first half. After Reggie Ho missed the extra point, Notre Dame led 20–7.

Peete stayed in the game, and the Trojans kept pressing even though they had only 41 seconds left in the half. Peete threw a deep pass to the Notre Dame 6-yard line, and safety Pat Terrell had the interception in his hands until USC backup flanker Gary Wellman broke up the play. Wellman patted Terrell on the head as the Irish defensive back got up off the ground.

On the next play, Stams flushed Peete out of the pocket and sacked the passer, planting Peete on his left shoulder. Showing no quit, Peete called time-out with 5 seconds on the clock. He had separated his left shoulder, but he'd only miss one play of the game. His backup, Pat O'Hara, came in to hand the ball off and end the half.

At halftime, Holtz went over to Alvarez.

"Are you okay?"

"Yeah, we're fine. I don't think they'll have any answer, because we haven't shown blitz all year."

Alvarez thought the blitz would be effective for a few reasons. With Peete's weakened voice, Alvarez figured, Notre Dame could stack men at the line of scrimmage because the quarterback wouldn't be able to bark out an audible to change the play. Certainly sending this many men after the quarterback would surprise the Trojans because no game film existed where Notre Dame had done it before. The reason Alvarez could send the fleet is because Notre Dame exploited a USC weakness. The Trojans did not have the speed at wide receiver to beat the Irish. The Irish lined up in man-to-man coverage and, by blitzing so many players, begged the USC passing game to beat them. Todd Lyght spent the game covering the wide side of the field on his own. Smagala played receivers on the opposite side, and safeties picked up the tight ends on blitzes.

"That was an offense no one had slowed down," Alvarez said. "Our kids played lights out."

The Notre Dame offense had gone dormant. "I'm having a bad day," Holtz told Alvarez.

The Irish gained 10 yards in the second quarter and didn't have a first down. The first-down drought continued through the third quarter. During a stretch from the first quarter deep into the third, USC outgained Notre Dame 254 yards to 7.

Late in the third stanza, the Trojans made their way to the Irish 4-yard line but had to settle for a field goal, making the score 20–10.

In a drive that took the game into the fourth quarter, the Notre

Dame offense awoke. Rice led a ten-play, 70-yard march to answer the USC field goal.

Mark Green leaped over the goal line to finish the drive with a 1-yard touchdown. The Irish took a 27–10 lead. Rice accounted for 52 yards on the drive. On the day, 177 of Notre Dame's 253 yards came from Rice runs or throws.

Green's second touchdown ended all the scoring, but Notre Dame's abuse of Peete didn't stop.

With a little more than six minutes to play, USC started a short-lived drive at its own 18-yard line. Peete dropped back to pass, and with solid coverage downfield, Stams smothered him for another sack and an 8-yard loss. The Trojans punted two plays later.

George Streeter, Notre Dame's hard-hitting strong safety, felt something he had never experienced before on the football field—compassion.

Oh my God, we are killing this guy, Streeter thought as the Irish continued to pummel Peete. *Will somebody take him out of the game?*

With 2:41 to play and down 17 points, Peete lined up in the shotgun and threw to Gary Wellman. Pat Terrell had been waiting a couple of quarters for this moment. The pat on the helmet in the first half infuriated Terrell. He kept his eyes on Wellman from across the field.

"I watched him get a sip of Gatorade. I watched him talk to his teammates on the sideline. I waited for him to come back in the game," Terrell said.

Wellman caught the Peete pass and ran across the middle, trying to turn it into a big play. Terrell lunged at Wellman, taking the receiver off his feet as he wrapped up his upper body and flung him to the ground.

"I tried to rip his head off," Terrell said.

On USC's last offensive play, Peete threw an incomplete pass before Wes Pritchett drove him into the turf. Summing up his day, the quarterback got up slowly with the help of one of his linemen. With his back to the field, he moved to the sideline, pulling a chunk of grass from his helmet.

Tony Rice stayed on the sidelines as the Irish ran the clock out. He garnered the game's most-valuable-player honors. It was another instance where Rice entered the game as the quarterback bridesmaid but left with a stellar performance and the win.

"From what I heard, there was only one quarterback in the stadium, and it was Rodney Peete. I didn't let it bother me because I knew what I was capable of doing," Rice said after the game.*

Before Notre Dame snapped it one last time, Holtz and Alvarez shared a joyous embrace on the sideline. Barry Alvarez, wearing the dark sunglasses, lifted Holtz off the ground and swung him around as the coaches hugged.

"Relief." That's what Holtz said he felt.

After the game, Peete had his left arm in a sling.

"He really took a pounding, and after the game he came over to me and was such a class, class act in every respect," Holtz said.

Tim Grunhard ended any storyline about division between the team and the jettisoned young stars. "Nobody's mad at Tony or Ricky. They learned their lesson. I'm sure they'll be ten to fifteen minutes early for meetings at the Fiesta Bowl," he told reporters.

"It's fantastic to go out this way. We struggled when I first got there. Now, to end up like this, it's awesome," Stams told ABC's Mike Adamle after the game.

The team visited Disneyland the next day. Photographers took pictures of the captains—Bolcar, Green, and Heck—with Mickey

---

*After the win, Rice took over the cover of *Sports Illustrated* for the second time that season. The underestimated quarterback and Los Angeles Dodgers pitcher Orel Hershiser were the only ones to appear on the magazine's cover more than once in 1988.

Mouse and Donald Duck. For his photo op Holtz stood between Goofy and Pluto, and a local newspaper sent the coach home with a parting shot.

"They ran a picture of me with Pluto and Goofy. And the caption said something like, 'Here's Lou Holtz, head football coach of Notre Dame, at Disney with Pluto and Goofy,' and then they put it in big capital letters that said 'LOU HOLTZ IS THE ONE IN THE MIDDLE,'" the coach said.

Back in South Bend, Holtz made sure the Irish didn't view the Fiesta Bowl as a reward like they did the previous season's trip to the Cotton Bowl.

CHAPTER 18

Carrying Them Off

For at least a decade, the Fiesta Bowl dispatched Bill Shover to Notre Dame to woo the Irish on the possibility of playing a postseason game in the desert.

In its pursuit to become a major player on New Year's Day, the Fiesta Bowl had spent years redefining the system of luring schools to games. The Fiesta scored a major victory hosting the No. 1–No. 2 Miami–Penn State meeting on January 2, 1987, and drawing the largest TV audience in college football history.

Two seasons later, the upstart group of Arizonans stood to host the highest prize in any bowl-bidding campaign—a top-ranked Notre Dame team.

"It changes everything. Notre Dame, love them or hate them . . . Once you get them in a bowl game, you bring fans out of the woodwork from every place," said Don Meyers, the Fiesta Bowl selection committee chairman in 1988.

Fiesta Bowl organizers hoped the relationships built by Shover, an Indiana native who had dreamed of attending Notre Dame, would payoff.

"Nothing would give me more pleasure than to see Notre Dame come out of the tunnel at the Fiesta Bowl," Shover, one of the men who helped create the event, told the *Indianapolis News* in late October.

During the first week in October, Meyers gathered his fellow organizers. Looking at the landscape of teams, he narrowed the number of schools that could play for the national championship in their bowl. Notre Dame, Miami, and West Virginia emerged as the candidates. The rest of the field had conference ties to other bowls, and Meyers hedged his bets on Arkansas, USC, and UCLA losing at some point in the regular season. With that in mind, the Notre Dame–Miami winner would become the most coveted team.

When the Irish prevailed against the 'Canes, the Fiesta Bowl had competition for Notre Dame among the bowl suitors. Like its southwestern counterpart, the Gator Bowl wanted to break into the big-boy club. Following the Fiesta Bowl model, the Jacksonville, Florida, bowl grabbed a sponsor in Mazda. It signed a television agreement with ESPN. It moved the date of the game from its typical late-December slot to New Year's Day. The Gator Bowl even promised a $3 million payout, which would be second only to the Rose Bowl, which paid each team $6 million.[*]

Even though official bowl invitations could not be made until November 19, everyone made deals and locked up teams long before that date. The Fiesta Bowl secured West Virginia in late October. They matched the Gator Bowl's payout.

In early November, during a call with top administrators in the athletic department, Fiesta Bowl executive director Bruce Skinner played poker with the Irish. Notre Dame wanted to somehow avoid playing West Virginia if the Mountaineers ended up losing after the Irish accepted the bid. Skinner made his move. "If you want a contingency plan ... then we're going to pass on you and take Miami," he said according to an article in *ESPN's TV Sports*, a newspaper supplement.

---

[*]The total bowl payouts for the seventeen postseason games played that year was estimated at $52 million, according to media reports.

A few days before the official invitations could be made, Notre Dame ruled out the Gator Bowl and said it would play in the Fiesta Bowl if asked.

The Irish never offered reasons for the Gator Bowl rejection. Instead, athletic director Dick Rosenthal said they had decided against the bowl and did not want its organizers to move forward thinking Notre Dame would play there.

The Fiesta Bowl had more advantages than the even money and the probability of playing undefeated West Virginia. While the Gator Bowl moved its date, January 1 fell on Sunday. Other bowl games, such as the Fiesta, moved their contests to Monday that year. The Gator Bowl would be played at night following a day of NFL playoffs. ESPN was still a growing network, and playing on a cable station that reached fewer than 50 million homes didn't compare to a network TV audience that could be seen in more than 90 million homes.

"It was extremely important for us to get that West Virginia–Notre Dame matchup because of what it did for our bowl game," Meyers said. "At the same time, you looked around the country and you could see that the other bowls did not have the game we had."

Holtz gave the Irish a few days to enjoy the USC victory. Then he held a team meeting and informed them the season was history. The focus shifted to West Virginia and fundamental football.

Before the team left campus for a few days of Christmas break, Holtz put them through a rigorous string of practices.

"All the little things that you're taught to do in spring practice and training camp, we went right back to them. We had some very intense practices all throughout the preparation for the bowl game," said linebacker and captain Ned Bolcar.

Holtz pumped the West Virginia fight song into the Loftus Center, playing it over and over and over again.

"It was so loud we couldn't hear each other," said sophomore linebacker Scott Kowalkowski.

If starters had thoughts about being complacent, Holtz erased them. "Every position is up for grabs," he said.

"Nobody was comfortable. That was one of the brilliant things about Coach Holtz, his ability to never let you be comfortable," said tackle and captain Andy Heck. "It wasn't particularly enjoyable going through it, but looking back on it, it certainly produced results."

Years later most players grew to appreciate Holtz's meticulous and disciplinary approach. In the moment, though, they struggled and sometimes commiserated about his methods.

None of the opining mattered to Holtz. He wasn't there to be liked. He was there to be their coach. Players being content or him being admired didn't matter. To Holtz, what mattered was being who he promised to be as a coach. That's what guided his words and actions.

"Your obligation is not to be well liked, not to be popular. Your obligation is to make them the very best they can possibly be," he said.

The team had confidence coming off a season with wins against Miami, Michigan, and USC, and that belief in themselves grew during the boot-camp-style bowl prep.

"There was no question. There was no teaching. It was 'This is what we're going to do. This is how we're going to beat them,'" Pat Terrell said. "I don't think I've ever been more prepared or more confident for a game than I was going into the Fiesta Bowl."

West Virginia headed into the national championship showdown after a season of breezing through opponents. They scored more than 50 points in five games. They averaged 42.9 points per game, good for second best in the nation. The Mountaineers' closest game was a 10-point win against Rutgers. They boasted an offensive line of all fifth-year-senior starters, clearing the way for a running game that averaged 293.5 yards a contest.

Sophomore quarterback Major Harris, who totaled 213 yards a game, powered the offense. Harris grew up in the Hill District of Pittsburgh. He played wishbone football for a bad team at Brashear High School. Arizona State was the lone college to show interest in him. The Sun Devils wanted him to play defensive back. Pittsburgh, West Virginia's archrival, never gave him a solid look.

West Virginia coach Don Nehlen first saw Harris at the Mountaineers summer football camp. Harris attended the camp with a group of his high school teammates. After each day of tutelage, the kids ate dinner and played touch football. That's where Nehlen made his decision to recruit Harris.

"Man, oh man, this kid has so much ability to stop and start," Nehlen said. "He looked awful good to me."

During the '88 season Harris pulled off what became known in West Virginia history as "the Play." Against Penn State, Harris called a belly option to the left. When he snapped the ball he went right and had no blocking. He laid a stiff-arm on a Penn State defender in the backfield and then put on a series of moves that made the Nittany Lions defense look foolish. One Penn State player lost his balance and ended up on his back looking skyward as Harris ran by him. The quarterback danced left and right. Defenders could barely get a hand on him as he made his way to the end zone on the 26-yard run.

"Coach, I'm sorry I went the wrong way," Harris told Nehlen on the sideline.

"I know. But the results were all right," Nehlen said.

Harris finished fifth in the Heisman Trophy balloting. Oklahoma State's Barry Sanders won the award, with Rodney Peete, Troy Aikman, and Steve Walsh finishing second, third, and fourth, respectively.

The Notre Dame players voted Tony Rice the team's most

valuable player, but Harris's dynamic season overshadowed Rice as the quarterbacks headed into the bowl.

The voters for the Associated Press All-American squad picked Frank Stams, Michael Stonebreaker, and Andy Heck as first-team selections. The honor included a trip to Miami and an appearance on the "Bob Hope Christmas Show," which aired each December on NBC.

Miami's Steve Walsh also made the AP first team. Being a Minnesota native, Walsh wanted to show his Midwest brethren some Hurricane hospitality. Walsh called his friend on the Notre Dame hockey team and gave him a message for Stams, Stonebreaker, and Heck.

"Tell those guys I'll be waiting with a limo. I'm going to take them out," Walsh said.

Walsh also included Michigan's All-American defensive tackle Mark Messner in the entourage. In Miami, the Hurricanes had celebrity status on the social scene, and this group hit the town with the leader of the 'Canes offense.

These men had fought each other for a shot at the national championship just a few months earlier. Now Walsh took them out for stone crab and to Little Havana.

"Oh, good Lord, we had cocktails, and we dang near didn't wake up on time for the shoot the next day because he kept us out so late," Messner said.

Whatever they drank, Walsh kept calling them Hurricanes, busting the visitors with the continual reference to his school's nickname.

"They were always these funky concoctions that tasted yummy and were designed to put you on your tail," Messner said.

The handful of guys got to know each other personally during the trip. They had been the players on the field during those classic games. Even though they were on opposite sides, they would always have a kinship through an experience only they and their teammates knew.

"That was one of my first times having an opportunity to meet guys like that," Heck said. "It was neat to realize and see these guys were just like us, regular guys."

Back in South Bend, fullback Anthony Johnson married his girlfriend, Shelley, on the day before Christmas Eve. He had proposed to her on her birthday in mid-November, and a few weeks later the couple found out she was pregnant. They decided to move up the date of the nuptials.

"We picked a date, a date that was not encumbered by Jesus' birthday or a bowl game, and said 'Let's get married.'" Johnson said.

The Irish were scheduled to arrive in Arizona on the day after Christmas. Players would fly in from all over the country, and Holtz had scheduled a practice for that afternoon. Backup senior safety Corny Southall arrived late, but he had a good excuse.

Southall boarded an Eastern Airlines jet out of Rochester. At 31,000 feet in the sky, en route to Atlanta, where Southall was scheduled to make his connection to Phoenix, a seam tore open in the fuselage near the tail engine. The oxygen masks dropped, but Southall's didn't work. The plane had to make an emergency landing in Charleston, West Virginia.

"The first thing I thought was *Am I going to make it?*" Southhall said in one of the many interviews he gave about the incident.

For all the confidence Notre Dame had, West Virginia showed up in Arizona with an equal batch.

"To be honest, I thought we'd win that game. I thought we were a better football team," Nehlen said.

The Fiesta Bowl was the first time the two schools met in football. Notre Dame retained its top status for the matchup, while West Virginia, the only other undefeated team, ranked third.* Both schools had 8-5 records in bowl games. While Notre Dame had played in every major bowl at least once, this would be the Mountaineers' first since the 1954 Sugar Bowl.

"We had played in a lot of bowl games, but we had never played in one like that," Nehlen said. "And the media absolutely drove me crazy. And Lou handled it so much better than I did. He was more experienced at that type of a situation."

Holtz picked what interviews to do, whereas Nehlen felt obligated to do them all.

"I was overwhelmed," he said. "I found myself running around like a damn chicken with my head cut off more than coaching a football team."

In circles of Notre Dame fandom, history predicted a win for the Irish. In the days leading up to the game, devotees pointed to Dan Devine's championship in his third year at Notre Dame in 1977 and Ara Parseghian's first championship in his third season in 1966. The concluding reasoning found that Holtz, in his third season and a calendar year divisible by 11, was destined to secure the national title.

Holtz thought Major Harris possessed great talent. He knew the offense had to protect against Renaldo Turnbull, who lined up at outside linebacker and defensive end for the Mountaineers. He wasn't overly concerned, though. When the West Virginia media corps played up the fact that the Mountaineers had an easier time beating Pittsburgh and Penn State than the Irish, Holtz let them run with it.

"West Virginia was good, but I didn't think they had played the caliber of competition that we had played. We were not going to be

---

*The Miami Hurricanes held the No. 2 spot in the poll.

shocked by their speed and their quickness and their execution," Holtz said. "Losing never entered my mind."

The Irish had been practicing at Scottsdale Community College, but on the day before the game, they walked through Sun Devil Stadium. Each player went to the spot where he would line up when Notre Dame took the field the following day. They had cameras and snapped photos of themselves, their coaches, and their teammates. The players watched the coaches play a touch-football game.

"I'd spike the ball and do all the things I didn't allow them to do," Holtz said.

Before the Irish left, Holtz did something he had never done as a coach. He assigned underclassmen to specific seniors to carry them off the field when Notre Dame won. Players had even practiced carrying Holtz off the field.

"There was just never any thought we might lose," he said.

Wes Pritchett had headphones on and tears pouring down his face when he stepped off the team bus at Sun Devil Stadium on game day.

"What's wrong, Wes?" somebody asked.

"I'm just going to kill somebody," he answered in a rage-filled howl.

Thoughts of his dad, who still lay in a coma, thoughts of the game's enormity, thoughts of his career at Notre Dame, had been filling his head.

"I absolutely remember being completely possessed," he said. "I can remember two or three days before that game feeling like I was being taken over."

A gray sky and 55-degree day covered the 70,021 fans in the capacity-filled venue. Notre Dame students traveled en masse to watch their team. Students purchased 3,958 tickets, equating to a shade under 40 percent of the total graduate and undergraduate population at the school.

In an about-face from having names on the back of the jerseys at last year's Cotton Bowl, the Irish didn't even wear the sunburst Fiesta Bowl insignia patches in this game.

Notre Dame had won the coin toss and deferred. West Virginia's high-powered offense started with the ball. The first two series quickly set a tone for the day.

After an incompletion and a 7-yard run, the Mountaineers faced a third down and 3 from their own 33-yard line. Harris ran a reverse option. Stonebreaker dove toward his midsection and looped around Harris's lower body, forcing the quarterback to stumble. As Harris headed to the turf, all 483 pounds of Jeff Alm and Frank Stams pounced on him.

On the same third-down play, cornerback Todd Lyght drew the assignment of the pitchman, halfback A. B. Brown. "I hit him right in the mouth," Lyght said.

"I don't even have the ball, why'd you hit me?" Brown asked.

"I'm going to hit you every chance I get," Lyght told him.

Harris's body contorted slightly and he favored his left side as he raised himself off the ground. He gained 2 yards, and West Virginia had to punt. He had injured his left shoulder and never recovered for the rest of the game.

On the punt, sophomore linebacker Scott Kowalkowski threw a block that knocked the helmet off a West Virginia player while Ricky Watters returned the ball 19 yards.

Rice handed the ball off and then pitched it on Notre Dame's first two plays. The Irish needed 7 yards on third down from their 37-yard line. Rice dropped back to pass. The pocket closed in on him and he took off, running out from under a West Virginia lineman's gloved-hand on his shoulder. Down the field, Rice sped past Mountaineer defenders who could only reach out a hand and watch the back of his jersey. He reached the West Virginia 45-yard line, where cornerback Willie Edwards broke down into perfect tackling form. Edwards crashed into Rice's thighs, but the Irish quarterback kept sprinting as Edwards bounced backward, falling away from Rice in what looked like slow motion. Rice picked up 13 more yards after leaving Edwards behind. A diving Mountaineer put a hand on his foot and the quarterback lost his balance, rolling to the ground at the 32-yard line. Rice picked up 31 yards on the play, the longest run in Notre Dame bowl history.

In the game's opening moments Notre Dame had shown itself to be the superior team. The Irish ran the ball on their first eighteen plays.

"We could tell people where we were going and they couldn't stop us," Rice said.

The Irish had trailed for 29 minutes and 25 seconds in the 11 hours of game time they had played. They never trailed in the Fiesta Bowl. Notre Dame took a 16–0 lead, scoring on three of its first four possessions. West Virginia failed to make a first down until more than a third of the way through the second quarter.

The Irish built a 23–6 halftime lead with rushing touchdowns from Anthony Johnson and Rodney Culver and a 29-yard touchdown pass from Rice to Rocket Ismail.

Major Harris had never been hurt before in his career. At halftime the West Virginia team doctor offered him a painkilling injection. Harris refused the shot.

"In retrospect, I think I should've put Major on the bench," Nehlen said. "He was just another guy that day, whereas the other eleven games we played he was a dynamite performer."

The Mountaineers came close to making it a game. With the lead cut to 26–13, Tony Rice threw an interception. West Virginia took over on the Notre Dame 26-yard line. A touchdown would have made it a 6-point game. On second down, Harris, avoiding a rush from Pritchett, put the ball on Grantis Bell's chest in the end zone, but Stan Smagala popped it loose for the incompletion. On the next play, Arnold Ale and Stams sacked Harris and pushed the Mountaineers out of field goal range.

Rice put the game away on the next drive. In an 80-yard march, the quarterback ran for 15 yards on a third and 7, connected with Ricky Watters for a 57-yard pass and finished it with a 3-yard jump pass to Frank Jacobs in the end zone and an option keeper for the 2-point conversion. Notre Dame led 34–13.

The Irish defense harassed Harris throughout the game. Notre Dame held West Virginia to 108 yards rushing, 185 yards below the Mountaineer average.

Flash Gordon, the fifth-year-senior linebacker who sat out the Miami and Air Force games, had worked his way back into a starting role. Bolcar, the captain, played most of the game, with Stonebreaker limited because of an illness. Stams picked up 2 sacks, and Pritchett played like the crazed man who stepped off the bus. Refs flagged him for late hits and he constantly drilled Major Harris.

"We all played to the whistle. Wes, in that game, played to the echo of the whistle," Stams said. "There were a couple times that game that I got close to Major Harris and all of a sudden the freight train would show up out of nowhere."

Stams even said something to Pritchett during the game.

"Dude, you better calm down out there. You're going to hurt somebody, and that person you're going to hurt, it's probably going to be me."

"That was probably the most fired up I had ever been in my life," Pritchett said.

In the closing moments, the Notre Dame defense drew a series of personal foul calls, including the ejection of one player. The Mountaineers added a meaningless touchdown and 2-point conversion to finish the scoring at 34–21.

Standing on the sideline next to Rocket Ismail, a smiling Tony Rice threw his No. 1 finger in the air as the seconds ticked away. The 12-0 Irish had become the national champions, and Rice was named the game's most valuable player. He tallied 288 yards, more than half of the Irish's offensive output. He rushed for 75 yards and threw for 213, completing 7 of 11 attempts.

As he had done throughout the season, Rice rose to the occasion, led the Irish to victory, and outdueled his highly touted counterpart.

"No situation was ever too big for Tony. He didn't get too high and he didn't get too low," Pat Terrell said. "There's no other quarterback in that situation with that team that could've won the national championship. A lot of people don't realize what a true leader he was."

ESPN analyst and college football historian Beano Cook agreed with Terrell's sentiment. "Without Tony Rice you don't win it," Cook said. "They don't mention him as a great college quarterback because he didn't play in the pros. He was a great college quarterback."

Spectators flooded the field to celebrate with the team that had returned Notre Dame to the top perch in college football. The band played the "Victory March," and underclassmen hoisted the seniors above a scene of waving Irish flags and swarming fans.

When the Associated Press released its final rankings, Notre Dame accomplished something no other team had done in the history of the poll. The '88 Irish remain the only national championship squad to beat four teams ranked in the top 7 of the final poll.

"One bad game, one bad play, one interception, one bad missed tackle and you don't go undefeated. It's that tough to do," said Mark Green.

The margin between being really good and etching a spot in history is thin. A made field goal in the season opener, or a completed 2-point conversion pass in a midseason tilt with the No. 1–ranked team, and greatness is forever out of reach. However, those are make-believe scenarios. What is true is that a disparate group came together and fulfilled a commitment to greatness. Led by a coach who preached a faith in the university's spirit, a quarterback whose abilities were constantly questioned, and a ferocious defense, Notre Dame answered every challenge the season presented. What is true is that the 1988 Fighting Irish were unbeatable.

EPILOGUE

The team visited the White House on January 18, 1989. President Reagan wanted to welcome the Irish as one of his last acts in office. It was the first time the players had been together since they left Arizona after the Fiesta Bowl. When the team returned to campus that evening, a group of players headed to O'Tays Nite Club in Niles, Michigan, a few miles north of campus.

Backup cornerback Bob Satterfield collapsed at the club.

"Hey, look, man, help is on the way, just squeeze my hand and let me know you're okay," said Mark Green, who held Satterfield's head in his lap, waiting for the ambulance to arrive.

"About five minutes before the ambulance came he wasn't squeezing my hand," Green said. "I felt the life leave the man's body. I'm holding this guy and by the time the ambulance got there, there was nothing they could do."

Satterfield was a well-liked walk-on player who had earned a scholarship in his reserve role. He suffered cardiac arrest and then a seizure, both the result of an undetected congenital heart defect, according to the medical examiner. There were no drugs or excessive alcohol in the twenty-two-year-old's system.

Green, who lost his mother during his freshman year and held Satterfield during his teammate's final moments, received word in

March that his father had died after suffering from pneumonia and a collapsed lung.

The Chicago Bears took Green with a fifth-round pick in the 1989 draft. He played four seasons and said the losses he dealt with in college made him fearless as an NFL player.

The 1989 NFL Draft gives further proof of the greatness of the 1988 college football season. Four of the top 5 players taken—Troy Aikman, Barry Sanders, Derrick Thomas, and Deion Sanders—ended up being inducted into the Pro Football Hall of Fame.

The one member of the top 5 who won't be enshrined in Canton is Tony Mandarich. He went from being "the Incredible Bulk" on the cover of *Sports Illustrated* to being billed as "the Incredible Bust" on the magazine's cover three years later. He became addicted to painkillers and washed out of the league after the 1992 season. After a three-year hiatus, a sober Mandarich made a successful comeback, starting thirty-two games for the Indianapolis Colts from 1996 to 1998. While being interviewed for this book, Mandarich said he had no regrets about taking steroids.

The Irish had five players taken in the '89 draft. In one college season, Andy Heck went from a tight end to an offensive tackle and became the fifteenth overall pick by the Seattle Seahawks. Frank Stams went to the Los Angeles Rams in the second round, Green to the Bears in the fifth. The Dolphins took Wes Pritchett in the sixth round, and George Streeter ended up with the Bears as an eleventh-round pick.

Pritchett was with the Buffalo Bills organization when his father died. Ken Pritchett had remained in a coma since the stroke.

The Los Angeles Rams used their sixth-round pick to take Michigan's Mark Messner. The team gave him a leave of absence so Messner could be with his dying stepfather. The man who influenced

Messner's decision to play for the Wolverines faced another bout with cancer. Messner would help bathe Del Petty. He would lift him in and out of a tub and flakes of Del's skin would be left on his stepson.

"It was horrible."

Messner was at home with his family when Del passed.

In 1989, the Irish winning streak reached a school record twenty-three games. They played another de facto national championship game at the close of the regular season. This time it was against the Hurricanes in Miami. Jimmy Johnson had moved on to coach the Dallas Cowboys, but one of the last things he told his team before leaving was to beat the Irish. The 'Canes prevailed 27–10, ending the Notre Dame win streak and eventually winning the national championship.

Tony Rice had an All-American season and came in fourth in the Heisman Trophy balloting. Thirty-four players from the 1988 Notre Dame roster went on to the NFL, but Rice never did. The quarterback who entered school with questioned academic credentials graduated with his class that spring.

Dean Brown, the offensive tackle who considered himself the player who benefited the most from being at Notre Dame, also graduated in '89. As part of a group of African American graduates on commencement day, Brown had the opportunity to meet Bill Cosby, the creator of his favorite TV show, *Fat Albert*. It didn't go well. Cosby asked him about his grade point average, then scolded Brown, telling him he had to do better than the 2.5 he had earned. The interaction made headlines across the country and eventually ran as a blurb in the *National Enquirer*.

"I went a lot of years feeling like I was a failure, one because I didn't think I played long enough in the pros," Brown said. "And, there were times that anytime I heard Bill Cosby's name—it wasn't a cringe, but it was a heavy uneasiness about what had transpired."

• • •

The tear-stained face of Chris Zorich on the field after the Irish's 1991 Orange Bowl loss to Colorado is one of the lasting images of this Notre Dame era.

He spoke to his mother, Zora, after the game that night. He returned to Chicago the next day, but Zora didn't answer the door when he arrived at the apartment. He kicked it open and found his mother had died.

She never saw him suit up for the hometown Chicago Bears, who picked Zorich in the second round of the 1991 NFL Draft.

In 1991, NBC began to broadcast all of Notre Dame's home football games. The move by the university to sign an exclusive deal with a network created a clear break with the College Football Association.

At the time, the NBC deal drew the ire of critics, partly because Notre Dame is always going to have critics and partly because Fr. William Beauchamp, Notre Dame's executive vice president, was secretary-treasurer of the CFA and a member of the negotiating committee for TV contracts.

The CFA had just inked its own TV deal when Notre Dame pulled out. The organization was able to reconfigure its contract, and the money lost in the new deal was the revenue slated to go to Notre Dame, said Chuck Neinas, who ran the CFA at the time.

Notre Dame striking out on its own was the first move in an evolution that was bound to happen. Soon after the Irish headed to NBC, the Big East and Southeastern conferences established network deals for their games. The CFA had done its job to enable schools to harness the power of football broadcast rights. The organization ceased to operate in 1997.

Notre Dame's arrangement with NBC has proven to be a major factor in the school's ability to remain independent while the vast majority of the twenty-four nonconference programs in 1988 have joined leagues.

College football TV contracts continue to explode. While technology allows viewers to watch shows on demand, sports provide DVR-proof inventory, which guarantees advertisers an audience and drives up the value of the broadcast contracts.

A sign that the TV money for college football isn't slowing down is the $80 million deal for the Champions Bowl. Before the game between the SEC and the Big 12 champions had a site, before it had ever been played, it took the Sugar Bowl name, and it grabbed as much money as the eldest statesman, the Rose Bowl.

Gerry Faust, the maligned head coach who preceded Lou Holtz, remains welcome on the Notre Dame campus. On many fall Saturdays he can be spotted in the press box during Irish home games.

Lou Holtz's Irish teams finished second in 1989 and 1993. He left Notre Dame after the 1996 season. He posted a 100-30-2 record with the Irish, five victories behind Knute Rockne's school record of 105 wins.

In his Hall of Fame career, Holtz led all six schools he coached to bowl games and four of those schools to at least one top 20 finish. He finished his career with 249 wins, 132 losses, seven ties, and one national championship. Every championship ring is inscribed with the words TRUST, LOVE, and COMMITMENT, the three words Holtz wrote on the board during his first meeting with the Notre Dame team.

Pat Terrell, the safety who batted down the Miami 2-point conversion pass, played nine years in the NFL. During his rookie year with the Los Angeles Rams the locker next to his belonged to former Miami Hurricane Cleveland Gary, the focal point of the controversial fumble play. After the NFL, Terrell, the aviation enthusiast, flew commercial airplanes.

While Notre Dame Stadium only held 59,075 fans in 1988, Terrell is pretty sure he's heard from about 70,000 people who say they were there, right there, in the corner when he made the play that ended up securing the national championship for Notre Dame.

NOTRE DAME 1988 ROSTER

No	Name	Pos.	Ht.	Wt.	Cl.
80	Alaniz, Steve	SE	6-2	196	Sr.
97	Ale, Arnold	LB	6-4	200	Fr.
72	Allen, Joe	OT	6-4	268	So.
90	Alm, Jeff	DT	6-4	248	Jr.
57	Anderson, Shawn	OG	6-3	253	Jr.
78	Balentine, Norm	OT	6-5	266	So.
39	Banks, Braxston	FB	6-3	211	Jr.
8	Belles, Steve	QB	6-4	211	Sr.
47	Bolcar, Ned	LB	6-2	232	Sr.
64	Brennan, Mike	TE	6-5	246	Sr.
41	Brooks, Tony	TB	6-2	218	So.
71	Brown, Dean	OT	6-3	283	Jr.
85	Brown, Derek	TE	6-7	235	Fr.
94	Callan, Mike	DT	6-4	249	So.
14	Connor, Sean	P	6-7	218	Sr.
77	Crounse, Mike	DT	6-2	264	Jr.
20	Culver, Rodney	RB/DB	6-0	212	Fr.
93	Dahl, Bob	DT	6-5	248	So.
26	Davis, Greg	SS	6-1	198	So.
4	Dillard, James	FL	6-1	180	So.
23	DiOrio, Doug	FS	5-10	187	Jr.
24	Earley, Rich	SS	6-0	181	Jr.
13	Eilers, Pat	FL	5-11	197	Sr.
83	Fallon, Patrick	SE	6-0	187	Jr.
46	Farrell, Joe	LB	5-11	214	Jr.
95	FitzGerald, Ted	DT	6-6	255	Sr.
92	Flannery, Bryan	DT	6-3	249	Jr.
32	Francisco, D'Juan	CB	5-11	187	Sr.

Hometown	High School	High School Coach
Edinburg, TX	Edinburg	Richard Flores
Carson, CA	Carson	Gene Vollnogle
Chicago, IL	St. Rita	Todd Wernet
Orland Park, IL	Sandburg	Tom Seliga
Omaha, NE	Creighton Prep	Tom Jaworski
Florissant, MO	Hazelwood East	Rick Gorzynski
Hayward, CA	Moreau	Tim Walsh
Phoenix, AZ	St. Mary's	Patrick Farrell
Phillipsburg, NJ	Phillipsburg	Philip Rohm
Severna Park, MD	Mt. St. Joseph's	Charles White
Tulsa, OK	Washington	Larry McGee
Canton, OH	McKinley	Thom McDaniel
Merritt Island, FL	Merritt Island	Gerald Odom
Ardmore, PA	Archbishop Carroll	Kevin Clancy
Zeigler, IL	Zeigler-Royalton	John DeNosky
Endicott, NY	Union-Endicott	Frank Angeline
Detroit, MI	DePorres	Ron Thompson
Chagrin Falls, OH	Chagrin Falls	John Piai
Hollywood, FL	McArthur	Roger Mastantonio
Columbus, OH	St. Charles	Tom Vargo
Worthington, OH	Bishop Watterson	Ron Shay
Lisle, IL	Benet Academy	Tim Cedarblad
St. Paul, MN	St. Thomas Academy	Jerry Brown
Pittsfield, MA	Pittsfield	Mike Murgo
Oak Lawn, IL	Brother Rice	Tom Mitchell
Wayne, NJ	DePaul	Joe Lennon
Lakewood, OH	St. Edward	Al O'Neil
Cincinnati, OH	Moeller	Steve Klonne

NOTRE DAME 1988 ROSTER

No	Name	Pos.	Ht.	Wt.	Cl.
38	Gordon, Flash	De	6-3	214	Sr.
87	Gorman, Tom	DT	6-6	255	Sr.
17	Graham, Kent	QB	6-5	228	So.
11	Graham, Pete	QB	6-3	207	Sr.
24	Green, Mark	TB	6-0	184	Sr.
36	Grimm, Donn	LB	6-2	224	So.
75	Grunhard, Tim	OG	6-3	279	Jr.
18	Hackett, Billy	K	6-1	184	So.
73	Hall, Justin	OL	6-5	290	Fr.
61	Hartweger, Pete	P	6-0	178	Sr.
56	Healy, Ted	OG	6-4	258	Jr.
66	Heck, Andy	OT	6-7	258	Sr.
55	Heldt, Mike	C	6-4	258	So.
2	Ho, Reggie	K	5-5	135	Jr.
25	Ismail, Raghib	RB	5-10	175	Fr.
88	Jacobs, Frank	TE	6-5	234	So.
33	Jandric, David	FS	6-2	192	Jr.
35	Jarosz, Joe	FB	5-11	205	Sr.
22	Johnson, Anthony	FB	6-0	225	Jr.
7	Jones, Andre	DE	6-4	215	So.
84	Jurkovic, Mirko	DT	6-5	270	Fr.
79	Killian, Chuck	OT	6-5	264	Sr.
54	Kinsherf, Jim	C	6-4	252	So.
37	Kowalkowski, Scott	DE	6-2	226	So.

Hometown	High School	High School Coach
Hillside, NJ	Hillside	Larry Coppola
Evergreen Park, IL	Brother Rice	Tom Mitchell
Wheaton, IL	Wheaton North	Jim Rexilius
Rumson, NJ	Rumson–Fair Haven	Joe Barley-Maloney
Riverside, CA	Riverside Poly	Mike Churchill
Scottdale, OA	Southmoreland	Bobby Thompson
Chicago, IL	St. Laurence	Mike O'Neil
Sarasota, FL	Riverview	Jon Sprague
Dallas, TX	Plano	Tommy Kimbrough
Creve Coeur, MD	Desmet Jesuit	Bob Christian
South Weymouth, MA	Archbishop Williams	Kevin McDonald
Annandale, VA	W. T. Woodson	Ken Poates
Tampa, FL	Leto	Barney Myers
Kaneohe, HI	St. Louis	Calvin Lee
Wilkes-Barre, PA	Meyers	Mickey Gorham
Highland Heights, KY	Newport Catholic	Robert Schneider
Omaha, NE	Creighton Prep	Tom Jaworski
Arlington Heights, IL	St. Viator	Jim Lyne
South Bend, IN	John Adams	Bill Farrell
Hyattsville, MD	DeMatha	Bill McGregor
Calumet City, IL	Thornton Fractional No.	Jerome Munda
Philadelphia, PA	Northeast Catholic	William Saybelt
Braintree, MA	Archbishop Williams	Kevin McDonald
Framington Hills, MI	St. Mary's Prep	Rob Hager

NOTRE DAME 1988 ROSTER

No	Name	Pos.	Ht.	Wt.	Cl.
37	Lark, Antwon	CB	5-11	177	So.
70	Lippincott, Marty	OT	6-5	284	Sr.
1	Lyght, Todd	CB	6-1	181	So.
68	Marshall, George	DT	6-2	243	So.
68	McDevitt, Dan	CB	5-10	167	Sr.
76	McGuire, Gene	OL	6-5	265	Fr.
76	McLoone, Mike	FS	5-11	183	Jr.
76	McNamara, Ted	FB	5-11	232	Jr.
91	McShane, Kevin	DE	6-3	219	Jr.
46	Mikhalko, Ryan	FB	6-2	234	So.
63	Prinzivalli, Dave	OG	6-2	247	Jr.
34	Pritchett, Wes	LB	6-6	251	Sr.
9	Rice, Tony	QB	6-1	198	Jr.
99	Ridgley, Troy	LB	6-4	255	Fr.
21	Robb, Aaron	FL	6-1	192	Sr.
96	Roddy, Steve	DT	6-2	237	Sr.
52	Ryan, Tim	C	6-4	245	So.
53	Sandri, Winston	OG	6-4	253	So.
53	Satterfield, Bob	CB	6-0	181	Sr.
3	Setzer, Rusty	RB/DB	5-9	180	Fr.
83	Sexton, Jim	P	6-0	188	So.
60	Shannon, Brian	DT	6-5	242	So.
29	Smagala, Stan	CB	5-11	186	Jr.
48	Smalls, Michael	LB	6-3	220	Fr.
28	Smith, Rod	RB	6-1	183	Fr.
31	Southall, Corny	FS	6-2	194	Sr.

Hometown	High School	High School Coach
Santa Ana, CA	Saddleback	Jerry White
Philadelphia, PA	Northeast Catholic	William Saybelt
Flint, MI	Luke M. Powers	Bill Tucker
Somerset, NJ	Franklin	Len Rivers
Chicago, IL	St. Laurence	Mike O'Neil
Panama City, FL	Mosley	George Cochran
Dunedin, FL	Clearwater Ctr Catholic	Nick Bravos
Dallas, TX	Frankfurt American	Carl Pachucki
Joliet. IL	Joliet Catholic	Gordon Gillespie
Pelham, NH	Pinkerton Academy	Brian O'Reilly
Kaneohe, HI	Punahou	Mike Pavich
Atlanta, GA	Westminster	Wyman Creel
Woodruff, SC	Woodruff	W. L. Varner
Baden, PA	Ambridge Area Woods	Frank Antonini
Coeur d'Alene, ID	Gonzaga Prep	Don Anderson
Harleysville, PA	Lansdale Catholic	James Algeo
Kansas City, MO	Rockhurst	Tony Severino
Raleigh, NC	Millbrook	Earl Smith
Encino, CA	Notre Dame	Kevin Rooney
Gary, IN	Hammon Noll	Jerry Vlasic
South Bend, IN	St. Joseph's	Phil Teegarden
New Wilimington, PA	Wilimington Area	Terri Verreli
Burbank, IL	St. Laurence	Mike O'Neil
Rialto, CA	Eisenhower	Tom Hoak
St. Paul, MN	Roseville Area	Clint Ewald
Rochester, NY	Rush–Henrietta	Werner Kleeman
	Sperry	

NOTRE DAME 1988 ROSTER

No	Name	Pos.	Ht.	Wt.	Cl.
30	Stams, Frank	DE	6-4	237	Sr.
42	Stonebreaker, Michael	LB	6-1	228	Jr.
27	Streeter, George	SS	6-2	212	Sr.
15	Terrell, Pat	FS	6-0	195	Jr.
12	Watters, Ricky	FL	6-2	201	So.
43	West, Rod	TE	6-3	234	Jr.
69	Williams, George	DT	6-3	282	So.
67	Wodecki, Darryl	OT	6-4	254	So.
89	Zackrison, Kurt	DE	6-3	230	Sr.
50	Zorich, Chris	DT	6-1	260	So.

Hometown	High School	High School Coach
Akron, OH	St. Vincent–St. Mary	John Cistone
River Ridge, LA	John Curtis	John Curtis
Chicago, IL	Julian	J. W. Smith
St. Petersburg, FL	Lakewood	Bob Stephens
Harrisburg, PA	Bishop McDevitt	Tim Rimpfel
New Orleans, LA	Brother Martin	Bob Conlin
Willingboro, NJ	Kennedy	Ted Kowal
Chagrin Falls, OH	Kenston	Paul Koballa
Elmhurst, IL	York	Gary Grouwinkel
Chicago, IL	Vocational	John Potocki

AUTHOR'S NOTE

For this book, I interviewed former Notre Dame players, coaches, administrators, and students; media members who covered the team; and opposing coaches, players, and administrators.

Unless attributed differently or noted in this section, the quotes, anecdotes, and dialogue in this book are taken from those interviews.

For Lou Holtz, I interviewed him and used material from two of his books—*The Fighting Spirit: A Championship Season at Notre Dame*, written with John Heisler, and *Wins, Losses, and Lessons.* I met with Holtz in New York City for two and a half hours in June 2012. With the two books already providing expansive details on many fronts, my interview with the coach focused on the uniqueness of being the head coach at Notre Dame, his thoughts about what it takes to be successful there, and his approach—to both turning around the program and to football games. He spoke about watching the 1985 Notre Dame–Miami game and gave extensive details on the 1988 Cotton Bowl and four critical contests in the 1988 season—the season opener against Michigan, the battle with No. 1–ranked Miami, the 1-versus-2 matchup with USC, and the Fiesta Bowl.

A handful of interviews occurred between October 2011 and January 2012. The majority of interviews, which took place in person or over the phone, were conducted between April and September 2012.

I interviewed Tony Rice eleven times, mostly in person and in the South Bend area.

I spoke with Barry Alvarez on the phone once and met with him for more than an hour in his office at the University of Wisconsin's Camp Randall Stadium.

Other notable interviews for the book include former Notre Dame president Fr. Theodore Hesburgh; former Notre Dame head coaches Ara Parseghian and Gerry Faust; former Notre Dame athletic directors Gene Corrigan and Richard "Dick" Rosenthal; Notre Dame assistant coaches on the '88 team Vinny Cerrato, Chuck Heater, George Stewart, and Tony Yelovich; former Notre Dame players Steve Belles, Steve Beuerlein, Ned Bolcar, Reggie Brooks, Tony Brooks, Dean Brown, Derek Brown, Pat Eilers, D'Juan Francisco, Darrell "Flash" Gordon, Mark Green, Andy Heck, Mike Heldt, Anthony Johnson, Mirko Jurkovich, Scott Kowalkowski, Todd Lyght, Wes Pritchett, Tim Ryan, Stan Smagala, Frank Stams, George Streeter, Pat Terrell, and Chris Zorich; former Miami Hurricanes Bernard Clark, Maurice Crum, and Steve Walsh; former West Virginia head coach Don Nehlen; former Michigan Wolverine Mark Messner; former Michigan State Spartan Tony Mandarich; former Pitt Panther Mark Stepnoski; former Miami sports information director Rich Dalrymple; USC sports information director Tim Tessalone; former head of the College Football Association Chuck Neinas; and Don Meyers former head of the Fiesta Bowl.

The media members interviewed for this book, and noted with their affiliation at the time, include Andrew Bagnato, *Chicago Tribune*; Bill Bilinski, *South Bend Tribune*; Tim Brando, ESPN; Beano Cook, ESPN; Jeff Jeffers, WNDU; Sally Jenkins, *Washington Post*;

Tom Lemming, *Prep Football Report*; Jack Nolan, WNDU; and Lou Somogyi, *Blue & Gold Illustrated.*

I watched every game of the 1988 season, sometimes multiple broadcasts of the same game. I also revisited the 1985 Notre Dame–Miami game and the 1988 Cotton Bowl between the Fighting Irish and Texas A&M.

The Sports Information Department at Notre Dame is a researcher's dream. I combed through player, coach, and game files filled with notes and articles. Beyond chronicling the history written by media members of the era, there are nuggets such as the player questionnaires filled out in the player's handwriting, as well as correspondence between university departments and with other athletic departments.

Beyond quotes in multiple media outlets, the sources used for Jimmy Johnson are the former players I interviewed and Johnson's book, *Turning the Thing Around* (as told to Ed Hinton).

Unless attributed differently in the text, the material used for Ricky Watters comes from his self-published autobiography, *For Who For What: A Warrior's Journey.*

For Raghib "Rocket" Ismail, the source material is noted in the text with the exception of an interview about the Miami game, which comes from an Internet video interview by Legends of South Bend.

Material for the anecdote about the PLAY LIKE A CHAMPION TODAY sign comes from the Holtz interview as well as reporting from the Associated Press and an archived feature story on Notre Dame's athletics Web site, *UND.com.*

The anecdote about Tim Brown's back-to-back punt returns for touchdowns in 1987 against Michigan State comes from a video interview conducted by Fighting Irish Digital Media.

Unless the publication is noted in the text, other quoted material, particularly statements previewing games or discussing them in present tense, comes from nonexclusive interviews with media members covering the team and Notre Dame's postgame statistics booklet for each game, which included player and coach quotes from both teams.

ACKNOWLEDGMENTS

At eleven years old I flew alone on Piedmont Airlines from Newark, New Jersey, through Pittsburgh, and to the Michiana Regional Transportation Center, where my big brother Rob picked me up on Thursday, October 13, 1988. I arrived for the weekend of the Miami game.

On Friday afternoon my brother had class, so a freshman a few rooms away in Fisher Hall watched me. LaPhonso Ellis, the 6'8" power forward from East St. Louis, Illinois, took me to media day for the Fighting Irish basketball team. I sat on the Notre Dame bench, next to Phonse, and held a tape recorder for a reporter as the media crowded around the prize freshman.

After the interview session, I sat in the locker room with the team as coach Digger Phelps talked to his squad about the upcoming season. He told them they were pure energy, and then he played Information Society's "What's on Your Mind (Pure Energy)." The players sat in silence, but to me it looked like some super-cool-athlete-intense thought.

We headed to the team dinner. On the way, Phonse introduced me to a balding man in slightly tinted glasses. "This is Roger, Jer. He'll take care of you. Stick with him." It was Roger Valdiserri, an associate athletic director and Notre Dame's legendary sports information director. The three of us sat together eating dinner with the rest of the team in a meeting room in the Joyce Center.

So I start with gratitude for three people. LaPhonso Ellis for introducing me to Roger, who stayed in touch with me through phone calls and mailed press releases on the Notre Dame football and basketball teams. As for Roger, who, on my first day on campus as a freshman, brought me to the Sports Information Office and introduced me to John Heisler, his successor, whom I worked for as a student.

My brother Rob paved a way for me. Standing on the wooden bleachers of the fifty-ninth row of a sixty-row stadium, my torso painted with a 42 and STONY across the chest, we shared a brothers' moment watching the Irish beat Miami 31–30 and rushing the field afterward. Thanks.

I thank and acknowledge Mrs. Elizabeth "Bette" Kleinfeld, my fourth-grade teacher at Gregory School. On the second Tuesday in January, she pulled me aside and admonished me for shoddy work. She then put my desk next to hers, sent home weekly progress notes, and, by the end of the year, forever altered the trajectory of my academic career.

Dennis Joyce of Joyce Entertainment—everyone should have someone in his life who provides as much faith, support, and care as you. Thank you.

This book doesn't happen without a core group of particular people who all played different roles. Scott Gould at RLR saw that the idea could be a book. Marc Resnick at St. Martin's Press took *the* step to make it a reality. Thank you, gentlemen. At Notre Dame, I owe an immense thanks to John Heisler for opening his office to me to do research and to Reggie Brooks for going above and beyond to help me reach interview subjects.

Carol Copley of the Notre Dame Sports Information Department answered every request I had and went the distance to find primary sources to verify minuscule details that I felt were important to the book. Thanks so much.

I am grateful to the Notre Dame Sports Information Department from the 1988 season and the current staff, including the invaluable student-assistants from both periods, who, among many duties, clipped and filed newspaper articles throughout the years.

A big thank-you to Jan Partain, who helped confirm multiple details included in the book.

I also thank Bernadette Cafarelli and Alan Wasielewski for their constant hospitality.

Thank you to Fighting Irish Digital Media and the University of Notre Dame Archives for granting me access to material used in this book.

Lou Somogyi of *Blue & Gold Illustrated,* Tex Noel and the Intercollegiate Football Researchers Association, and Art McDermott—thank you for providing fact-checking and research that underscored important aspects of the book.

My ability to tell this story was greatly aided by the work of the newspaper beat writers who covered the team and provided a tremendous chronicle to research and study, and those same sentiments are true with regard to *Sports Illustrated*'s coverage of college football and the Notre Dame program throughout the publication's history.

I have to recognize the great resource that is the Monmouth County Library, which provided space for me to write, and holds the access to a trove of archived newspapers, which contributed to my research.

A special thanks to Scott Kowalkowski, Tom Lemming, Sue Shidler, and Annie Duffy.

I have to acknowledge the support from Brian Lucas, Calley Duffey Westerlund, Joyce Jang, Tony Faber, and Steve Davis.

To Ron Bennington as well as Fez Whatley, Chris Stanley,

and everyone at *The Ron and Fez Show,* thanks for giving me opportunities to come on the air and talk about sports and college football.

Thank you to Jeff Pearlman, Michael Weinreb, and Scott Raab, veterans of the book-writing world, who were kind enough to throw some guidance my way as I researched and crafted this story.

On the home front, it took a small brigade to help out as we attempted to maintain some sort of normal life while this book was written. I am forever grateful to Elizabeth Barca, Mary Derin, Fran Keane, June Zeringue, Kevin Keane, and Matt Keane.

This story came alive because of the people who were willing to be interviewed—some multiple times. I am humbled by your generosity of time and information, and I will always be extremely grateful to you.

To my wife, Beth, a high school English teacher, who read and edited the pages first, dealt with my mood swings, and spent too much time alone taking care of our children, I can't thank you enough for your unending love and support.

To my son Jerry, who sacrificed a ton of playtime but was kind enough to mock me for gaining weight and drinking too much soda during the writing process; to my son Bryant, who checked in daily to ask how many pages I had left; and to my twin daughters, Bella and Grace, who learned to say the word "football" and recognize its image after waddling into my office to blow me kisses good night, thank you.

INDEX